Turkey Hunting
with Charlie Elliott

TURKEY HUNTING
WITH
CHARLIE ELLIOTT

*The Old Professor Tells All About
Hunting America's Big-Game Bird*

CHARLES ELLIOTT

Foreword by William E. Rae

David McKay Company, Inc.
New York

Elliott, Charles Newton, 1906-
Turkey hunting with Charlie Elliott.

Bibliography: p.
Includes index.
1. Turkey hunting. I. Title.
SK325.T8E44   799.2'48'61   78-13775
ISBN 0-679-51377-9

1 2 3 4 5 6 7 8 9 10

Manufactured in the United States of America

Contents

Foreword

When I retired from *Outdoor Life* in 1973, I carried a farewell message in my last issue that was really an appreciation of the many wonderful people with whom I'd worked at the magazine during the twenty-two years I was editor-in-chief. Since it is peculiarly appropriate, what follows is essentially what I said about Charlie Elliott at the time.

I always think of Charlie Elliott, Southern field editor, as the last surviving pioneer and woodsman in the likeness of Daniel Boone. I did more hunting and fishing with Charlie than with any other member of the staff—in all corners of the country and for practically anything you can name.

I have known Charlie to put a guide right on direction in dramatic fashion. It was in Alaska. After a day's hunt, the guide motioned to Charlie and said, "Let's head back to camp."

"Where you goin'?" Charlie asked. "Camp's this way."

The guide insisted on his way, but Charlie had been checking his compass periodically and making note of the landscape.

"You go any way you want to," Charlie told the guide, "but I'm going this way."

"Well, no damn guide can leave his dude," said the guide resignedly, and he tagged along.

They hit the camp within 100 yards.

I think of the time Charlie and Wiley Hadaway deliberately set out to live off the land in the Piedmont Area of Central Georgia. They took with them only .22 rifles, some fish hooks, and salt. They lived on crows, snakes, catfish, and squirrels. They could have killed a deer, but felt it would be a waste at that point since their six days were all but up.

I have known Charlie to be trapped in a canyon in the Gila Wilderness of New Mexico on a lion hunt when his horse refused to climb farther in the treacherous footing. Charlie climbed out himself, got back to the ranch at 4:00 A.M., and returned for his horse in the daylight.

I think of a time in Wyoming when Charlie made an incredible stalk over a mile-long expanse of sagebrush—and cactus—to get within 100 yards of an unsuspecting antelope. I watched the show through binoculars as he crawled, crouched, lay motionless, or disappeared in unseen draws or behind folds in the terrain, until he finally took his shot—one hour and thirty-five minutes after he first left our place of concealment.

I can't leave Charlie without thinking of the spring turkey hunting we've done all over the South. I can't begin to talk with the gobblers the way Charlie does, but I'm always flattered when a certain friend greets me with, "How's the ol' turkey shooter?" I think I like that title better than editor-in-chief. Anyway, there are many who think turkey hunting's the greatest hunting in the world.

Right, Charlie?

Right, Brooks Holleman?

Right, Turkey Johnston?

Right, Dwain Bland?

You'll meet them all in the following pages.

Bill Rae,
Orleans, Massachusetts

Introduction and Acknowledgments

No one ever wrote a book of this kind completely on his own. He could devote a lifetime to the subject and cover all of his personal experiences—but what would he have without the help of scientists and other technical people who have studied the wild turkey from its gizzard to its gobble, setting down details of its feeding habits, range habitat and behavior? Then, too, there are parts of this continent where turkey hunting has been quite limited for even such a dedicated outdoorsman as I.

Many fine books have already been written on the wild turkey. One of the first, detailing the technical aspects of the bird, was *The Wild Turkey in Virginia,* authored by Henry S. Mosby and Charles O. Handley, and published by the Commission of Game and Inland Fisheries in 1943. By then I had been chasing gobblers for several decades; and that book, which contained such fascinating facts about the life history of the bird, served as my turkey bible for a number of years.

Then someone loaned me an old book by Tom Turpin, one of the early master hunters of the wild gobbler, called *Hunting the Wild Turkey.* This was more along the lines of how the hunting should be done, and I must have read it half a dozen times. I fully intended to steal it, but the friend who had loaned it to me finally remembered where it was and came to retrieve it. Much, much later, in 1966, Penn's Woods Products copyrighted and reprinted the Turpin book, with an introduction by Roger Latham, and Roger himself sent me a copy.

Back in 1956, Roger Latham had written *The Complete Book of the Wild Turkey.* This excellent volume has been in such continuous demand that it was finally revised and reprinted in 1976.

Brady's *Modern Turkey Hunting,* Lewis's *The World of the Wild Turkey,* Hanenkrat's *The Education of a Turkey Hunter,* Whittington's *Tall Timber Gabriels,* Harbour's *Hunting the American Wild Turkey,* Kelly's *Tenth Legion,* and

Lignon's *History and Management of Merriam's Wild Turkey* all added special flavors of their own to what many of us consider the finest game bird—not only on this continent, but on this earth.

The two finest technical books I have found on the subject are Arlie W. Schorger's *The Wild Turkey: Its History and Domestication,* and *The Wild Turkey and Its Management,* edited by Oliver H. Hewitt. Hewitt's book, published by the Wildlife Society, is a series of chapters written by many of the most informed people on the wild turkey in this land. Together, these two books contain priceless information for both the student of the turkey and the hunter. (Particulars concerning all of the above-mentioned works can be found in the Bibliography at the end of this book for any interested reader.)

Faced with this wealth of information and experience and delightful accounts of gobbler chasing, a fellow feels that anything he puts down on paper might be only duplication, or at least maybe a bit redundant.

Yet this is not quite true. Each man's turkey-hunting life has its own aura of excitement, drama, romance, and humor. Each story is different—and yet many times similar, too. In his fascinating *Tenth Legion,* for example, Tom Kelly makes a profound observation about something that has happened to every turkey hunter I know, although I'd never seen it expressed before in the writing of any other gobbler chaser.

Tom Kelly says that although no wild turkeys have been seen in the heart of New York City since around 1720, if the Audubon Society there wants to add a turkey to their list of sightings, all they have to do is invite him into Central Park some morning about daylight, with his gun and a roll of toilet paper. If he follows his usual procedure about that time of day of leaning his gun against a tree, lighting his pipe, and pulling down his pants to answer a call of nature, a turkey gobbler will immediately fly out of the tree overhead.

There's not a turkey hunter I know who hasn't had that happen to him in turkey woods somewhere over these United States. All of us recognize it as a fact of life. But it took Tom Kelly to set it down on paper.

How would a book such as this ever be complete without my also including the partners of literally hundreds of hunts over so many years? Or the tales told around a campfire or in a motel room on the night before a hunt? That's where you get some of the most colorful and dramatic facts you'd never find in any reference book.

Those outdoor partners of mine are the characters in many of these stories and have made much of this presentation possible. Many have contributed directly or indirectly to the finest gobbler hunts I ever had. Such men as Phil Stone, Lamar Westcott, George Shuler, Bill Rae, Brooks Holleman, Tom and Hugh Howard, Ray Barnes, Turkey Johnston, Jimmie Shirley, Billy Arthur, Doc Hines, Bob Card, Dempsey Cape, Robert W. Woodruff, Bob Balfour, Goodwin Tuck, Jack Dudley, Charley Dickey, Earl Groves, Ben Rogers Lee, Roscoe Reams, Tom Shanks, Tom Rodgers, Jerry Allen, Lea Lawrence, Ralph McDonald, Monk Montague, Glenn Titus,

Bruce Brady, and Dwain Bland—to name only a few with whom I have hunted regularly over the years. There are many, many more.

Two of these men, Bruce Brady and Dwain Bland, collaborated with me on some of the chapters in this book. Bruce helped put together the information on equipment and guns, while Dwain concentrated his efforts on calls and calling, with which he's had vast experience. These collaborations, coming from two of the top turkey hunters in the country, were of great help to me.

Turkey hunting is basically a lone man's game, but it's the outdoor partners and friends who make it really worthwhile.

Many of the stories and anecdotes in this book have appeared before in national and regional magazines and in newspaper columns over the years. I appreciate the approval of Tom Rodgers and Editor Gene Smith for use of material I prepared for *Turkey Call,* the magazine of the National Wild Turkey Federation. I'm indebted to John Fry and Lamar Underwood for their permission to recount stories and incidents originally published in *Outdoor Life,* where I have served as field editor for more than a quarter of a century, and to which I contributed for a dozen or more years before becoming associated with the magazine. To these men and to many others I am grateful for the privilege of being able to use again various stories and incidents to illustrate certain points I have made on the where, why, and how of gobbler chasing.

You will find some repetition of material on calls and calling, guns, equipment, and behavior in the field. This has been done deliberately to emphasize certain basics of turkey hunting and is not a by-product of my softening skull, as you might be led to suspect.

I have only one wish. I hope you find a fraction of the enjoyment in your fifty hours of reading this as I have had in the fifty years that have gone into putting it together.

Charles Elliott
Covington, Georgia

1

A Bearded Legend: My Best All-Time Trophy

From the time of man's creation until he steps beyond the shadows, his life is not so much a matter of years, or seasons, or days as it is of moments. A vast majority of these are so vapid and humdrum that the mind makes no attempt to file them away in its incredible storehouse. Many others remain as memories or facts available to our mental computers. A few of the latter stand out bright and vivid and, in spite of the years, never lose one sparkle of their original brilliance or beauty.

One of those highlights in my life had to do with a wild turkey gobbler. I have avoided saying *the* highlight for fear of domestic or other repercussions, but my moment of grandeur with that magnificent bird stands close to the top of the list. There's not a sound or movement or spot of color in that high drama that I've forgotten, or will ever forget.

When I first met the Cohutta gobbler, I had no faint suspicion that he and I were embarking on such a splendid outdoor adventure. The woods were dressed in pastel shades of greens and golds and splotched with chalky clumps of dogwood, making them seem almost unreal. This was spring gobbling season in the mountains, and I was hunting alone in the Cohutta Range on the Georgia-Tennessee line.

For me, this is one of the most stimulating hunt seasons of the year. The forest floor is bright with flowers, tree buds are bursting with new life, and the vitality of the woods and its creatures make it seem on the verge of erupting into some unbelievable fantasy of sound and color.

At dawn I'd walked out the backbone of an isolated ridge and paused to listen for resonant notes that might indicate a big buck turkey on its roost or on the prowl. For an hour I stood there with my back against an oak tree, while the dawn woods came to life and the sun touched a distant mountain with burnished copper.

About flying-down time, when there's light enough for a turkey to distinguish the bushes from the bobcats, I yelped the cedar box in my hand,

1

making notes like those of an amorous hen. This sound will sometimes set a silent old tom's genes to percolating and motivate him to reply with a lusty gobble to tell his intended that he's in the mood to solve her problem—and his.

When, after fifteen minutes, my yelps brought no response, I strolled another quarter-mile along the ridgetop to try again.

There I first heard him, somewhere beyond the wild jumble of ridges and valleys sprawled out below me. His notes, high-pitched and vibrant, denoted an old gobbler. From long experience I knew that the closer I could get without spooking him, the better my chances would be to put him in the bag. So I struck out in a beeline across the ragged series of ridges, navigating the rough valleys and pausing on each ridge to call and get an answer.

On the fourth ridge I sensed that he was somewhere near. When I clucked my yelper and didn't get an answer, I considered that the bird and I were at close range. I stood motionless, straining my ears, and after a few minutes heard some creature working in the dry leaves that blanketed the shallow cove just beyond the hilltop. The crest of the summit was thinly clad in laurel, and the ground around the thickets was reasonably bare of leaves. In a half-crouch to keep my head below the narrow backbone of the ridge, I circled to a point directly above where I could hear the parched leaves rattling.

After listening for a moment, I concluded definitely that the sound was made by turkeys scratching for sustenance in the brown carpet, though they hadn't made a note of any kind to verify their presence. I stood perfectly still, trying to determine what my next move should be.

I have little doubt that I'd have concocted some scheme to get a look at those birds over my gunsights, if a gray squirrel hadn't chosen that exact moment to make a trip through the scrubby timber. When I heard him rattle the bark on a tree above me, I instinctively glanced up. The squirrel was so close I could have touched him with the tip of my gun barrel. I had my camouflage clothing on but had neglected to smear my face that morning with bowhunter's paint, preferring instead to use a gauze mask when the time came to sit in a blind and call up a gobbler.

When the squirrel saw my white face and identified me, he seemed to go berserk. He made a flying arc to the next tree, another long leap, and then in his third jump he either misjudged distance or broke a limb in his headlong flight. I got a glimpse of him in midair, then heard him hit the leaves on the slope below.

If those startled turkeys had taken to the sky, I could have killed one. They were scratching within 40 feet of where I stood. When I heard them running in the leaves, I charged through the laurel, hoping for a shot. But by the time I spotted the birds, they were sprinting up the far slope, out of shotgun range. One was the tallest gobbler I'd ever seen in the woods. He simply dwarfed the two jakes with him.

The season was running out, but I spent my last eight days on the trail of that big turkey. I still feel that if all those slopes were piled on top of one another, I must have climbed a hundred miles high. Joel Biggs, a local wildlife officer, told me that turkeys often range as far as 4 or 5 miles, and I must have looked in every cove and on top of every ridge in those 20 square miles.

I hunted through the open seasons in Georgia and Tennessee and on the Ocoee Wildlife Management Area. On five different occasions I could have put a young gobbler in the bag, but I passed up each one. One had a raspy voice I thought belonged to my old bird. He gave me a few hair-raising moments. Yet when he walked around the end of a log, 50 feet away, I saw that his beard was no longer than my index finger.

I was stricken with big-turkey fever. That huge gobbler had my tag on him and I wanted him more than any big-game trophy I'd ever brought home—and that included sheep, bears, elk, and caribou.

Before the hunt was over that spring, I met one other mountain man who was on the trail of this same bird. Gobbler hunters have a special feeling of camaraderie. If they happen to meet on a high ridge or isolated woodland trail, it's like two Daniel Boones bumping into one another. They exchange cordialities either by sign language or in whispers, briefly swap plans so they won't conflict in choice of territory, and trade bits of information on fresh scratchings or other sign. They might even take a few minutes off to compare the tones of their turkey calls. Then, for the remainder of the day, each man will listen for the sound of the other's gun—hoping all the while he won't hear it.

This grizzled mountaineer I met came down the trail as softly as a forest cat. After the usual ritual of greetings, he showed me his call and I yelped my box for him. The old fellow listened with a slightly cocked ear to the notes, then nodded.

"Gobblers around here shore oughta like that Southern accent," he commented. Since he seemed a very affable and gracious fellow, I took his words with a grain of saltpeter.

During the three seasons that I devoted my full attention to this long-bearded old patriarch of the forest, I learned all over again that killing a large wild gobbler presents perhaps the greatest challenge in hunting. It doesn't take the courage needed to coldly face a charging grizzly or the stamina necessary to climb for a mountain goat or trophy ram. But nothing else requires more in woodsmanship, patience, and ingenuity.

As I said, I stayed on the trail of the Cohutta gobbler for three seasons. I filed my license in my home state of Georgia and took birds in Alabama, Mississippi, Oklahoma, and New Mexico, and could have added Tennessee to the list with a lesser gobbler, had there not been only this one I was truly interested in.

To make the cheese more binding, as they say in Crackerese, I learned that my old gobbler had already acquired a reputation in both the Cohutta Mountains and around Ocoee. Several of the local sportsmen had an eye on him, and more than a few had devoted most of their spring gunning to the bird. So I approached each April season with the growing apprehension that one of those mountain men might get to the gobbler before I had another chance at it.

I saw the bird a number of times. It seemed to lead a charmed life. Only once could I have blown the whistle on him. He walked across the road in front of my car. He was only a few yards away when I stopped, jumped from behind the steering wheel, and threw a shell into the chamber of my gun. The huge gobbler walked unhurriedly and almost majestically up the slope, as though he knew just as well as I that I wouldn't shoot. To bushwhack that old patriarch would have been as heinous a crime as ambushing my best friend.

Once I called him to within 75 yards of my blind. For thirty minutes he stayed in one spot, strutting and gobbling. Then he vanished as suddenly and completely as if he had been erased. It made me wonder if I'd seen him at all and should seek psychiatric help.

On another occasion I ran into him at least a couple of miles from where we'd first met. He was on the Georgia side of the line, on the last day of the Georgia open season. I was traveling a long "lead" (which is the local term for a main ridge) just after daylight. When I paused on the brow of a slope to call, he answered. At least, I was almost certain I recognized his voice.

I made a breathless detour of more than a mile to the ridge above him. But before I could get into position, half a dozen crows spotted the tom. Ganging up on and harassing a lone wild turkey is a favorite crow pastime, and from their language I knew they were really working this one over.

I crept downhill as close as I dared to get to the melee and set up my stand for business. For more than an hour we maneuvered around on that point of the ridge. Finally the crows, or an unknown intruder, or something I said on my wingbone call or cedar box spooked him. Or maybe he just got tired of playing games. He turned away and crossed a shallow cove to the thick laurel on the next ridge. The crows apparently lost him in the laurel, but when he hit the open ridgetop they found him again. Finally the whole side show continued out of hearing over the crest.

The foreboding that someone else would get to that gobbler before me grew acute when, on the third season of our acquaintance, I had to miss the first three open days. My only consolation was that spring came later than usual that year and those first legal days were rainy and cold, which might somewhat dampen the ardor between toms and hens, normally in full blossom by then. As for the dedicated gobbler hunters, I knew they'd be in the woods even if we were in the middle of a second ice age.

On the morning of the fourth day, I was on the mountain half an hour before daylight. The brown carpet of leaves was white with frost, and a cold blanket of air lay across the hills.

I wasn't exactly pleased with the way my plans had been disrupted on this particular morning. Phil Stone (an old hunting partner) and I had decided to hunt together through the gobbling hours, then separate and scout out a tremendous territory for signs. My wife Kayte refused to stay in camp alone and insisted on coming with us.

Three's a crowd, even at turkey hunting, so when we parked in a little gap, Phil took off down a dim logging road that skirted a narrow valley. I'd have sent Kayte in the other direction, but she gets lost even in our backyard, and I knew we'd then have to spend the rest of the season looking for her. So she stayed with me, which meant confining my hunting to the more gentle terrain around the car.

As the first dawn light turned the woods from black to gray, a ruffed grouse flashed across the road. Farther down the valley we flushed two more of these colorful birds out of a branch bottom. The dawn was bright and cold as we climbed the point of a low ridge overlooking the valley. From this spot I knew we were high enough to hear turkeys on any of the half-dozen ridges sloping away from that massive range around Big Frog Mountain. Kayte and I got settled and waited until the noise we'd made in the frozen leaves was forgotten by the forest creatures around us and they began to move about once more.

On my box I gave the low, plaintive notes of a hen. After a few minutes without an answer, I called much louder. A quarter of an hour later, I rattled the box with the throaty call of a gobbler. All this activity produced exactly no results, except for the raucous notes of a crow across the valley and the loud drumming of a woodpecker on a hollow stub nearby.

Kayte and I climbed over the crest of the ridge into the next valley to repeat our performance. The sun spotlighted the tops of the highest hills and the line of light gradually crept down the mountains until it touched and warmed our half-numb hands and cheeks.

We moved from one ridge to another and heard nothing that resembled the notes of a turkey. At 8:30 A.M. we made our way back over the trail to where we met Phil Stone, who'd also gone through an unproductive session.

The three of us discussed the situation and decided that, with the season so retarded, the birds were not yet courting and probably not even speaking to one another. This evaluation gave me a vast sense of relief, along with some assurance that my big gobbler had not yet been disturbed and that I'd see him again somewhere in these mountain woods.

Kayte and Phil were already in the car, impatiently waiting for me while licking their chops in anticipation over the Bloody Marys they would be soon having at breakfast. I don't know whether it was impulse, instinct, or some strange intuition that suddenly impelled me to step away from the car to the edge of the road with the turkey call in my hand.

I clucked a couple of times, gave the low, breathless notes of a hen, and then listened. No response. I'd expected none. Still, merely to complete the routine, I half-heartedly rattled my box to simulate the call of a gobbler.

There was nothing half-hearted in the challenge that bounced back from the next ridge, almost quickly enough to pass for an echo.

I have no idea how my two partners got out of the car and beside me so fast and so noiselessly, but they now appeared to have lost all interest in breakfast or Bloody Marys. I touched my finger to my lips.

"Stand here a few minutes," I whispered, "and let's see which direction he's headed."

When the buck turkey gobbled again, he was 100 yards farther down the ridge. That was enough for me. My partners agreed that I could travel faster and get ahead of the gobbler if I went alone, and that I also might have a better chance of seeing and definitely identifying him as the one bird I wanted. As for myself, I already knew.

I climbed the slope and circled the side of the hill in a half-run. At the spot where I hoped to intercept the gobbler, I zipped up my camouflage suit and sat down at the base of a big tree with emerald vegetation growing before it.

I wasn't sure yet who it was the tom answered, but he gobbled again shortly after I'd given him the soft, gentle notes of a hen on my slate-type call. Minutes later a second gobbler, this one with a younger voice, set the woods to ringing off to my left.

The smaller tom definitely was coming to me, but the turkey I had planned to intercept walked off his ridge, crossed a rivulet in the hollow, and climbed to a cove that angled away from where I'd taken my stand.

I left the young buck turkey decoying to my squeal and took off across the slope. I didn't even try to convince myself I was acting foolishly in giving up a bird in the hand for a try at that old boy with the rusty pipes. The big tom had already cost me at least five gobblers since I'd first met him. I figured he should be worth at least one more.

By midmorning the leaves had lost their frosty coating. The drying forest floor became much noisier underfoot. I had to pause every few minutes to get another fix on the gobbler, who continued to answer my calls. We were walking at about the same speed. By the time I reached the road that separated Georgia's Cohutta Range from Tennessee's Ocoee, the tom had crossed the road and climbed the side of a massive mountain into the forbidden area.

This appeared to be the end of the trail. The Ocoee area was closed except for five two-day periods in April, and I wouldn't have another chance at him until then. It looked like old long-beard had once again given me the shaft.

By all sane criteria, I knew it was hardly possible to entice that cagey gobbler to backtrack so late in the day over the route he'd just taken. Especially since he had been intent on going the other way from the moment we'd first heard him.

One thing for sure. I had nothing to lose by trying. I whacked my cedar box with a couple of lusty yelps. Almost instantly, he came back with a high-pitched gobble. I settled down in a little clump of pines in legal territory to wait. At least ten minutes went by before his resonant tones again rolled down the mountain—and this time they seemed to come from farther off. I waited. His next call came from near the top of the mountain. There wasn't any doubt in my mind now that he was walking out of the picture. In desperation I gobbled my box as loud as I could make it quaver.

For a full twenty minutes, complete silence. Then he sounded off again from approximately the same spot where I'd last heard him. My heart gave an extra thump or two. At least I'd stopped his flight . . . momentarily.

I waited. And waited. And waited. I have no idea how long I sat in that one spot, trying to convince myself he'd already gone on and over the mountain. I suppose the only thing that kept the seat of my pants pressed against the unfriendly rocks and roots was the knowledge that many times when a tom stops gobbling, but hasn't been spooked, he's coming to investigate. If so, there wasn't any harm in giving him my exact location. Stealthily I reached for the slate and cedar stick, touched them softly together for a few dainty clucks, then dropped them beside me on the ground. Most novice hunters are likely to call much too much.

To wait—and keep on waiting—requires an enormous amount of patience. Even more so, when there's no hint of any kind whether you are on the verge of success.

At last I gave up. The rocks and roots now seemed to be actively attacking my hindquarters. My legs felt numb from sitting in one position. Phil and Kayte—and beyond them the Bloody Marys, country sausage, eggs, and biscuits—were waiting. I hadn't heard a peep out of my gobbler for three-quarters of an hour. By now he could be in the next county. With disappointment welling through me, I shifted my position to reach for the slate and cedar stick I had dropped to the ground.

Suddenly somewhere a limb or twig cracked; the sound a deer makes as it tiptoes through the woods. I came to full attention again, straining my eyes for a glimpse of feet or head or brown deerhide. For a dozen minutes I sat motionless. At last I decided that the animal or whatever that had cracked that stick must have drifted on by.

Once more I relaxed and prepared to gather up my gear and call it a day. I was on the verge of standing up to give my numb muscles some relief when I heard footsteps in the leaves. The cadence was exactly that of a man who slips stealthily along, stalking unseen quarry.

Again I froze. I couldn't see a man or make out movement of any kind, but at the moment there wasn't anything I needed less than a load of high brass No. 4 or 6 pellets smack in my face.

I had been straining so hard to see some deer or human form that my first glimpse of the gobbler now came as a distinct shock. He was beyond and walking parallel to a contour that dropped off like a terrace about 20 yards in front of my blind. The contour hid all but the meaty, wrinkled top of his head above the wattles. I couldn't see enough yet to definitely identify him as the old patriarch who had led me on a merry three-year chase, but that one glimpse still had me all shook up inside.

He took two more steps, bringing his head higher up above the contour, but I still couldn't see his beard or judge his size. He put his head down to

The most-exciting turkey hunt I've ever had was the one that led me to this gobbler, the largest I've ever killed.

peck at something on the forest floor, and while his eye was out of sight I quickly raised my gun. On its way up, the gun dislodged a dead Y-shaped stem. It straddled and lodged on the gun barrel in such a way that I couldn't see the sights. The bird continued to walk, growing taller and taller as it came up the shoulder of the hill, and I moved the barrel slowly to keep it in line with his head.

It was purely a matter of luck that at the same moment my gobbler walked behind a large tree trunk, a protruding twig suddenly flipped the Y-stem from my barrel. When the tom stepped past the tree, my sights were directly on his head.

My 12-gauge Winchester pump gun was loaded with shells holding No. 6 shot. Some hunters like large shot—No. 4 or No. 2—but I know I have a better chance of hitting the vital parts of a bird's head and neck with a denser pattern. Most shots in this type of hunting are at a bird's head and neck while he's still on the ground. I often back up my first round of No. 6 with a No. 4 and then a No. 2 load, which gives me a reserve of progressively larger pellets to break down a turkey that flies or runs after the first shot.

There he stood for all of five seconds with his head up in a patch of sunlight, as tall and majestic as I remembered him from two springs before. He was so close it seemed I could reach out and touch him with my gun. The sunlight on his feathers made them ripple in a display of copper, green, and gold so resplendent that I caught my breath. What a beauty. Then I saw his heavy beard and knew beyond any doubt that he was indeed the old patriarch I'd dreamed about for so long.

It was almost sacrilegious to shatter that magnificent moment with a shot—but the powerful impulses developed in a lifetime of hunting triggered the gun. It was a clean, one-shot kill.

That's when all the excitement of the past two hours finally hit me. My hands shook as I tried to unstrap the camera from my shoulder. When I hefted the bird for weight and saw how far I had to lift his feet so that his head would clear the ground, I got the shakes all over again.

He pulled the hand on the corroded old camp scales up to 25½ pounds—the largest mountain gobbler I've seen, and one of the biggest turkeys I had ever killed, including the heavier breeds from some of the Southern plantations.

Phil peered wonderingly over his glasses at the scales.

"There just ain't no telling," he said, "what this critter might have weighed, if these scales weren't so rusty." (We checked them later on and found that the scales did, in fact, read almost 1½ pounds too low.)

At that moment, though, the gobbler's weight didn't make too much difference. He had given me my finest hunt in turkey woods, and he still remains my most highly prized big-game trophy.

2

The Turkey in American History

The more a person knows about any game bird or animal—its background, habitat, and habits—the greater will be his appreciation of both the individual and the species to which it belongs.

Genealogy of a game species may interest hunters somewhat, but they know it's the knowledge of habits and habitat that puts meat on the table. No old mountaineer or swamp hunter I ever met could tell you the scientific name of the wild turkey, or that its ancestry dates back a million years to the Pleistocene epoch. But he knows how to bring home the makings of a fine Christmas dinner.

And while we're at it, we can be just as certain that an old patriarch gobbler couldn't care less about his ancestral lines, or what happened in the past million years, or what will happen in the next. When he lets his eyes range over the woods like a radar beam, searching out unusual signs or movement, his immediate concern is to stay as far away as possible from being the main attraction on that Christmas dinner table.

That part, however, we'll get to later. For the present, let's take a peek at the bird's ancestral history and his relationship with man down through the ages.

No doubt the turkey is little impressed that, in the order of things, he's considered the world's largest gallinaceous game bird. Or that he is even more American than the American Indian who, theoretically, came here from Asia across the Bering Strait and spread himself over this continent a good many millenniums before our European ancestors sailed across the Atlantic and took the country away from these so-called "savages."

What we know about the wild turkey in those times comes mostly from historical accounts. These were presented quite graphically in Arlie W. Schorger's great and comprehensive book, *The Wild Turkey: Its History and Domestication;* in *The Wild Turkey and Its Management,* prepared by some of the top wild turkey experts in the country under the editorship of Oliver H. Hewitt and published by the Wildlife Society; and in various other books

11

that go into far less detail concerning the wild turkey. Since it won't be long until first light breaks across the horizon and that old tom out yonder will be gobbling on the roost, I'll touch only briefly here on what's known about our turkeys in those early days. Then I'll pull on camouflage, grab turkey calls and gun, and go hunting.

Schorger thinks it possible that the first European to lay eyes on the wild turkey was Columbus when he came over on his fourth voyage and landed on a group of islands off the coast of Honduras. He called these birds *gallinas de la tierra,* or "fowl of the earth," a name also later used by the Spanish explorers who followed him to this side of the world. In fact, all our ground-dwelling game birds that scratch for a living are known today as *gallinaceous* birds.

Columbus was, of course, followed by hordes of Spanish conquistadors who penetrated deeply into the mainland of the continent looking for gold.

Some of the most interesting accounts of the abundance and domestication of the wild turkey came out of Hernando Cortez's army, which reached Mexico in 1519. The bird they found there was the Mexican turkey, with a range generally south of the Merriam and the Rio Grande turkeys, both Southwestern U.S. species.

Apparently the Mexican turkey was easily domesticated. The Aztecs raised them by the hundreds of thousands. They were prominent in the marketplaces of Mexico City, afoot, dressed for cooking, and cooked. In those days, though, no Spaniard thought to bring back to Europe a Mexican recipe.

Emperor Montezuma maintained a very large zoo of carnivorous animals and birds, and part of the vittles fed them included some 500 turkeys a day. These were part of the tax he imposed on his citizens. It is said that, in one Mexican state, Montezuma collected as a portion of his tax one turkey from each person every twenty days. Some mathematician counted heads and estimated that from this one state alone the Aztec ruler collected a toll of more than 100,000 turkeys annually.

But even before Cortez, around 1511 or earlier, Mexican turkeys were brought back to Spain by royal decree for breeding.

Wherever it ranged and whatever the species in pre-Columbian days, the population of wild turkeys in what we now know as the United States was almost unbelievable. One authority says that in the one-and-a-half million square miles covered presently by thirty-nine states, the turkey population was estimated at 10,250,000 birds.

There are accounts of the Eastern turkey's being domesticated by a couple of tribes, but these were only a small fraction compared to those raised in captivity by the Central Americans. Generally, domestication was unnecessary in the eastern half of the United States. Because of the bird's abundance and tameness, an Indian hunter could get his wild-turkey dinner out of the woods almost any time he wished. Evidence of that abundance can be found in so many place names like Turkey Knob, Turkey Run, and

Turkey Creek; not to mention, of course, our annual Thanksgiving feast that was established entirely around the big bird.

There are diverse accounts of the Indian's relations with the wild turkey. It is said that certain tribes would not touch the meat. Others looked upon the turkey with contempt, as a creature fit only for budding warriors to train their hunting skills upon. Still other tribes considered the turkey a basic wilderness-food item.

Even those Indians who found turkey meat tasty and nourishing hunted it for other reasons as well. Awls, beads, and spoons were fashioned from its bones. Turkey spurs were sometimes affixed as arrow tips. Turkey feathers were used for many purposes—as fans, as headdress, as fletching for arrows and woven into garments. Dr. John W. Aldrich, noted authority on turkeys, points out that the Cheyennes were known as "the striped-arrow people" because they feathered their arrows with the barred wing feathers of the wild turkey.

Many of these ornaments must certainly have been considered "trophies" by the Indians. In the same manner, we today save the beards and spurs to show our prowess as hunters, and sometimes we even turn the turkey tail into a colorful fan.

A lot of guesses have been made, of course, but no one knows exactly how the turkey got its name. There are various logical—and illogical—explanations.

One suggestion is that the word came from an Indian tribe which used the word *firkie* to designate this bird. But this, perhaps, is too simple an explanation.

Another similar story is that when the peacock was imported from India into Europe, it brought with it the name *togei,* a word taken from one of the Asian dialects. Over the years this became pronounced as *tukki*—and, eventually, *turkey*. Since the bird brought back to the Continent by the Spanish explorers somewhat resembled the peacock in size and appearance, and in courtship spread its tail and feathers in a similar fashion, it also may conceivably have been called a *togei,* a term that by this time had been corrupted to mean "turkey-cock." (This was, historians tell us, a word combination used in Europe long before Columbus ever saw his first gobbler.)

Turkey-cock was also applied to a very large, dark North-European grouse known as the capercaillie, almost as large as the American bird, and possibly to various other birds that spread their tail feathers into a fan as part of their mating rituals.

Paradoxically, the most logical—and yet most erroneous—explanation is that the bird's name originated by association with the country of Turkey. Schorger says that "in the Middle Ages, nearly everything exotic was obtained through Turkish or Arabian territories and . . . the belief persisted that this bird came from Turkey, long after it was known that the New World was its origin."

Aldrich states that the confusion over this one name used to describe several completely dissimilar birds continued until Carolus Linnaeus, the Swedish botanist, came along in the eighteenth century to give us our first taxonomic classification of all living creatures.

But even Linnaeus was confused. To the North American wild turkey, he gave the Latin name *Meleagris gallopavo*. (The first word is an ancient Roman name for the guinea fowl, and the second a Latin compound of chicken and peafowl.)

The domesticated Mexican turkey made the rounds from Mexico to Spain to Central Europe and was introduced into England in the early 1500s. It finally got back to America through the early colonists.

Then, as now, the domesticated bird was easily identified. It is smaller than the native Eastern turkey and the tips of the domesticated bird's tail feathers are white, or almost so. The tail-feather tips of the Eastern run from a chestnut brown to almost chocolate.

I remember one experience in identification. During a snowstorm, I met a gobbler on a forest trail in North Carolina's Snowbird Mountains. He seemed as surprised as I was. We were no more than 40 feet apart, and I put my gun sights on his head. But he was facing me. In the storm, I couldn't tell whether the tip of his tail was brown or white.

Earlier, I'd seen a cabin with its garden plot in a cove not too far away, and I had no intention of starting a feud with some mountain family by doing away with what might be the makings of their Christmas dinner. The gobbler quickly solved my problem of identification. As he vanished into a laurel thicket along the trail, I caught a glimpse of his white tail feathers. I quickly lowered my gun.

When white men invaded this continent, they found four main species of wild turkeys in what we know today as the United States: the Eastern, Florida, Rio Grande, and Merriam's. Some were thought to be in various stages of integration, such as the Eastern and Florida (or Osceola) turkeys, and the Eastern and Rio Grande, but no one knew exactly where one such line began and another ended. Mainly, each of the four species had its own range, and each was abundant almost beyond the comprehension of the men who came into contact with the huge flocks.

The original range of the Eastern turkey covered all or part of the states ranging from Maine to Texas and South Dakota, plus a portion of Ontario; the Osceola was predominant in southern Florida; the Rio Grande was seen mostly in Texas and western Oklahoma, with a small corner of its range reaching up into Kansas; and Merriam's wild turkey generally occurred in New Mexico, Colorado, and Arizona. Both the Rio Grande and the Merriam's also spilled southward into Mexico.

Documentary evidence presented by Schorger as well as Hewitt indicates that there once existed tremendous flocks of all four species. "Hundreds in flocks," some observers reported; "so numerous that it might be said they appeared but one flock, universally scattered through the woods;" and, in the upper Ohio Valley, "as many as 5,000 in one flock."

The Eastern gobbler.

One hunter reported from a settlement in Kentucky that "it was a poor sportsman who could not shoot a dozen in a day" and that he could have killed 40 had he been so inclined. Luckily, he didn't elaborate on that word "sportsman"!

Wild turkeys were common on the food market, bringing as low a price as six cents each, and one hunter filled an order of 100 turkeys in one day. To those of us who now look hopefully to bagging one gobbler per season, this sounds like the stuff out of which fairy tales are made. We can only assume that the hens and gobblers were a bit more plentiful then—and certainly a lot less wise and cagey than they are today.

From every corner of turkey range, the records are laced with accounts of the tremendous flocks seen and of the incredible number of birds killed as the westward march of pioneering America went on. Schorger gives us some examples:

"Two men in Scotland County (Missouri) had their rifles with them while husking corn, and killed 132 turkeys in one day."

"In the fall of 1870, Bertram (in Kansas) saw as many as 1,000 turkeys daily over a period of ten days to two weeks, in and about the junction of the North and South Forks of the Soloman River."

"The winter of 1868-69, (General) Sheridan was camped in the vicinity of the Antelope Hills, Ellis County (Oklahoma) where the trees were black with turkeys (no doubt on the roost). They were so plentiful that the soldiers had all they wanted—and according to Lane, flocks containing 3,000 turkeys were seen as late as 1877 by hunters."

"Bingham hunted in Frio County, Texas, in November 1878 and states, 'I will assert that I saw in one roost, the night before we left, in 500 yards' distance, over 1,000 turkeys. I killed at least 25 in thirty minutes. Our whole kill of turkeys on the tramp was over 100.'"

The list goes on and on—from Maryland, North Carolina, Georgia, Illinois, Iowa, and many other states.

Schorger's estimated pre-Columbian turkey population in the United States added up to 10,250,000. Texas led the list with more than 2,000,000 birds, while some of the colder northern states, such as Maine, Minnesota, and Vermont, were thought to have had less than a thousand turkeys each.

The white man, with his guns, abused this tremendous resource. As he has done with the bison, passenger pigeon, and many other birds and animals considered as game, he practically wiped out the turkey population in little more than half a century. One Midwest sportsman's account tells of almost 9,000 turkeys being killed in a single year.

An interesting sidelight is that back in those days, even as today, this large bird stirred the imagination more than any other winged creature since the roc. Hunters reported wild turkeys weighing up to 50 or 60 pounds. (I can only assume that these were birds brought back to camp over a steep mountain trail and slung across some sweating hunter's shoulders. Believe me, I myself have felt the same way about their weight sometimes!)

The slaughter went on. The range of all turkey species decreased along with the number and size of the flocks. Aldrich provides a telling example when he quotes Frank B. McMurry that all of the original turkeys in the Wichita Mountains of southern Oklahoma were exterminated during the three decades leading up to 1900. This was not too far from the same region that, a few years before, had reported tree roosts black with turkeys.

It was the same story almost everywhere. Wild gobblers disappeared from New England in the middle 1850s and from much of the Ohio Valley later on in the century.

When I first started hunting turkeys in the early 1920s in my home state of Georgia, only a few pockets of the big birds were left in the coastal region, on the extensive shooting plantations in the southwest corner of the state, and in the depths of two or three of our large river swamps. The remote regions of our mountainous North Georgia contained a few scattered turkeys.

Those that had become wary of man's intentions and smart enough to escape the gun were wilder than wild. I spent a lot of days in the Savannah

River Swamps below Augusta, my scattergun loaded, my face daubed with mud, trying to meet up with the old gobbler out of a flock I had located.

In those days, I knew very little about turkey calling and even less about the turkeys themselves. The only bird I ever brought home from that drowned and remote region was a young gobbler that had been flushed by a fisherman at one of the hidden swamp lakes. It winged its way over where I stood against a tree and wondered what my next move should be.

Not until a few decades ago—when the game departments in most states where the wild turkey had once lived at its peak of abundance finally began to take an interest and a hand in the restoration of turkey flocks—not till then did the turkey population trend take an upward curve over the entire country.

The game departments made mistakes at first. One was in trying to hatch wild turkey eggs in an incubator, raise the poults on wire, and later release these as stocked birds. There was no way to wean either young or old turkeys off growing mash or scratch feed and switch them to wild seeds, fruits, insects, and berries, or to teach them which predators to avoid, including man. Each turkey would have needed its own personal security guard to keep the wildcats, wolves, foxes, and gunners off its back.

Recently I made an attempt to establish a flock with about two dozen of these pen-raised birds. The location and terrain were perfect—wild-river swamp with old channels cutting through it, crowded with oak, beech, and other food-bearing trees, and bordered by rolling upland of pine and hardwood forest providing abundant food and cover.

I released the birds at an old house site and, as I had been told to do, fed them a few days until they could learn to shift for themselves. This feeding may have been a mistake. The birds came back regularly for their handout of vittles. Every time they appeared, one or two more were missing. If I'd been more optimistic, I'd have concluded that at least some of them were beginning to make their own way. But I knew better. The swamps and hillside critters were picking up some very tasty meals.

After I stopped feeding the birds, I heard that they had appeared at tenant farm houses in the vicinity to dine with the chickens. The last report of my attempted stocking came from a doctor friend who lived a couple of miles up-river from my release point.

"One of your gobblers roosts on our patio every night," he told me, "and craps all over the place. You'd better come and get him before I decide to wring his neck and subject him to some microwaves."

"Kill and eat him," I suggested, "before some *other* varmint does."

My classification of him didn't seem to bother him, and I suppose he followed my advice. I didn't ask, and he never told me.

One state raised thousands of birds on wire and then banded and released them in choice locations. Not a single band was ever recovered.

The game departments universally decided that turkeys hatched and raised in the wild were the only solution to restocking. A few unsatisfactory methods of taking the wild turkeys, such as stationary wire pens, were tried, but birds trapped inside these setups hurt or killed themselves by flying against the wire.

One of the most effective methods of taking the wild birds was by netting. Earlier, this approach had been found satisfactory for capturing ducks and geese for banding. The birds are fed liberally in an area until they lose at least some of their suspicion. Tremendous nets, large enough to cover a whole flock, are arranged so that the corners and middle can be shot out of a placement of three or four cannons, thereby covering the feeding turkeys. Surprisingly enough, the net pins down the powerful birds in such a way that there's little chance for them to struggle and break a wing or leg or otherwise injure themselves.

Florida developed another system of capturing turkeys for telemeter research and for stocking, which also injured the birds in no way. The biologists in the Sunshine State baited with treated corn that put the birds to sleep, or at least immobilized them enough to be picked up by hand.

To me, one of the most interesting observations of this program was how it affected the other kinds of birds that joined in the feast of treated grain. Crows walked around listing sideways as though they had just staggered out of Joe's All-Night Bar. Once I picked up a mockingbird and sat it on a log. Trying to maintain its balance, it looked up at me and opened its mouth. I think it was trying to entertain me with music, but the sounds that finally came out didn't resemble any song I'd ever heard.

According to James S. Lindzey, an authority, the use of wild-trapped stock for planting on both formerly occupied and new ranges throughout the country is the most important technique now being used to restore the wild turkey in the United States.

Most states, aside from a few to-be-expected political ripoffs, stocked their captured turkeys in areas they could protect, could supply with at least a part of the nourishment through feed patches, and could constantly observe the birds' progress. A very large percentage of the stocking went to wildlife management areas, scattered throughout the United States, with expanding acreage in every state. Here the turkeys had maximum protection and could be managed along with other game species.

In most instances, even the game men were amazed at how fast the turkey flocks grew and spread out when they had enough food and the proper cover. After a few years, many states were able to open areas and even whole regions for hunting.

Thanks to this stocking program, the range of all species of the wild turkey has been greatly expanded. Today, the big bird is found in many states where it did not occur originally. It has been successfully stocked in Wyoming, Montana, and California, as well as in other regions well beyond its historical range. Some species have been substituted for the original stock, as in South Dakota, where the Eastern bird once thrived; the new plantings there in recent years have been Merriam's wild turkey.

Populations have gone up, too, far above that of a dozen years ago when Aldrich reported a count of approximately 750,000 turkeys in forty-two states. But because most of our wilderness has deteriorated into urban development, or been transformed into farm or pasture land, or is now covered with pine pulpwood forests, there's still little chance that we'll ever approach the 10,250,000 turkeys estimated for the pre-Columbian days.

The hope is that, with the proper management of both public and private areas, the number of wild turkeys will reach a plateau that can accommodate the growing number of hunters. Thirty-nine states, at this writing, have fall or spring seasons, or both.

Many states claim that a sizable percentage of their wild turkeys are from the original stock, which somehow managed to survive in wilderness pockets through all those decades when gunners were taking an unhealthy toll of birds out of the flocks.

It wouldn't be fair to a lot of magnificent old gobblers to pass over those early days without recalling what most of us already know—that the wild turkey was once a candidate for the honor of being made our National Bird. Such was the proposal of Benjamin Franklin, and when the votes went in favor of another bird, the author of *Poor Richard's Almanack* wrote:

"For my part, I wish the Bald Eagle had not been chosen as the representative of our country; he is a bird of bad moral character . . . For in truth, the turkey is in comparison a much more reputable bird, and withal, a true, original native of America. Eagles have been found in all countries, but the turkey was peculiar to ours . . . He is, besides (though a little vain and silly, it is true, but not a worse emblem for that), a bird of courage, and would not hesitate to attack a grenadier of the British guard, who should presume to invade his farmyard with a red coat on."

Possibly Ben Franklin was speaking of the barnyard turkey; still, it could just have easily been the wild turkey, which was so abundant then that you could knock one over with a rock. One thing for sure—Old Ben had no experience of hunting those cagey needle-witted gobblers that you and I encounter in the woods today. Otherwise, he never would have used that word "silly."

3

From Egg to Trophy: A Turkey's Life History

Let's take another day off from hunting and carry a turkey through its life cycle, or at least what an amateur such as I—with help from the pros who have studied this bird—know of it.

Books—and some very detailed and interesting ones—have been written by knowledgeable authors who delved deep into the life history of the wild turkey. These, along with dozens of reports, pamphlets, and magazine articles, as well as talks with the authorities, have been invaluable in helping me get a close-up view of this fascinating game bird. What follows, then, should help you and me as hunters to understand what makes an old gobbler tick.

One of the best places I know to start at is gobbling time. We suppose any turkey's life span begins from this point, in a way.

The show starts before daylight, while the birds are still on the roost. Early in the season, or when the weather is acting up, a tom may gobble only once. But as the days slide into spring and his ardor increases, he will often sing out several times from his tree limb, then periodically on the ground until the mating time of day is over and he loses interest in the women. Depending on the latitude, on the wildness of the turkey, and on how often he is hunted, this gobbling sometimes lasts until well up into the day.

How often a gobbler sings depends partly on his personality. For several seasons, Brooks Holleman had an old tom on his place in South Alabama. At the height of breeding season, he would make the woods ring for several hours after daylight, as though he found a special pleasure in his own music.

Brooks had no intention of trying to bag this gobbler, nor would he let any of his more accomplished turkey-hunting guests go after him. He saved him for his novice hunters, and seldom did one come back to camp without an exciting story. This was probably the most talked-about gobbler in the entire South. It was a sad day on the farm when one of the tyros happened to say

21

the right thing in yelps—and later brought the loquacious tom into camp, swinging him over his shoulder.

Some of the people who study such things say that when a tom turkey is in good health, its gobble is high and shrill. In poor physical condition, its voice is more likely to be hoarse and cracked. My experience with toms indicates that the high-pitched note is more likely to mean an old bird with sharp spurs and long beard.

A real young gobbler is like a boy with a changing voice that cracks in the middle. He gives only a half, incomplete gobble, as though he were trying—but not quite able—to impress the surrounding world with his manhood.

Any number of sounds can set a bird to gobbling. I've heard them answer an automobile horn, a train whistle, a bull bellowing in a nearby pasture, the scream of a chain saw, thunder in the distance—an unbelievable variety of noises. In Alabama one morning I killed an old gobbler in a downpour of rain, while lightning played and thunder roared all around us. That bird was gobbling so often and so fast, I thought he'd either choke or drown.

Every turkey hunter knows that under normal circumstances a tom can't resist replying to the hoot of an owl. Often a hunter locates the roost tree of a gobbler when the owls are calling their farewells to the night. If no owls are singing, a knowing hunter mimics these owl calls and usually gets an answer.

Then, of course, there's the yelp of a hen to set him off, or the call of another gobbler. I've had many an old bird answer my box when I rattled it in the dawn woods.

Some experts seem to think that an active gobbler's voice grows coarser and deeper as the mating season advances.

A few words here about the other sounds made by the big birds. No one has ever been able to put down turkey talk in words. Since we're human and prone to think we know it all, we still try to make human words out of turkey music. Some of the calls we've written down in English are *cluck, tuck, putt, pop, clock, clop, yuck, yowk, yowlk, ke-ok, cuick, cuionk, phutt, purt, keow, kee-kee, he-oh, kew, k-eee, kee-e-e-e-ok, yeedle, brr-r-r, tukah, gul-lobble, gi-obble-obble.* It must be the way each hunter or biologist hears it. We try, somehow, to put it into prosaic words. I'm sure there's no way we could ever re-create it in musical notes.

Each of those sounds means something, and the hunter who knows what each is meant to say usually has the most success in bringing home the bird.

For instance, the low, sleepy *putt* . . . (pause) . . . *putt* . . . (pause) . . . *cluck-cluck-cluck* of a hen on the roost means that she is waking up for the day, will soon fly down, and will probably be in a receptive mood. That sets a gobbler's genes on fire.

The *kee-kee-kee-kee-kowk-kowk* run of a young gobbler means that he's looking for company.

The *kee-e-e-e-e-e-owk* (with a rising inflection) of an old gobbler in the fall, often known as the wildcat call, is an indication that he's been separated from some of his companions, is roosting separately, and wants them to know his location so they can get back together in the morning.

The cackle of a hen—*kowk-kowk-kowk-kowkkowkkowkkowk—kowk-kowk*—in answer to a gobbler means she wants him to know that she's excited and ready. This often brings an old tom in on the run.

By the loud *clop! clop! clop!* of a gobbler, you know he's close by and looking for you. Then if he says *phutt! phutt! phutt!* in an alarmed tone, you know he's seen and identified you, and the odds are that you'll never get another glimpse of him.

The sweet, dulcet *kee-lu* of a hen will often bring a buck turkey running. As with many turkey calls, this is a two-toned note that requires a lot of practice on whatever turkey call you use.

Tuck-uh is the sharp order a gobbler gives to a hen when he is ready for her to squat and pull up her feathers.

I once ran into a mixed flock feeding up a valley in the Cohutta Mountains of northern Georgia. They were gossiping among themselves, all talking at once as some people say the ladies do in a sewing circle—though I've never belonged to a sewing circle. These birds were *clock-clock-cluck, cluck-ca, cac-cac-cacking* with one another. I tried to get into the act, but they would pay me no attention.

George Shuler, a mountain friend, told me later that they were "cacking," a term familiar among the Southern highlanders. Over the years, I've heard this several times.

I could go on and on about turkey talk, but the chances are that you wouldn't always agree with my translations. Nor is there any way to learn the language, except by belonging to the flock or being in the woods with the birds and gradually, over many years, becoming acquainted with the message each of the various calls means to convey.

The courtship display an old gobbler goes through to impress his hens is something to behold. When he flies down off the roost, he is likely to pick a little opening in the woods or to land on the rim of a large field or meadow. Often he has a favorite trysting place near where he roosts.

When a gobbler goes into his strut, he drops his wings until the ends of his wing feathers scrape the ground. Then he spreads his iridescent tail into a huge, round fan that stands up at right angles to his body, at the same time drawing his head down almost out of sight into the feathers between his "shoulders." His body feathers are extended outward until he seems almost twice his normal size. Sometimes he'll make a sort of shuffling little dance, which may or may not denote anticipation. When his head is drawn down in this manner, any veteran gobbler hunter will tell you not to shoot, no matter how close he is. You are more likely to cripple the bird than to kill it.

You'll hear a little sound then, as though the bird had said: *Whuff!* At last he takes a few steps forward, dragging his wings on the ground, and suddenly throws his chest so far forward you'd think he'd lose his balance and topple over. This is followed by a sound that goes something like *va-roo-om-m-m,* as he seems to expel his air and collapses back to normal size like a suddenly deflating balloon.

He'll stick his neck up then and look around, probably to see whether his display has attracted a hen or predator—two-legged or otherwise. His sharp eye misses nothing. Then he'll sound his ringing gobble through the woods.

A gobbler may follow this complete ritual a number of times. He expects the hen to come to him, and she usually does. If two or three or even more hens are in a group, one will break off and go to the gobbler. How they decide among themselves which hen gets this honor would be interesting to know. If the hen pulls the universal feminine trick of appearing uninterested or stand-offish, he may walk toward where he sees her or has heard her yelp or cluck, and go into his strut again. When she is ready, she squats down and raises her tail. He steps upon her back and gets into position, and then they go into the mating procedure.

The people who study such things believe that although the act of mating may take place a number of times, a single copulation is enough to fertilize an entire cluster of eggs. They say that when a hen becomes "broody," her ovaries shrink and she loses all interest in sex.

When turkeys are in a nuptial mood, they may exhibit at least a few human traits. I once saw a mountain boy who was so good with a brier leaf that he called a gobbler to him when the gobbler already had a hen waiting nearby. The tom became so excited by the notes of the brier leaf that he didn't walk or run—he flew a hundred yards from one hillside to another, across a shallow cove! But the hen refused to be deserted. She flew with him, making noises all the way like a jealous wife.

One observer declared that he watched a gobbler so impressed with his own display of vigor that he continued to strut while two or three hens close-by were being served by younger gobblers that had been lingering on the fringes of the show.

"He sure must have had some powerful medicine," the fellow said.

The hunter with a lot of experience knows how important it is to get as close as possible to a gobbling tom before setting up shop and beginning to call. Often a buck turkey will travel a long way to get to a hen, but the closer a hunter is, the better chance he has to bag his bird.

I saw my companion, Hoyt Pippinger, a Tennessee game warden who'd taken the day off to hunt with me, call a gobbler from two ridges away. It took a while, but the bird finally walked within range.

Some hunters say that a gobbler is easier to seduce after his harem has laid eggs and gone on the nest to begin the period of incubation. All other conditions being normal, late in the season is often the best time to find a gobbler still on the prod.

Old gobblers that live together in harmony through the fall and winter will suddenly fight like fury in mating season. A big tom collects his harem and is a jealous husband. He wants no infringement on his territory. If another gobbler trespasses, the interloper is likely to find himself involved in a fracas. Accounts have been given of gobblers that knocked other gobblers off hens even during the act of copulation. The resultant fight was not for fun.

This territorial impulse of gobblers will often help a hunter bag one of the forest patriarchs. I have taken advantage of the trait myself a number of times when an old tom simply paid no attention to my hen calls, no matter how seductive *I* thought they were.

I was once with Bill Rae and his son Billy in Tennessee's Ocoee Wildlife Management Area. We sat down 20 or so yards apart on the crest of a ridge that dropped off into a shallow valley. About 150 yards below us in the valley, a buck turkey gobbled, but only occasionally. This routine had been going on for more than an hour.

I tried every seductive note I knew. I was sure the turkey could hear me, for when he gobbled, it was usually in response to one of my calls. But this seemed as far as his interest would go. Several times I rattled my box at him, and this too usually got a reply—but the tom stayed in one place.

Finally he stopped gobbling. I couldn't even get him to answer a call. When this happens, he's either lost interest altogether or is on his way in to make a silent investigation.

We sat another forty-five minutes, waiting him out. Now and then I'd try a cautious cluck, hoping he might be close enough to reply. He never did.

The day was drawing on toward the middle of morning, at which time most gobblers have percolated out and simmered down. After we'd had no word from the big boy for about an hour, I figured the show was over, but I made one last attempt. I clucked, yelped low, then yelped louder. I guess it was more exasperation than anything else that made me grasp the handle of the lid on my gobbling box and beat it back and forth against the two upper edges of the box. It was simply too loud and too harsh to be a good gobble, but it must have had the right rhythm. The tom turkey came right back, not far from the spot we had last heard him. His tone was so fierce that he sounded as though he were trying to match the noise I had made on the box.

Before I had a chance to make another call of any kind, the bird gobbled again, this time on the crest of the ridge about halfway up from the valley. He couldn't have reached that place in such a hurry unless he'd been on a dead run. I laid down the box and put my gun into position. Seconds later the turkey appeared. He'd come up behind some brush no more than 30 yards away, and his head shone through it like the red light on a traffic signal. His angry *clack! - clack! - clack!* rang like a mallet on a wooden washboard.

I had the gun sights on his head. I started to squeeze the trigger, and then the bird took a couple of steps to the right as though he'd walk right over the top of Bill Rae. I wanted Bill to kill him, so I held my fire. In another couple of steps he'd have been under Bill's gun, but something happened. The gobbler backed off and made a long detour around us on the ridge. He was still angry and clacking as he went, and we heard him cross a little cove above us to the next ridge.

I called my two hunting companions and followed. When we reached the cove, the gobbler had gone out of hearing. To relocate him, I hit the box with the same stroke I had used to stir him up. He answered immediately from far out on the ridge. We climbed to a brush heap above us, but I suppose we were too long in getting there. We didn't hear the tom again, and I could only surmise he had come back along the second ridge to meet us, had seen us climbing the slope, and figured he'd been duped. When he identified us, church was out.

No doubt about it. That was one angry gobbler. And though the hen calls failed to interest him, he'd come looking for a fight with the stranger that invaded his domain. I was at fault because I hadn't given it to him when he was close enough.

The mated hen builds her nest, but she doesn't go to much trouble. About her only preparation of a spot in which to lay her eggs is to scratch out a shallow cup on the ground and pull a few leaves into it. It may be beside a log or under a fallen old treetop, within a honeysuckle thicket, canebrake, palmettos, mesquite, or other such cover that forms a part of the country in which she lives. Almost always the nest is close to water and has an umbrella of vegetation concealing it from above. The Merriam's hen likes more open sites, preferably in tall grass and generally at elevations from 7,000 to 9,000 feet.

Depending on the species, the weather, the location, and the longitude, hens may lay their eggs anytime from the middle of March into June. In most sections of the country April is ordinarily the prime period for laying.

The number of eggs in a clutch usually averages around a dozen—but may vary from 6 or 7 to 20. Sometimes two or more hens will lay in one nest and then the clutch is multiplied. One nest was found with more than 40 eggs. Another held 26. This nest was being incubated by one hen, while a second hen stood close by, possibly to see that the job was well done or to wait her turn. Large broods have been found, mothered by two hens.

The incubation period generally extends through four weeks. Because of weather, predators, and other conditions, only about 35 percent of all eggs laid will hatch.

The turkey hen is a good mother. During the last days, when her eggs are close to hatching, she remains faithfully on the nest. She hovers nearby while the young pip their way out of the shells. The newly hatched chicks don't stay in the nest. As is true of most gallinaceous birds, they are immediately active. The eggs, which may be laid over a two-week or longer period, all begin the incubation period at about the same time and hatch out over some twelve to eighteen hours. The hen then groups them together and moves them away from the nest.

One thing the mother hen fears is rain. The chicks are covered with soft down that soaks up water like the tufts of a sponge. Although a turkey may be one of the toughest birds in existence after it approaches maturity, the chick is a fragile fragment of life. Veteran outdoorsmen have told me that raindrops will fill the exposed openings of a young turkey poult's ears and drown it. I don't know. The authorities never mention this. They say that a mere soaking is lethal to the very young turkey chick and that, in extremely wet springs, a new crop of turkeys hardly ever comes along.

Until they begin developing a better coat of feathers, the mother hen broods her chicks. At night or when a few raindrops start to fall, she calls her brood together for protection beneath her wings and body.

Woodsmen who have watched the turkey crop along with the seasons will tell you that when the spring is dry, you can count on good hunting for the next year or two. Extremely wet springs cut drastically into any increase in the turkey flocks.

As the poults grow older, they become less susceptible to the rain. As with their smaller cousins, the quail, turkey chicks start out in life on a diet of soft insects, which won't injure their tender insides. The growing turkeys graduate from insects to berries, fruits, shoots, and other vegetation, then to seeds and a variety of vegetable and animal matter, which includes almost anything they can find, subdue, and swallow. A mature turkey can gulp down a whole hickory nut and crush or grind it up in his gizzard.

The hen keeps her family together during this most dangerous period of their lives. She has words in turkey language to instruct them in the various arts of survival. She introduces them to foods they do not already know by instinct. They respond to her notes, which tell them when to assemble and when to flatten in order to escape detection. Following her instructions, they will remain frozen in one spot, even though an intruder walks through or steps on one of them.

For the first four or five weeks, the hen broods her family on the ground, until they are able to fly and begin roosting in trees. Some young turkeys are able to fly before this time. Most develop strong wings by the age of six weeks.

Various authorities have estimated the survival rate of turkeys from newly hatched chicks to maturity. This rate averages from around 20 percent to about 40 percent, depending on weather, disease, and predation.

The males and females in a brood generally remain together through the summer months and into the fall. Occasionally two broods live together as one. The mother hen calls all the signals, and the young turkeys seem to know instinctively that by following her instructions they have a better chance of escaping the creatures that aim to feed on them.

The family breaks up in late fall or winter. The young males leave the mixed group and form flocks of their own. In the fall and winter, especially in areas where turkeys are plentiful, the gobblers generally range together in age groups. You'll find the yearlings in one bunch, the two-year-olds in another, and possibly the three-year birds in a third. Older gobblers seem to prefer the company of other older gobblers and usually don't separate until mating season begins in the spring.

People who study such things list many "enemies" of the wild turkey—

though I think the word enemy does not apply anywhere in the wild. An enemy is one that kills or maims out of revenge or hatred, and "with malice aforethought," as the word technicians put it. Enmity is more of a human trait. But even we two-legged critters don't feel any animosity toward the quail we gun down or the outsize gobbler we put a bead on. I'd have to presume that other predators feel about the same way. With them, killing is a matter of food and nothing else.

Predation naturally starts with the eggs, which are on the ground and easily accessible. The egg-eaters include a wide range of creatures. Some of the most persistent are skunks, raccoons, ringtails, opossums, armadillos, foxes, gray wolves, coyotes, badgers, feral dogs, rats, crows, ravens, jays, and snakes. Some researchers have found that only about one-fourth of the nests are undisturbed and have eggs that are allowed to hatch. The highest rate of egg survival under the most favorable circumstances is generally less than half.

Each year, many nests are abandoned for various reasons. Man's activity—agricultural and otherwise—is one. Others are low temperatures, snow, and flooding. Then, too, turkey hens are often killed on the nest by such predators as coyotes, bobcats, and feral dogs.

A critical time for the turkey flock is from the poult stage until the birds are almost mature. Many creatures that do not molest grown gobblers or hens still find the poults easy to capture and a tasty meal. Among these selective predators are the hawks, with the Cooper's and sharp-shinned hawks perhaps the most persistent culprits. Several kinds of owls also take their toll of the growing turkeys.

Of our eagles, the golden is the one most likely to take a turkey poult or even a full-grown adult. This magnificent bird is one of the few predators that does not hesitate to attack a healthy, mature gobbler. Most of the smaller meat-eaters pass up gobblers and concentrate on less pugnacious meals. Fortunately for the turkey populations, golden eagles are not too abundant and their range is rather limited to the lofty remote sections of the West, where they prey on a large variety of winged and furred animals.

Nor is the bald eagle, whose home is continent-wide, too much of a threat. As a rule, our national bird prefers to set up housekeeping near large bodies of water. The bald eagle's diet consists chiefly of fish, ducks, marsh rabbits, and other such life around its home. This bird is listed as one of the turkey predators, but because of its relative scarcity and nest-site preference, the odds are that the bald eagle does little damage to turkey flocks.

Since turkey met man, man has been one of its worst "enemies." The Indians, with their crude weapons and their wisdom of never killing for the pleasure of pure slaughter, wreaked little damage on the wild-turkey populations. But the arrival of the white man on this continent almost marked the beginning of the end for this grand American game bird.

Over a span of two centuries, uncounted millions of wild turkeys were whittled down to scattered remnants, hidden in isolated pockets of wilderness. The European immigrants, with no closed seasons or bag limits to hinder them, killed hens, gobblers, and poults the year round, not only for family meals but also for the market. According to Edward Howe Forbush, author of *Birds of Massachusetts and Other New England States,* for a hundred years after 1730 the price of dressed wild turkey went through uninterrupted inflation—from half a cent to twelve-and-one-half cents a pound. The flocks continued to be decimated.

On top of this, the magnificent hardwood forests, home of the wild turkey, were gradually cut, piled, and burned to make way for cultivated lands. Later they were logged for profit. The wilderness went down before man's "progress," and many game species, including the wild turkey, went down with it.

Even in these modern times, man remains one of the worst predators. He continues to destroy the hardwoods and replace them with pine trees for a quick profit in pulpwood. The creeping cancer of urbanization overruns much of our land. But no wild turkeys are sold in the market today, and most sportsmen value this game bird too much to take it out of season or otherwise violate the regulations. Nowadays the worst two-legged predator of turkeys is the game outlaw and cheater who is also woodsman enough to avoid being seen by game-law officers.

Many of these outlaws have no compunction about slaughter or how it's most easily done. Recently I've heard stories of turkeys caught on "trot-lines," similar to the kind set out for catfish. A long, strong nylon thread is tied close to the ground between two trees. Attached to this at intervals are shorter lines with fishhooks that are baited with kernels of corn. The trot-line is placed where the outlaws have earlier fed the wild turkeys with corn, and so the birds are not suspicious. The turkey swallows a grain of corn with a hook embedded in it, and there's no way for him to escape. An outlaw can wipe out a whole flock of the big birds this way. The thought of such poaching makes at least some of us want to sink a hook into the gizzard of the murderer and hang him by it to the nearest tree.

Turkeys are also baited by pouring corn into a shallow trench. When the birds become accustomed to feeding there, the man with the shotgun stations himself nearby. When the heads are all together, eating in the trench, he opens fire, killing many and wounding more—that get away only to die elsewhere.

Another breed of outlaw concentrates on shooting poults in the spring. He waits until they are "frying size" at 2 or 3 pounds. He finds a flock, scatters it, then sits down nearby to give the call of the mother hen. One by one the poults come to him, and he kills them with a small gun—usually a .22 rifle with a short-short cartridge that doesn't make enough noise to attract the attention of a game warden. This kind of outlaw will also wipe out an entire flock of young birds. The only way to describe him is as one of nature's worst predators.

Though a number of meat-eating predators feed on the eggs, fledglings, and poults, few have the temerity to tackle a healthy, mature turkey. The hen with poults will often put up a battle for her brood. Woodsmen and experienced biologists tell many a story of foxes and other predators that back off from irate hens and gobblers, and of actual combat between predator and prey. One Merriam's gobbler was seen to stand off a coyote, which finally gave up and went its way.

Not so, though, with either the great horned owls or bobcats, which are big, strong, and fast enough to take on turkeys of any size. The owl, with much better night vision than a turkey, attacks when its prey is on the roost. The trick is to knock the big bird off its limb, catch it on the way down, and kill it on the ground. One eminent biologist, who spent years with turkey flocks, opined that the possibility of an owl attack was one reason turkeys prefer to roost over water: an owl trying to subdue one of the big birds it has knocked off a limb would probably drown trying to kill it below.

One and a half centuries ago, Audubon named the great horned owl and the bobcat as the two predators that accounted for the heaviest toll of the wild-turkey population. Most biologists agree that this appraisal holds just as true today. The bobcat, like its winged counterpart, is fierce and aggressive. There is little that will cause him to back away from any creature.

Such wild cats move with amazing speed and agility. Few of them can be domesticated, even when captured as kittens, but a friend of mine once owned one that was tame, and I spent many hours playing with it. One game it liked involved a tennis ball. Standing a few feet away, I was never able to throw the ball past him. When I'd feint and keep the ball in my hand, the cat wouldn't move a muscle. As soon as the ball left my fingers, however, he was on it. I could only imagine how deadly that bobcat would be with any bird or animal in the woods.

The bobcat can blend into its surroundings with all the invisibility of a motionless quail. David Morris, who runs a shooting plantation, told me recently that he saw a bobcat drift into a brush pile and disappear. He walked toward the brush with his gun ready, studying it intently. He stood there for five minutes, peering into the brush, trying to make out the outline of the cat. He didn't see it until it moved, less than 10 feet from where he stood. Then it was gone so fast he never got a shot.

Possibly the worst enemy of the turkey clan, though, is bad weather. From the birds' egg stage to adulthood, weather is a critical factor of survival. Not only does it affect eggs and poults; it is also capable of practically decimating entire populations over large regions.

Drought and floods may take a toll of the young, but these two hazards seldom affect old birds. Nature's most destructive forces against old birds are subarctic temperatures, deep snow, and freezing rain. Schorger, in his great book on the wild turkey which I've already referred to, says that freezing rain is the worst condition a bird can encounter. It not only puts a heavy glaze over seeds and other rations on which the turkeys depend but also often freezes on the feathers of the birds, causing them to lose their maneuverability and thus become an easy meal for any predator. If the rain and ice are followed by subarctic temperatures, the birds often freeze on the roost.

Another disastrous condition is an icy wind that drives a snowstorm before it. Snow is hammered into the feathers of the bird. Then it melts on the turkey's head, runs down its neck, and turns into an ice that covers the nostrils and suffocates the bird.

Schorger cited example after example where extremely low temperatures and deep snows, crusted over, kept turkeys away from their food. Since food is the source of heat, prolonged periods of intense cold will cut severely into flocks.

The severe winter of 1976-1977 stands as an example. Hunters sent me photos from the more northerly portions of the turkey ranges, showing hens and gobblers frozen and hanging lifeless in the trees.

Some turkeys, apparently more hardy than the others, nevertheless survive these conditions. In sheltered areas they may stay on the roost for days. Under experimental conditions, healthy turkeys have been found capable of living without food from one to two weeks, though during that time they lost from one-fourth to more than one-half their body weight. Some turkeys have been known to live for even longer periods without sustenance. They're a rugged breed.

Once I spotted a turkey on the roost at one o'clock in the afternoon. The day before, we'd had a mild sleet storm. In spite of plummeting temperatures, the skies remained dark and twilight hung in the forest all day. Whether the gobbler saw and recognized me as a man, I don't know. I backed off and called spasmodically for half an hour. Since I got no response of any kind, I left him. Next morning I found him on the same limb. How long he'd been there I have no idea, but I can reasonably assume that he spent at least one day and two nights in that tree.

The food supply of a wild flock usually determines where you'll find it. The flock may range one type of terrain in the spring and an entirely different type in the fall and winter. There seems to be no limit to what a turkey will eat, as long as it's small enough to swallow. The turkey diet includes hundreds of kinds of spiders and insects as well as the larvae of many of these, plus snails, salamanders, crabs, crayfish, frogs, worms, and snakes. The bird also forages on grass, plant leaves, clover, buds, wild fruits, berries, ferns, flowers, and seeds of almost every kind. A turkey will venture into agricultural lands to help harvest such man-made crops as corn, wheat, cowpeas, soybeans, and peanuts. Where the bird is under management, strips or small fields of chufa, peas, and rye are often planted specifically for the turkey in some open corner of the woods.

Where you'll find turkeys at any season is where one or many of these foods is most abundant. In the spring, you might locate a turkey in a creek or river swamp or bottomland where he grazes on patches of tender young grass, scratches for grubs and worms, and picks up such tidbits as crawfish and salamanders along a water course. Or if the acorn crop was heavy the fall before, he might be up on the hillside trying to uncover some acorns left over from the winter.

In the fall, a turkey is sure to spend part of his time under the more productive oak trees. You know he's been there when you find the carpet of leaves literally torn to shreds, especially around the bases of the trees. Where one or more birds range hopefully through the woods, trying to pick up some of the endless variety of autumn seeds, such as beech, pine, grape, and cherry, the wide V-scratches will point like an arrow in the direction in which they feed. If the sign is fresh enough, there's always a chance that you can circle and get ahead of a gobbler or a flock.

By knowing the food habits of the turkey in your territory and where he is most likely to find the best buffet at any season, you give yourself quite an advantage.

The question most frequently asked by a turkey hunter making his first try for one of the big birds must certainly be, "How can I tell a gobbler from a hen?"

To a veteran turkey hunter, telling the difference is as easy as distinguishing between a naked man and a naked woman. The hen and gobbler are almost that far apart in appearance—though not necessarily for the same reason.

You can hardly make a mistake when you see a turkey strut and hear it gobble, but the curtain goes up and comes down on this show at only certain hours of the day. Identification becomes a bit more difficult in poor light or when you get only a glimpse of the bird. Another difficult time is when a turkey sets your blood pressure soaring by suddenly materializing before your eyes, so close you wonder whether it's an apparition or the real thing.

The hen is a smaller bird, normally no more than two-thirds the size of a full-grown gobbler. But when you don't have the two together to make this comparison, they all look as tall as an ostrich. The head of a bird is perhaps your most certain means of identification, and many times this is about all you can see. The hen's head is small, bluish gray, and covered with feathers. Dr. John W. Aldrich describes it in more technical terms: "Head and anterior portion of neck bare, except for a sparse covering of small dusky-tipped white downy feathers from which rise small black hairlike bristles. A band of small chestnut-tipped fuscous feathers forms a continuation of body plumage up back of neck to crown of head."

The gobbler's head is broader and appears to me flatter on top. Except for short, scattered black bristles that are hardly noticeable, the head is bare above the lower neck and adorned with fleshy wattles that hang down from the throat or chin to the feather line, and with a carbuncle (a warty projection) on top of the head. There is also a thin, pencil-like attachment of flesh near the upper edge of the bill. The color of the head and of these appendages ranges from a bluish gray in winter to a bluish white during breeding season. Sometimes the hue seems to me to be even lighter, with a sort of yellowish cast. This color is normal until the gobbler becomes excited by the mating ritual or is ready to tackle another gobbler encroaching on his territory. Then the head color turns a crimson red.

I've called up long-bearded toms with my gobbling box, and they came in so angry and determined to whip the trespasser that their heads looked as though they had been dipped in red ink.

A turkey that has a beard is probably a male, but not definitely. Many old hens grow beards, although these beards are generally smaller and more stringy than the tassel of hairs hanging below the throat of a gobbler. A few times I've seen novice hunters come in with bearded females—an honest mistake.

Earl Groves, one of the top turkey hunters I know, says that, from a distance, a hen seems squatty compared to a gobbler. Her tail seems almost to touch the ground. She stands and walks with her head at a much lower angle than that of a gobbler's. His legs are longer, his tail has more clearance, and he stands much more erect.

It's obvious that as a male turkey grows older, his beard grows longer and his spurs become longer and sharper. The beard of a first-year gobbler is a short, blunt tuft, and his spurs little more than knobs. The spurs on a four- or five-year-old are long, keen, and sometimes almost as sharp on the ends as a thorn. Spurs rarely exceed 1½ inches.

There's a lot of discussion among hunters about turkey beards. A very good one measures 11 or 12 inches. News of one longer than that may raise an eyebrow or two. I've never taken one longer than 13 inches, but have seen and measured others that exceeded 12 inches. The longest I ever saw was a fraction under 17 inches. As the years passed, and I became more acquainted with turkeys, I began to doubt my eyes, measurement, and memory. So I wrote to my friend Tom Howard, with whom I covered a sizable portion of Georgia's big Altamaha Swamp over many years, looking for turkeys, deer, squirrels, and other critters. Here is Tom's reply:

"To the best of my memory, I traced a beard of the length you describe to a hunter friend of mine, the late Henry Parker of Ludowici. Herman Parker, who lives near me, substantiated the fact that Henry killed one somewhere between the Old Camp and the Hickory Tree Old Field, that had a beard which measured 17 inches long. He said the gobbler only weighed 12 pounds and was so old that you could hold all of his feathers in a double handful."

And so—more raised eyebrows and more discussion. Well, anyway, it's good exercise.

There's no doubt that the back country in which the wild turkey gobbler lives, his uncanny sense of survival, and his almost unbelievable powers of sight and hearing make him one of the most prized trophies on this continent. Though no authority has ever looked through the live eye of a turkey, authorities seem to agree that, compared to man, the wild gobbler has about eight-power vision. Considering this, you might want to try a simple experiment: look at the woods around you with your naked eye, and then through a pair of 8X binoculars. Now you'll understand why a gobbler can see so much better than you. It's also remarkable how far he can hear your softest yelps and clucks.

About the only survival faculty you can't credit this bird with is a sense of smell. One of my mountain friends was convinced that a gobbler could smell as well as a deer or a boar. The man wouldn't even smoke before breakfast when he was going out for turkeys. I asked another mountain man his opinion, and he snorted.

"If a gobbler had a sense of smell to go along with his ears and eyes," he said, "nobody would ever kill one."

Add to the gobbler's physical characteristics his habitat, which I think helps make him our most fascinating game bird.

One of the first things a man who has never hunted turkeys would probably like to know is where to find them. Worded more technically, the question might be: What kind of habitat do they prefer?

All species I've encountered, and especially those with which I'm most familiar, prefer forest land or territory that borders on forest land.

The gobbler and his family are birds of the woods. They may range away from the woods to feed in open pasture, grain fields, planted patches, or the scrub, but they run or fly for cover as soon as danger threatens. They also go to the woods when they are ready to find a roosting place for the night.

I learned some of my first lessons in turkey hunting about half a century ago in the Savannah River Swamps below Augusta, Georgia. The people who were supposed to know claimed that this wilderness region, because it was a perfect habitat, had carried over one of the original wild strains of birds, unmixed with domestic stock. Many localities lay claim to original turkey strains, and no doubt some of these are truly so blessed. If so, they were probably rediscovered in pockets such as the Savannah River Swamps, known to few but the local citizens.

There, in those swamps, I got acquainted with the wild turkey on his home grounds for the first time. Perhaps that's one reason I thought then—and still think—that these turkeys were the cagiest and spookiest birds I could ever meet.

At that time, the Savannah River Swamps were primal wilderness—one of the most beautiful and isolated places close to my home. It was a land of long, curving lakes that had once been the run of the river but were sealed off at both ends when floods clogged the course of the stream and it cut a new course. Its forest was largely an open, virgin stand of oak, hickory, ash, poplar, and other tall species. The forest floor was generally clean but here and there was splotched with higher "islands" of dense underbrush.

The swamp was a game paradise that had deer, turkeys, squirrels, raccoons, and rabbits. Wood ducks lived there year-round, and flocks of mallards and other ducks spent the winter months in the area as well.

Occasionally we took a deer and some lesser game out of the drowned wilderness in season, but our most highly prized quarry was the turkey. My hero in those days was Barney Smith, who taught me at least some of the tricks of turkey hunting. Barney was a rugged and deeply tanned individual, and he spent many a night in the swamp not far from where he had heard gobblers and hens fly up to roost. When he hunted, part of his camouflage was the dark swamp mud. He rubbed it on his face and hands to blend with the natural colors of the lowland forest. I like to think that Barney's mud pack was the forerunner of the grease paint some turkey hunters and bow hunters use today.

I must admit that I did not learn my lessons very well. I am sure I concealed myself from the turkeys artfully enough, and I used enough mud to start a fair-size brickyard. But apparently my calling left a lot to be desired. The only turkey I ever killed in the swamp was a bird some fisherman or bootlegger flushed. It just happened to fly over me.

This swamp was typical of many Southern creek and river bottomlands I have hunted since those early days. Portions of the great Altamaha Swamp were one such area. Before it was logged over two or three decades ago, a man could lose himself in the dark interior, where he might encounter a turkey almost anywhere. In many places the towering trees, their branches woven into an almost solid canopy, would shut out all but scattered shafts of sunlight. This twilight shaded out the lesser vegetation, except the mossy carpet, leaving long vistas visible through the columns of tree trunks. Sand ridges angling into the swamp forest were choked with palmetto clumps and scrub-oak thickets sporting titi and lesser vegetation, much of which furnished acorns and other mast for the wild denizens. The turkeys also ranged out of the big swamp and up the creek and branch heads, which were crowded with magnolia, sweet bay, gum, pine, and many food-producing plants. A few flocks, although not as many, could also be found in the swampland of the Ocmulgee and Oconee rivers and other tributary streams.

Similar swamps throughout the Deep South states from North Carolina to Arkansas and Texas made up some of the last strongholds of the Eastern wild turkey and of the Osceola turkey during those years of decimation before the state game departments took over, got some teeth into the game laws, gave the wild turkeys needed protection, and began to bring them back to some semblance of their former abundance.

As with the swamps, civilization flowed around the rougher mountain ranges. Some of the isolated coves and hollows contained backwoods families that had been there for generations. These wilderness families lived off the land, much as had the Indians before them. Game birds and animals were their main source of meat, but these scattered settlers were never numerous enough to wipe out any of the game species, even though they hunted them in all seasons of the year.

Throughout those years, which ran well into this century, tremendous reaches of mountain wilderness had no families living in them. With no roads, those areas were too isolated for even the "peckerwood" sawmills. These were regions that also helped save the wild turkey from complete extinction. The virgin hardwood forests were ideal turkey range, and they

Habitat like this is where you can expect to find the Osceola (Florida) turkey.

contained one tree species that provided an abundance of food for a host of wild creatures. Even in the 1910s and 1920s, when I was growing up, chestnuts were plentiful in the Southern mountain forests, but the creeping blight left more chestnut-tree skeletons each year.

Typical of this range before the loggers began to peck away at it was the Ocoee region of East Tennessee. Most of it is now established as national forest land, but vast areas have long been devastated by logging operations. Steep hillsides are gashed by roads and washed off into what once were clear, clean trout streams. Hardwood trees too small for lumber are girdled and left to stand as skeletons, their rich crops of fruits and nuts lost forever.

I give thanks that I saw this land before its devastation began. I can remember the still, clear mornings when the voice of a gobbler traveled long distances. I'd stand on a high ridge and listen. If I heard a tom, I'd go to him. If I heard no bird within a reasonable period after their flying-down time, I traveled from ridgetop to ridgetop, clucking, yelping, gobbling my box, and trying to get an answer. I brought back many an old long-beard—and short-beards, too—following this routine.

Most of these isolated mountain regions that helped to save the Eastern wild turkey have since gone down before the logger's saw. They are checkered with highways of the U.S. Forest Service or pulp-and-paper companies. Where the mature timber is removed and smaller hardwoods are left standing, turkeys begin to drift in again and re-establish themselves after a few years. Where the whole terrain has been bulldozed flat and planted to pines, you can write off most species of wild game there.

Throughout the Southern mountainous regions, some of these hardwood pockets have been left undisturbed for one reason or another. Where you find them, you'll usually also find a good population of turkeys.

Most of my turkey-hunting experience has been in the South. And one type of terrain I have hunted with excellent results, in between the vast river swamps and the mountains, is the pine-hardwoods-scrub piedmont area, which usually has winding or narrow creek swamps transecting it. Typical of this type of woodland, which you'll find almost throughout the range of the Eastern turkey, is one section that embraces a number of middle-east Georgia counties. Dempsey Cape, an old hunting partner, and I have hunted one of these counties each season for years. It has become a sort of ritual with us.

The region is veined with creek swamps, some of which have been logged in recent years. Pine and hardwood forests grow on the steeper hills that flank the swamps, and behind these hills—on the upper, flatter slopes—a sizable percentage of the country has been converted to pasture and agricultural lands. Turkeys find the pasture grasses a supplement to their wild diet of fruits, seeds, and other food, but the birds seldom venture too far from the heavy forest cover, or away from the creeks and beaver ponds, which for them are safety features. Here the wild birds, with plenty of cover, have adjusted themselves to the encroachment of agriculture.

Typical of such rolling-hills, creek-bottom regions was one I hunted for many years with "Turkey" Johnston and Jimmie Shirley were the old Allison Lumber Company lands in western Alabama. There was no agriculture. Over many years, we found some of the best turkey hunting here. Time and land practices changed that. When the Allisons owned the property, they selectively cut the largest trees to feed their sawmill. Except for the removal of old, ripe hardwoods and pines, the country remained much the same.

The paper company that acquired the Allison holdings embarked on a different program: harvesting all larger hardwoods, bulldozing down and burning the rest, and replanting the vast acreage to pines for its paper mill.

The country below Hayneville, in south-central Alabama, had a different history. Once the center of a cotton empire, it fell before the onslaught of the boll weevil. Cattle came next, and some acreage was converted to pasture. Much of the rest went back to natural hardwoods and pines, with a generous sprinkling of cedars. As with much good Southern turkey terrain, the country was veined with small streams running into larger creeks.

A few years ago Brooks Holleman, a Montgomery businessman, bought a few acres below Mount Willing, leased thousands more acres around it, and embarked on a program of restoring the flocks from a remnant of the wild turkeys that had survived there.

Brooks sank a lot of effort into his project. He cleared and planted food patches all over the area. He eliminated some of the overabundance of opossums, raccoons, and foxes that break up turkey nests, as well as bobcats that prey on the turkeys.

Thanks to these and other assists, and with Brooks's outstanding range,

A Southern inland swamp, seen here early in the season before heavy vegetation has developed, is typical terrain for the Eastern turkey.

the wild-turkey population was brought back until it overflowed the boundaries of his place and became established in much of the surrounding countryside as well. Brook's guests now harvest many dozens of the big birds during gobbling season each spring without harming his abundance of buck turkeys. Turkey Hollow, as Brooks calls it, is one of the most attractive piedmont ranges I have ever seen for the big birds, and almost every knowledgeable hunter to Turkey Hollow gets his gobbler.

From swamp to highland, productive Eastern turkey lands are basically the same throughout the South to far beyond the Mississippi River, where the heavily forested regions run out and the character of country begins to change.

Western Oklahoma, for example, where I hunted several seasons with Dwain Bland, has excellent turkey range; but it is vastly different from that in the East. Here another species, the Rio Grande turkey, takes over.

Where Dwain and I hunted, the acreage was about equally divided between grain fields and shin-oak thickets (known as shinnerys, although they might contain a variety of other vegetation).

An amazing number of creeks, wet and dry, cut through this country. In these draws and along the streams, cottonwoods grow as lone trees, or in scattered clumps, and make some of the best roosting sites. The shin-oak hillsides and flats are usually so open that a hunter has no chance of stalking within shotgun range of a bird. Nor is it possible, as a rule, to get close enough to a lone bird or a flock feeding in the grain fields. For this reason, many Oklahomans I met in those days with Dwain hunted with high-powered rifles and counted on long-range shots to bring in the bird. (Hunting turkeys with deer and varmint rifles will be discussed fully in Chapter 13.)

Dwain is one of the fellows who introduced turkey calls and calling to western Oklahoma. If he knew of a good turkey roost, or series of roosts—for the birds often change sleeping trees—he would set up a blind in the vicinity and remain until after the hour of gobbling. If he couldn't get a reply to his yelping or gobbling his box, he'd shift to another of his blinds.

Those Sooner turkeys with which we became acquainted spent the greater part of the day in the shinnerys. On several occasions in the middle of the day, I sat down in the heart of an extensive thicket and called at intervals. Sooner or later a bird came up to investigate. This was usually after I had taken my limit of one gobbler, so I had just as much fun teasing the bird as if I had been serious about putting it on the table.

We found the best places to hunt were those shinnerys bordering a creek or around the edges of the grain fields. Much of the private land in this part of the country is posted, and any hunter is wise to get permission before going on it.

As far as I remember, the first time I ever saw a Merriam's turkey was during a mountain-lion hunt in the Gila Wilderness of New Mexico. The size of the flocks amazed me. One flock we encountered must have con-

Midwestern and Oklahoma landscape such as this is a good bet to harbor the Rio Grande turkey.

Many hunters, when searching for the Rio Grande turkey, use binoculars, as Dwain Bland is doing here.

This stand of Ponderosa pine is one of the places you might expect to find a Merriam's turkey.

tained 100 birds or more. Most of the birds we saw were grazing on open slopes, not too far from forest cover.

Later I hunted the Merriam's in northern New Mexico. There the turkeys are forest birds, just as elsewhere. They range above 5,000 feet, where the pinyons grow and produce an abundance of food. Most of the turkeys we saw were above 7,000 feet in the forests of western yellow pine. The birds may be found from that elevation to timberline. These forests are generally open and are often patched with small parks that have luxuriant stands of grass. The transition zone of the western yellow pine ordinarily contains a number of other fruit and seed-bearing trees, which are prime sources of food for the turkeys.

The wild turkey is mainly a forest bird. He lives in and around its edges where his food is most plentiful. That is where any hunter in unfamiliar territory should concentrate his activity, searching for tracks, droppings, dusting places, and other such signs.

The ability to recognize proper habitat is a considerable asset for any aspiring turkey hunter.

4

How to Prepare for Your Gobbler Hunt

I sat in the saddle of my tractor lawn mower, hurrying through one of those domestic chores that plague the existence of every suburbanite. The motor under me roared like a British tank on its way up the last hundred feet of Mount Everest. To ignore its blast, I was trying to concentrate on the opening of gobbler season a few days away. Suddenly a horrible thought hit me with the impact of a high-brass buckshot load.

I reached for the key and switched off the motor. The sudden dead silence left my eardrums vibrating.

"Why, you damned fool," I said aloud. "If you keep this up, by next week you won't be able to hear a gobbler thunder in your very ear pans."

Here I was, violating one of my own rigid rules on how to get ready for a gobbler hunt. I climbed off the tractor and went inside to my gun room. I picked up a pair of ear muffs, which were given to me by Tom Shanks—a turkey-hunting partner and airline mechanic—to protect my hearing on the target range. Then I returned outside.

With these on, I heard the lawn mower as a purr instead of a blast, and I went about completing my unsavory job in comparative peacefulness. While I guided the mower between trees on the front lawn, I had time to think about the week ahead and to wonder how many hunters ever consider taking such seemingly insignificant precautions ahead of time to ensure a successful gobbler hunt.

In this intensely precise sport of outwitting a cagey old long-beard, the ear is one of the most necessary of your physical senses. Yet most people spend a lifetime abusing their ears. We live in a world of souped-up sonic intrusions. The decibels we get from everyday living include high-frequency radio and TV broadcasts, the horrendous roar of traffic, the din of both jet and prop-driven planes, and the mad beat of so much modern music. All these tend to overwhelm and harden the eardrums long before old age has a chance to take over.

Recently I was with a fellow twenty years my junior. His job takes him daily through the din of a modern machine shop. A few seasons ago he could hear a turkey gobbler almost twice as far as my own ears would reach. Last spring in the woods, I identified sounds that registered not at all with him. I was amazed how so much of his hearing had gone in such a short period.

I have no idea of the physical mechanics involved, or whether the ears can be repaired. But I feel certain that when I go into my period of training for turkey season, my hearing improves. If blaring music erupts in a room, I get out of there as though someone had taken a shot at me. If I must be in a noisy place I can't avoid, I wear small rubber plugs that some swimmers use to keep water out of their ears. These may make conversation a bit difficult at times, but usually a fellow hears more than he wants to, anyway.

I spend as much time as possible in a quiet stretch of woods, far from traffic noises, straining my ears to hear and identify each separate sound. After a few days of this practice, I begin to distinguish movements of small birds and animals and the quiet chirp of insects that I apparently missed at first. This result may be more a matter of concentration than of any actual improvement in my auricular apparatus, but it certainly helps me in my turkey hunting.

Such sessions in the woods also prove beneficial to my eyes. Most people with no hunting experience walk through the fields and forest without seeing anything but trees and grass. If they are ornithologists, they see birds; or they see flowers if flowers are their first love. Yet most wild places are full of movement—the flash of a bird's wing, the darting of a hornet out to inspect the neighborhood around its nest, the twitch of a squirrel's ear as he flattens out on a limb with only his eyes and the tips of his ears visible. Many times there's only a flicker of movement—but often that's all you'll see when an old gobbler comes prowling around, too. Most turkey hunters know enough to look for this almost imperceptible motion. Being able to notice it and guide my action accordingly has helped me bag many an old long-beard.

Training your eyes is a conscious thing. Instead of just looking off through the woods, you learn to concentrate on any unusual motion. Finally, the proficient observer even notes the natural movement of leaves that stir with the breeze, wisps of clouds drifting overhead, and the sparkle of water as it trickles along a tiny rivulet.

If he concentrates on being observant, a man learns over many years to see everything that goes on around him. Most of us, however, tend to notice only what interests us. It may be automobiles, or women's shoes, or the articles of whatever business we're in. This is why it's valuable practice ahead of turkey season to get away from familiar objects and readjust our eyes to the outdoors and the creatures in it.

You can do a number of other exercises to ready yourself for the gobblers. One of these, if you are in a sedentary job, is to strengthen your legs. Some outdoorsmen keep in shape through the winter hunting season by going after deer, quail, pheasants, grouse, and other game that require a lot of walking. But the man chained to his desk by a relentless time clock—including his boss—would do himself a big favor by walking around the block, or many blocks, every night after getting home from work.

Gradually increase the distance until you can walk a fast mile or two without discomfort to your legs or lungs. Turkey hunting aside, it's one of the best things you can do to yourself for your health.

The heart requires exercise just as much as the other muscles in your body. I know a few hunters who jog slowly to keep their heart muscles in shape. They know that once in a while they must run to get close to a gobbler before dawn is bright enough for it to fly down off the roost. Any doctor, however, will warn you not to run a marathon the first time out. He will also suggest a physical examination before you start on any rigorous exercise program. If you are sound, then you may gradually and safely build up your stamina to the level you often need for a long walk or quick action, which could put a strain on unaccustomed legs, lungs, and heart.

One way you can help tighten up those human drumsticks and thighs is to scout out the territory you plan to hunt. This should be one of your preseason exercises. Not only is knowledge of the terrain important, but tracks, droppings, and other signs will often give you a pretty good idea where the big birds are feeding and roosting. If you have firmly in your mind the layout of the land, with its ridges or swamp creeks and sloughs or dense brushy areas, you have a much better chance to find your way in the predawn darkness without getting yourself mired up to your knees in a morass, or having to fight your way through almost impenetrable brush.

One precaution every scattergunner should take before season is to pattern his gun. This applies to the turkey hunter especially. Whatever the barrel length or the bore, is the shot pattern better with No. 6 or No. 4 shot? At what maximum distance is the shot string thick enough to ensure several pellets in the head of a gobbler?

You'll need some shells to find these things out; but, believe me, they won't be wasted. I'll trade a box of shells anytime for a sure chance at a sharp-spurred old tom. I'm sure you would, too.

Square out a number of sheets of brown wrapping paper, 3 feet by 3 feet. Newspaper pages are acceptable in a pinch, but they don't show up the shot holes as well as a smooth brown surface will. Tack up your square sheets; and then from distances of 20, 30, and 40 yards, put in loads of No. 4s and No. 6s, using a separate sheet for each shell. On each sheet, mark the distance and load. You may want to try a target or two at 50 yards if you shoot a 10- or 12-gauge 3-inch magnum that is capable of such a range. Some guns pattern better with one size of shot and some with another.

When I get into my blind, I want to know how far my shot string is lethal. Then I can select the bases of trees at maximum range from where I sit. I'll wait until my bird is well within that range before I pull the trigger. If possible, I want no cripples. Being certain of how effective the pattern is at each range helps me establish my shooting distance in the woods.

If you don't touch your turkey call from one season to the next, you may find your calling technique a little rusty, too. All year long, whenever I think of it, I pick up one of my favorite calls and walk outside to test it. This drives the dog next door crazy, and a few curious jaybirds always come around to see what's going on. But this periodic practice helps keep me acquainted with the various notes of my call, and how to avoid the sour sounds.

If you're new at turkey hunting, your best bet is to select, out of the dozens of calls on the market, one or two from which you can most easily learn sounds reasonably close to those a turkey might make. Buy any one of the several turkey-calling records on the market and try to imitate the clucks, yelps, gobbles, and other notes you hear. Work on this until you are familiar with every note that reflects each particular mood of the turkey. Practice on your call until you can imitate each exactly and know what it means.

You won't become an expert in a day or a week. I know hunters who practice from one season to the next. But the critical time to tune up is in those weeks immediately preceding turkey season.

The more experience a man has at chasing gobblers, the more he is convinced that his equipment plays a large part in helping him be successful. I've missed some birds because I did not pay enough attention in advance to certain details. That's why I now keep a checklist to make sure I won't leave any item behind.

Among other things, my list includes: camouflage clothes (plus spares in case these get wet); boots to fit the type of terrain I will hunt; a 30-inch full-choke Model 12 pump gun with sling (the gun is browned instead of blued, to reflect less light); a small flashlight for predawn travel; light rain gear; bowhunter's camouflage net gloves; a compass (this has brought me out of flat country more than a few times when the day was overcast); a waterproof matchbox; small hand-pruning shears (with which I can make a quick blind); about 2 feet of thin rope (to help me bring my turkey—if any—out of the woods); a small plastic bag for the turkey liver, gizzard, and heart; my turkey calls; a small camera; a shoulder bag (to carry the smaller of these items in); and, of course, my hunting license.

I start going over my list and gathering my gear at least a week before opening day; and I carefully check the working condition of such things as the flashlight, camera, and waterproof matchbox. I look over my list again on the morning of the hunt to make sure I have everything. My friend Doc Bob Hines, from Cleveland, Tennessee, told me that once he had gone into the woods before dawn, heard his turkey gobble, set up a perfect blind—and then discovered he'd left his gun back in camp.

My list of equipment sounds like quite a load, I know, but really it's not. Most of the items are small and don't even crowd the shoulder bag or the space in my pockets.

Another thing you can practice ahead of season is patience, possibly the most valuable asset any turkey hunter can have. In this high-speed world of ours, patience is a virtue that few of us grow up with or ever acquire any more. Until a turkey hunter is shot through with it, though, the chances are that he'll have to put his sights on his Thanksgiving dinner only at the supermarket meat counter.

The turkey, like most other wild creatures, has infinite patience. If he can't quite make up his mind that you are a bona-fide lady love, he'll stand hidden in the brush until your own tail feathers begin to collect calluses from pressing against the ground. The only way you'll ever see him is by having patience to match his.

Since patience is not one of modern man's natural traits, we who go after the long-beards must learn to develop it. When we make a conscious effort at relaxing and waiting without fuming or fretting, a lot of stress magically disappears from our daily lives. Our efforts to simmer down are always easier, too, when we realize that a huge, bronzed gobbler might be its eventual reward.

How do you develop patience when the world goes at such a mad pace? All day long I run into situations that would have me tearing out what few strands of hair are left on my marble pate if I didn't give myself some reason to calm down. Say I'm late for an appointment and get bottled in behind a stalled car, with traffic on both sides so heavy I can't pull into another lane. Or I'm waiting in a doctor's office. I sit there watching people who came into the waiting room much later than I did going in ahead of me. Or I select the shortest line in a bank. All I want is to cash a ten-dollar check. On both sides of me the lines flow past the cashier windows like a precision-drill team. The lady customer in front of me goes through more financial transactions than a minority stockholder and, on top of that, has to tell the cashier all about her brother's hernia operation.

Such occasions always pumped my systolic pressure up beyond the danger mark—until it occurred to me that they were some of the best opportunities I could ever get to train for turkey hunting. Where up to now I had considered those periods of line-waiting as nervous voids between dashing hither and yon in my futile efforts to outrun the rest of the world, I suddenly began to see each one as a step toward conditioning my mind and muscles for the even longer periods of waiting in the woods when moving at all might spoil my chances. With this objective in mind, my frustrations gradually gave way to relaxation—and even amusement—at the human antics that had previously kept me so upset.

If you can turn such stumbling blocks into stepping stones, you've made a giant stride toward relaxed and gracious living. What's more, patience pays off better than any other quality you might have, while you wait for that supreme moment when your feathered trophy stands in front of you. When that happens, you'll know that whatever preparations you've made have all been worthwhile.

5

The Iridescent Ghost

Before he's hatched, a male turkey lies in his shell, thinking up ways to outmaneuver the human hunter. This is a scientific fact to which any gobbler hunter will attest. There is simply no way any wild creature could develop such wariness and ingenuity to cope with what goes on around him unless this awareness had begun to develop in the pre-kindergarten stage.

Before he gets through pecking his way out of the capsule, the half-saturated little fellow pauses from time to time to look behind every bush, studying every leaf for movement by some unsuspected danger. Even before he becomes a fledgling, he is already developing his sense of survival.

A male turkey keeps at this sort of thing as long as he lives. As a poult he learns to flatten out against the gound and disappear before your very eyes, or to blend into a sprig of cover that wouldn't hide a grasshopper.

The longer he lives, the more this ability increases. It's simply incredible how little cover is needed to hide a 20-pound gobbler that stands 3 feet or taller with his neck stretched upward for a look around.

We were hunting quail on an island off the South Carolina coast. The grassy flats and open woods had an abundance of bobwhites that gave us some excellent shooting, both with coveys and with singles. We were told that the island also contained a sizable population of wild turkeys. We'd seen plenty of signs, yet in two days of hunting quail we never encountered one of the big birds until late one afternoon. We had a dozen or more bobs and hens scattered out on a grassy flat. The grass was no more than ankle deep, with widely scattered clumps of very low sedge tufts.

Our two pointers had been working that day as though charmed by some canine fairy princess and we were fast approaching our limit of quail. I was a bit miffed at myself because I'd missed the last two easy, straightaway shots, and when the two pointers came to attention in a completely open stretch of meadow, my hunting partner said with a sly smile, "Try this one. If you miss, I'll back you up."

I refrained from making some dignified reply, like "Go to hell, will you," and we walked in behind one of the pointers that seemed to be certain he was on a quail.

I couldn't have been more startled if an Army bomber had flushed out of the grass right in front of the dog's nose. The gobbler that came off the ground looked *that* big! I was so tense and so ready that I couldn't have stayed my trigger finger if I'd tried. At such close range the shot string almost tore the head off that big tom turkey.

The gobbler weighed about 19 pounds. How it could have remained completely invisible in that ankle-deep grass until we almost stepped on it was a question that had both me and my shooting buddy shaking our heads in disbelief. I didn't think of going back over the ground at the time, but the grassy flat must have contained a shallow depression into which the bird had flattened itself when he first heard us make our appearance on the meadow. There he would have remained and let us hunt on by, if one of the dogs had not caught his scent and pointed. Later I saw a number of old toms pull this very same trick.

Bruce Brady, a Mississippi outdoor partner, relates an experience to show how effectively a gobbler can disappear when it is apparently standing on bare ground.

He and his son, Bruce Junior, were crossing an old roadway through turkey woods. When Bruce started up the far bank of the road, the boy—from a few steps behind him—suddenly hissed at his dad. Bruce Senior froze, then asked in a barely audible whisper, "What is it?"

"Big gobbler," the boy said, "standing in the road."

Bruce held his awkward position and turned his head as slowly as the minute hand on a clock, until he could see for a hundred yards down the roadway. It looked as flat and clean as a stretch of Interstate.

"You've got an imagination," he whispered.

"No, sir!" the lad declared under his breath. "He was there. He didn't run or fly. He just sort of melted into the ground."

Big Bruce's decision came from years of experience with the big birds.

"Don't move. We'll stay here for a little while and see what happens."

His son crouched in a clump of brush where he'd gone down when he'd glimpsed the gobbler, and Bruce remained flattened against the bank, his eyes never leaving the length of roadway below him. For a quarter-hour or more they waited. Bruce was just about deciding that his son had seen an apparition and was tensing his muscles to get to his feet again when a gobbler seemed to materialize out of the earth in the middle of the road, about 75 yards from where he lay.

"I see him," he whispered. "Don't move."

The gobbler stood up slowly, stretched its neck, and looked all around. It remained motionless for long minutes. Then, apparently satisfied that its intruders were gone, that turkey walked slowly into the roadside brush. The two Bruces gave it a few minutes longer, then circled to get in front of it. An hour or more later, it came to Bruce's call.

They went back and examined the road where Bruce Junior had first seen the gobbler. A logging truck must have gone through a soft spot there, leaving a rut no more than 8 or 9 inches deep. That tom turkey had crowded its body into this depression and literally disappeared while young Brady was watching it.

Bill Rae had a variation of that experience when he and I hunted at Brooks Holleman's farm in South Alabama. This was years ago and Bill still refuses to believe it. "Even though I saw it with my own eyes," he says.

In the corner of a wide meadow along the creek, Brooks had planted a rye patch on which his deer and turkeys could graze. Both used it, too, especially in the early spring before the first wild grasses were high enough to become succulent forage.

Brooks built a blind on the woods side of his field, surrounding it with enough cover so that turkeys could approach the patch from any direction, which they usually did. You never knew whether one would come in from the wooded hillside or from the fringe of brush along the creek in front of the blind. A few very small scattered bushes grew in the meadow between the planted patch and creek, and these made up the only cover for a hundred yards.

Brooks and I left Bill in the blind one morning and went off down the creek to find a gobbling turkey. Bill has a lot of patience, even for a Yankee editor, and he remained quiet with only his eyes and ears busy, shifting his weight occasionally to relieve the numbness that crept into his posterior padding where the ground had poked at it too long.

Not until midmorning did he see a turkey. He admitted it was possible that one might have come up noiselessly behind him, then retreated when he moved to shift his weight. The gobbler he first saw was approaching across the open meadow from the creek. It came warily, as turkeys do, stopping every few yards to listen and to examine the premises with an eye that apparently missed nothing.

The tom was standing near one of the thin, scraggly bushes when something in or around the field caught his attention. Bill didn't believe he had moved, though he said he might possibly have blinked an eye. The bird made a step or two and went out of sight behind the bush, though that bush didn't seem large or thick enough to hide a jaybird. Bill estimated that the gobbler was almost within range of his shot string and decided he'd try it when the tom made another two or three steps toward him. He put his gun against his shoulder and waited. After a few minutes when his arms began to shake under the strain, he put it down. The gobbler had not appeared.

Bill sat for more than an hour, concentrating on that bush. The field was open all around it and he could see the meadow beyond it all the way to the creek. Brooks and I found him thus transfixed when we came up on his blind from behind, after a long examination of the field and fringes around it to make certain no turkeys were in sight.

When Bill heard our footsteps close by, he whispered without turning his head, "Sh-h-h! There's a gobbler over there, right behind that sprig of bush."

"Which bush?"

He pointed it out. "He just walked behind it and never came out."

"How long ago was that?"

"More than an hour ago."

Brooks and I exchanged glances.

"He's probably on the other side of Wolf Creek by now," Brooks opined.

"There's no way he could have left that bush without me seeing him," Bill insisted.

He stepped out of the blind and we walked out to the sprig of bush. Bill kept his gun ready, as though he expected the gobbler to take to the air any second, but the field around us was as barren as if no turkey had been there in generations. Bill couldn't believe it. "There just ain't no way!" he kept saying to himself.

It did seem to be an impossible feat, even for a wise old gobbler, but I've seen them pull many such maneuvers that are not in the books. This must be one of the tricks a turkey conceives while he's still curled up inside his eggshell. More times than the number of hairs on my head—well, more than that because these days I'm getting to look a little like Kojak from the hat brim up—I've seen a gobbler step behind a tree or bush . . . and disappear. Once he has that body out of sight and out of danger, he turns and keeps the tree trunk behind him and runs straight away, as though the very devil were on his tail and jabbing at him with a pitchfork.

Any turkey can move along a depression so shallow that you hardly understand how even a packrat could get by without being seen. Probably the most striking example I've had of this habit took place in the Ocoee Management Area of Tennessee, where I've been after gobblers for more than three decades.

I once told the following story to illustrate an entirely different point. It appeared in another book originally listed as *The Outdoor Observer,* but later revised and titled *The Outdoor Eye.* Forgive me for repeating it here, but it seems entirely appropriate.

Most of the gobblers in isolated regions such as Ocoee have virtually the same routine. It seldom varies. If all conditions are right, a tom will gobble on the roost, maybe several times. He wants the hens within hearing to know the vicinity in which he plans to operate. After he hits the ground, he keeps on gobbling until one or more hens cozy up to him, or his ardor either cools or carries him under the sights of a hunter's gun. Whether or not he trades satisfaction with one or more of the hens, he usually shuts down his gobbling about midmorning, loses his interest in sex, and begins to take on vittles.

A tom may satisfy every desire, but he never loses his curiosity. At any time of day, he may answer a yelp or cluck—especially if he's alone. Both toms and hens are very gregarious characters. Many veteran turkey hunters I know spend the entire day in a blind, calling now and then to attract any gobbler that comes by or happens to feed within the sound of a yelper.

I've stuck out a few full mornings in a blind. But as much as I preach about patience, I've never had enough of the stuff myself to keep me there for a full day. I remember one morning when I remained rooted until time to gulp down my noon sandwich. Then I grew restless. I had heard nothing that even remotely resembled a turkey, and my every bone and muscle ached from long contact with the ground. The flies had eaten me once and were going over me a second time for dessert. So I decided to wander and look for fresh scratching and other signs that might help me locate a gobbler the next morning.

The rest of the day was ahead of me, and I was in no hurry. I made my way from one high cove to another, stopping on most of the backbones of the ridges to relax in a cool breeze and work my yelper, hoping for an answer. One of these spots seemed so pleasant that (after I'd tried a few tentative notes) I put my cedar box into my shoulder bag and just sat back to enjoy the shade and the breeze.

When, after an hour, the log I was on began to grow a new assemblage of knots, I picked up my gun and went prospecting for some more territory. I was on my way into a narrow cove at the base of the ridge when my eye caught a movement near a decaying treetop not more than 25 yards away.

It could have been a packrat, a towhee, a squirrel—almost any creature. I stood still, trying to see it a second time. The floor of the cove was so clean around the tree I could have seen anything that moved away from the mass of limbs. Whatever had caught my attention had to be still there. I walked over for a closer look.

I've never been any more startled than I was then when wings roared on the crest of a little knoll to my left. I swung just in time to get a glimpse of a big gobbler pitching over the contour. He was gone before I had even thought to bring my gun around.

I was even more surprised when I investigated that ground thoroughly and finally figured out what had happened. A depression no more than 12 inches deep ran down that knoll to the treetop. No vegetation of any kind grew around it. The gobbler had flattened himself into the shallow ditch and—to stay out of sight—must have gone up that gully like a snake. I just didn't see how that was possible—but he did. When I reached a point where I could have seen him had I not been watching the treetop so intently, he took a chance and flew over the crest.

A gobbler will pull all sorts of such stunts, and every man who has hunted tom turkeys over a period of years has his own list of experiences in which he was outwitted by one of the iridescent ghosts. Any turkey hunter will tell you about those times, too, if you're willing to sit down and listen and not keep interrupting to regale him with similar experiences of your own. Every turkey hunter I know finds as much enjoyment in telling about the one that got away as he does in recounting his successes. Somehow a gobbler chaser takes special pride in the wisdom of an old tom that's smarter than he is.

Brooks Holleman told me about two large gobblers he once saw feeding along the bank of a ditch that ran through one of his open fields. The ditch was deep enough for him to crouch slightly, walk up it, and yet remain out of sight all the way to where he could stand up and get a shot at the gobblers, which were on the north bank.

He tried to crawl to the open lower end of the ditch without being observed by the birds. Just before Brooks reached the point where he could duck completely out of sight, first one turkey and then the other stopped feeding and put his head up. Brooks lay still until the birds went back to grazing again, convinced that they were not afraid but just being cautious.

In a crouching position, Brook moved up the cut as fast as possible. Then, just at the point where he knew the turkeys should be, he stopped and very slowly raised his head until only his camouflage cap and eyes showed through the tall grass that grew along the edge of the ditch bank.

He couldn't seen them, but he knew they were very close. One of the turkeys gave a questioning *putt* in a low voice. Holleman strained his eyes, trying to find them. The bird putted again, and this time the sound came from a little farther away. Brooks let his eyes range the meadow and examine every clump of grass in detail. Not a living creature seemed to be in sight.

Seconds passed and the bird made another note—not an alarmed *phutt!* but one more inquisitive than the others, as though the gobbler were not quite certain what the movement at the edge of the ditch had been.

It suddenly dawned on our veteran turkey hunter that the two birds had completely outfoxed him. Slowly he swung from his scouting of the field north of the ditch and looked behind him. While he was stalking up the ditch, the gobblers had pitched over the narrow opening through the field, reached the south side, and were now walking unhurriedly toward a wooded creek nearby. They were just at the outer edge of his shotgun range, so he wouldn't take a chance on wounding one or both. Brooks crouched there helplessly and watched them walk out of sight.

"Those birds changed directions on me," he said, "and I'll bet my last load of No. 6s it wasn't by accident. When they spotted me before I entered the ditch, they were grazing toward the hill. When I got there, they were headed for the creek swamp, like they knew exactly what I was going to do."

A gobbler counts a lot on his ability to remain motionless, whether or not he is concealed. Maybe he learned that from the gyrations of hunters he has spotted in blinds or elsewhere who attempt to hide when they are afflicted with the fidgets as though they had fleas. He seems to know instinctively that movement attracts the eye.

Once in North Florida's piney woods, I watched a gobbler that had no idea he was being spied on. He was feeding in vegetation that grew about as high as his shoulders, if he'd had any shoulders.

That gobbler would scratch and peck at something on the ground, then straighten up until only his neck and head were visible. After a long look around, he'd scratch and peck again.

A farm wagon came down the woods road that ran within a few yards of where the gobbler was feeding. He kept his head up, listening to the sounds of the wagon and the driver, who was carrying on a conversation with his mule. When they came into sight, the gobbler pulled his head down, probably crouching in the low brush, and remained hidden until the wagon had gone on down the road.

When all was quiet, he went back to feeding again, in the same spot. My bet is that most of us have been close to turkeys any number of times and never knew they were there. We'd have walked past that aforementioned tom on the South Carolina island, probably within yards, if the dogs hadn't smelled and pointed it.

Another example I had of this gobbler trait was in Georgia's Cohutta Mountains, up against the Tennessee line.

Shortly after dawn I heard a gobbler, and as usual I tried to get close to it before the bird flew down off its roost. The woods were open. And though I didn't get as close as I would have liked, I had a feeling that the tom turkey had either seen me or otherwise knew I was there. He'd gobbled just once on the roost. I tried a variety of calls but couldn't get another peep out of him.

I worked at this calling for an hour, with no response. Then it dawned on me that, for some reason, the gobbler I had heard was in no way interested. If I wanted to look at a turkey over the sights of my shotgun that morning, I realized I'd better stir around and try to find a more agreeable bird. There was also a chance that I might get closer to the tom I'd heard on the roost and make him curious enough to investigate my calls.

I left my hastily constructed blind and moved cautiously toward where I thought the turkey might have flown down. Every hundred yards or so I'd stop and go through my usual routine of low cluck, a wait of a few minutes, a louder cluck, another wait, a low yelp, wait, louder yelp, wait, and then a gobble on the box. After a quarter-hour in each place, I'd move again.

I passed within 50 feet of a heavy treetop where a giant oak had been felled by the wind. I remember thinking that it would make an excellent spot for a blind. Thirty or forty yards beyond it, I stopped to call again, leaned my gun against a tree, and reached for the wing-bone call that I carry on a thong around my neck.

I swung around at the explosion of heavy wings, just in time to see a huge gobbler clear the treetops and roar away through the woods toward a mountain slope across the valley. I could only figure that the tom, silent though he had been during the early-morning hours, was also curious and had been on his way to investigate my calls. When I met him on that open forest floor, possibly within gun range if I had seen him, he had ducked into the treetop. He'd crouched there and let me walk close by and on out of the danger zone. Maybe he'd even seen me lean my gun against the tree trunk. Anyhow, at exactly the right moment, he took off for the distant slope.

I could only surmise that this was one of those maneuvers he had conceived years before, while he lay curled up in his shell, waiting to be hatched.

6

Why You Should Not Become a Turkey Hunter

If you are *not* a turkey hunter already, and have read this far without deciding to stow this book away in some dark corner of your library, I have a suggestion. Give it up now and proceed on the placid course of your existence, or the even tenor of your ways—whichever comes first.

If, however, one of your ambitions in life is to be a hunter of gobblers, give the subject some serious thought. You must be dead sure about your goal. For, once you make that decision, you're stuck with it. It's like having a glass eye or a wooden leg.

One of my friends asks: "Well, what the hell is wrong with that? I got both."

No offense meant, pardner. Those don't change a man's character or his personality. Turkey hunting does. It's an addiction more binding than barbital, more tenacious than alcohol—more serious, even, than fishing. People occasionally overcome those afflictions. No one has ever been known to get over the disease of wild-gobbler hunting. There's no help anyplace—not even a Turkey Hunters Anonymous.

The addiction will cost you time and money and alienate those close to you. I can give you the names of a dozen addicts—myself included—whose wives begin to get their hackles up a week before turkey season starts and stay mad until a week after it closes.

You must fully evaluate your present status against such future dire possibilities.

An old Cracker hunter in South Georgia once told me, "I sort of half fooled around with them dag-nabbed birds for a few years, and then one day I decided I was going to take enough time to learn to call a gobbler, no matter what. That decision cost me a house, a farm, a good bank account, a wife, and a family—but I'm now the best danged turkey hunter in this part of the country."

57

He was right proud of his achievement, too, and apparently considered that his gain far outweighed his loss.

Gobbler hunting is more than a habit; it's an obsession. No matter what other vices a man may have, they pale into insignificance when the first bright days of spring roll around and both the tom turkey and tom-turkey hunter begin to get that same wild look in their eyes.

My friend Jim Dean, from up North Carolina way, once told me, "I have one turkey-hunting friend who says that the best two days each year are when the turkey season opens and when it closes.

"By the time it's over," adds Jim, "he's lost 20 pounds and is on the brink of divorce. Of course, I know some folks who might like one or both of these consequences—and turkey hunting is at least a good way to bring them about."

Even before the season opens, the human tom wakes up around 3:00 or 4:00 A.M. He walks outside, looks up at the stars, sniffs out the direction of the wind, and glances at the eastern horizon as if to hurry that first faint glow of daybreak.

A strange excitement percolates through him, and he is fortunate that the men in the white coats don't come along and catch him out at this hour and in this mood.

He belongs to a tenacious breed. Over the twenty-two years that Bill Rae was editor-in-chief of *Outdoor Life,* he and I hunted gobblers almost from one end of the country to the other. We've seen example after example of what the gobbler addiction does to otherwise sane, strong men.

Once, while traveling a mountain road to camp in Tennessee's Ocoee Management Area, we stopped to give a lift to a couple of walking gunners. When we paused to let them out at their parked car, I noticed that the vehicle bore an Ohio license plate.

"You fellows are a long way from home," I said.

"We come down here each spring for the turkey hunting," he replied. "In fact, this is our twelfth season."

"Got this year's gobbler yet?" Bill asked.

The guy grinned.

"Truth is," he said, "neither we nor our two buddies—they're hunting over on the next ridge—have ever killed a turkey. We've talked about giving up the hunting, but there just ain't no way."

That quartet of scattergunners very quickly found a spot in my book of dedicated gobbler hunters.

The man who takes up tom-turkey chasing becomes a hermit of sorts. In season, this guy lives in a world all his own. He is out from long before "can't-see" until long after the rest of the world has gone to bed. Whether he sets up camp, lives in a mechanized camper, or tries to operate out of a motel, his hours are such that he remains out of contact with civilization, except for the all-night restaurants into which he pops for coffee and a hurried snack.

I remember one such trip taken with Glenn Titus, outdoor editor for *The*

At least a few gobbler hunters I know have bagged "trophies" such as this sapling in Bill Rae's hand. When you're following a turkey's head with your gun barrel, you may not notice if the bird walks behind a bush or small tree.

Oklahoma City Oklahoman and Times. We hurtled by automobile through the greater part of the nights from one choice territory to another. We slept in snatches. We ate on the run. After four days of this routine, we arrived back at Glenn's home in Norman long past the time when sensible people had gone to bed.

After a drink and a steak with all the trimmings, we retired to Glenn's study and sat down for an interview around which to build one of his columns. Glenn got out his pen and note pad.

"What," he asked, "do you think of turkey hunting in Oklahoma?"

I remained upright in my chair and kept my eyes open, but they must have been glazed over. All the rest of me was unconscious.

"Er, uh," I said. "What was the question?"

"I'll be damned if I can remember," Glenn said.

We gave it up and went to bed. Suffice to say, we had our interview the next morning.

Bill Rae and I had a similar experience one spring in Oklahoma. We hunted with Dwain Bland of Enid. Dwain is one of the worst turkey addicts I know. We covered a sizable segment on the west side of the Sooner State, grabbing a bite here and there, catching a few winks of sleep whenever we could. A fellow just never had time to get acquainted with a bed.

"You know," Bill said to me after the hunt, "I'd like to come back one day and see this country in the daytime, meet some of the folks here, and maybe go into a store and shop for a postcard and a pair of socks. Not even a dyed-in-the-ringtail coon hunter uses up so much of the nighttime as we do chasing those gobblers."

Oklahomans don't have a corner on that kind of living during turkey season. It's that way everywhere. Dempsey Cape and I spend about half the hours of darkness riding to turkey territory—and the other half riding home again. Then we catch a catnap before repeating the performance once more.

Sometimes it's most difficult to believe what a man will put himself through in order to bag an 18- or 20-pound chunk of meat, the near equivalent of which he could buy over the counter of a supermarket for $10 or $15, depending on where you live and the whims of inflation.

Yet, in spite of the frustrations and disappointments—such as when an old gobbler walks silently up behind you and says *Phutt!* to let you know he has seen your head or hand move and is about to exercise his passport for some other part of the world before you can swing around—and in spite of the sleepless hours, the bugs that chew on your carcass, and other attendant tortures, gobbler hunting still remains one of the most fascinating and rewarding of all outdoor activities.

A few details of the hunt Bill Rae and I made with Dwain Bland may help you decide one way or the other whether you really want to become a gobbler hunter.

At the time, Dwain, when not off somewhere hunting or fishing or guiding hunters, was electrical inspector for the city of Enid, Oklahoma, where he lived. I'd had a most memorable hunt with him the previous year. In fact, I'd been so impressed by the country, its people, and Dwain's ability as a turkey hunter that I'd convinced Bill Rae he should make a spring hunt with me in Oklahoma.

We arrived at the Bland home in Enid the afternoon before season opened and had dinner with Dwain and his family. Then we drove to the western part of the state, where one of Dwain's rancher friends had invited us to try our luck and skill with the big birds.

The Rio Grande turkey had been properly stocked, and it flourished in most of the western-Oklahoma counties. We knew that the state conservation agency maintained, over much of this range, a series of public shooting areas where many of the birds were harvested. A large percentage were bagged on private ranch lands, where hunting was by invitation or permission only.

After leaving Enid far behind, Dwain, Bill, and I launched into what you might call a typical spring gobbler hunt with all the trimmings. We arrived at a motel in the quaint little city of Waynoka, where we had reservations. By the time we had unpacked the car, made plans for the next day, compared the shape, size, tone, pitch, and performance of our various types of yelpers, laid out our hunting clothes, and turned out the lights, the hands on my watch were well past midnight. It seemed like I had just about closed my eyes and taken one deep breath when Dwain began pounding on the door.

"Three o'clock!" he called. "We'll have to hurry."

Anything can happen at this time of day. Dwain was taking a last look around the room when a drunk staggered through the door.

"I been waitin' all night for you to get out," the guy said, "so I'd have a place to sleep."

"You make arrangements with the hotel management?" Dwain asked.

"I will when I get up," he said.

With that, he pulled a bottle of shaving lotion out of his hip pocket, took a swig, and lay down on the bed, still wearing his hat.

Before we drove away from the motel, Dwain woke the owners and reported the drunk. They called the town constable. While we were downing ham and eggs at the local all-night café, the officer came in.

"About ten o'clock last night," the policeman said, grinning, "I drove that same fellow to a crossroads about a mile from his place, which is eight miles out of town. But he must have gotten his wires crossed. Instead of walking home he walked back to town."

The first faint light was showing on the horizon when Dwain, Bill, Dwain's son-in-law Tom Preston, Max Olsen (who had gotten permission for us to hunt one of the ranches), and I scattered out along a creek swamp that flanked a series of low sandhills patched with thickets of shin oak.

Bill hunkered down in a group of trees at the base of a hill, and I picked a spot in a clump of sagebrush across a narrow swale from his blind. The light grew brighter, and gobblers began to serenade us from large cottonwoods along the creek.

From the different locations and tones, I was sure I could distinguish at least a dozen tom turkeys in the narrow swamp. That kind of music makes your hair stand on end. The only disconcerting element at the moment was something chewing lustily on my rear end.

In a turkey blind, you're supposed to remain motionless. But I cautiously looked down. Not seeing any movement that might indicate ants or similar pests, I ran my hand over the seat of my thin camouflage trousers. They were covered with sand spurs (small spiny burs from bur grass), several of which attached themselves to my fingers. When I rolled over slightly to dislodge an especially vicious spur, my sleeve picked up another load of them.

Tom turkeys began to fly down off the roosts, and I tried to forget the burs, which were gouging me in a dozen spots. I yelped on my call, and two birds came into sight, walking directly toward me at such an angle that they would pass well within range of Bill Rae's shotgun. One gobbler stopped to strut, and then both birds moved a few steps nearer Bill.

As camouflaged and well-hidden as Bill and I were, those sharp-eyed birds must have spotted one of us. Suddenly they stopped, and then they stood with their heads up for half a minute. Next they began a slow retreat, making a wide circle that would bring them by us, but beyond shotgun distance.

Just a moment before, I'd cut a quick look in Bill's direction. He was just a shadow among other shadows, but I thought I caught a flash of white. I remarked on this later, and Bill said ruefully, "Yeah, it must have been my hand. I was bringing my gun up as slowly as I could, but in all that repacking this morning at the motel, I forgot the camouflage gloves."

To add to the misery of the sand spurs, one of my legs had gone to sleep. Furthermore, a mixed cloud of mosquitoes and gnats had found me and were taking advantage of the fact that I dared not move. My forehead, the back of my neck, and my hands all felt as if they were on fire.

Though the big gobblers were not yet out of sight, I was on the verge of some active scratching. Then a movement off to the right caught my eye and the head of a buck turkey showed through the brush. He stepped cautiously. Finally he came around a sage clump and into full view.

By its lack of beard I knew the bird was a yearling. I had my mental sights set on a long-bearded tom, so I allowed this one to walk within a dozen short steps of me before I barked an alarmed *Phutt!* on my mouth yelper. I had no idea whether he identified me, but he sure got the message. He ducked behind a sagebrush clump. When I saw him again, he was 100 yards away and running.

I went immediately into a series of gyrations, trying to slap off the mosquitoes and gnats, scratch all the spots that itched, and dig out the sand spurs at the same time. Bill left his blind and came across the flat at a fast trot.

When he was close enough to see what was happening, he stopped and burst out laughing.

"I thought you were having a running fit," he said. "But I'll join you. I've been wanting to get at these mosquitoes and sand burs all morning."

We spent the remainder of the day ranging the sandhills, looking for both turkeys and sign, digging out burs every time we sat down, and carrying on a running battle with the gnats. Late in the afternoon, Dwain and Bill passed up a yearling gobbler. After that, we stayed in the woods until 7:10 P.M. which was legal quitting time during Oklahoma's spring season.

During the next three days, we spread out over what seemed like several thousand miles in three western counties. The general pattern was to hunt until dark, drive 30 or 40 miles to a motel, and get a room. That last part was not always easy, for in our turkey-hunting duds and dusty boots, our faces dark with camouflage paint, we could have passed for the "wild bunch" in a shoot-'em-up western.

We would take a quick shower and then set out to find an all-night restaurant, which often meant driving many more miles. Almost before we had time to turn over in bed, the alarm clock would clang and it would be time to get up and hit the turkey trail again.

"I used to stay up all night," Bill said wearily, "but I was a lot younger then—and it wasn't for gobbler hunting."

"We've both come a long way from tom-catting to tom-turkeying," I commented slyly.

"Hey!" Bill said. "What I meant was that I used to work the lobster shift on a Boston newspaper."

During this period of little sleep, we were joined by two U.S. Air Force officers, Colonel Worth Clarke (retired) from Placerville, California, and Captain Don Miller, whose home was in Belleville, Kansas. They had driven to western Oklahoma to hunt with Dwain and Dick Bland. Dick, Dwain's twin brother, was chief electrician at Vance Air Force Base, but he took time off in hunting season to help Dwain as a professional guide.

Both officers bagged fine gobblers, and Don was especially pleased with his big tom since it was his first turkey.

Bill and I missed shots at two gobblers, but they had been spooked and were airborne and climbing out of there as though they'd been cleared for a scheduled flight to the West Coast.

Dwain was a hard taskmaster. He intended for Bill and me to fill out our turkey licenses even if we had to roost with the birds, who I'm sure got more sleep than we did. When we woke up one morning in the middle of a heavy thunderstorm and downpour, I had the mistaken notion that Dwain might let us catch a few extra winks. But his schedule called for a 3:00 A.M. wake-up, and that was that.

We drove 40 miles over soaked roads, stopped for eggs, toast, and coffee, then just before daylight turned off into a giant mud puddle that was supposed to be a road. My new automobile slid sideways and disappeared up to its bumpers. Not even a four-wheel-drive rig could have gone through that spot.

"This is another thing a gobbler hunter can expect," I lamented.

"Daylight'll be here soon," Dwain said heartlessly. "Let's leave the car and get to that creekbottom. We can get the rancher to pull us out after the hunt."

While we were still inside the car, we went through the contortions of getting into our rain gear. Then we sloshed out of the mud hole and into a wide creekbottom.

"If we hear more than one gobbler, we'll split up," Dwain whispered. "Otherwise, we'll stick together and try to surround a single bird."

As we moved slowly through the swamp in the day's first translucent light, Dwain stopped so suddenly that I bumped into him.

"Listen!" he hissed.

The shower had slackened to a drizzle, and above the patter of water dripping from the trees onto the swamp floor we could make out the faint call of a gobbler. Our guide motioned to Bill and me, and we followed him at a half-trot over the sodden ground. In a low swale he paused.

"Can't get too close," he whispered. "I believe he can hear a yelp from here."

Bill sat down with his back to a tree, and I moved to an old log heap on the opposite side of the swamp. While we waited for the tom to gobble again, I slid the diaphragm yelper into the roof of my mouth just in case I needed to use it, though I intended to let our Oklahoma host do most of the calling.

Dwain is a top hand with any of a dozen kinds of calls, but at that time his favorite was the Turpin yelper developed by Tom Turpin, one of Pennsylvania's most famous old-time turkey hunters. This call is difficult to master, but in the hands of a pro it's one of the most effective. Dwain was a maestro with it.

Dwain sounded the low, plaintive notes of a hen, and the buck turkey answered immediately. After that, our partner was silent until the tom had gobbled a couple more times. Then he clucked so quietly that, though I sat close to him, I could only faintly make out the note. But the gobbler heard, and he made the swamp ring.

We heard him fly down. And then—from when he hit the ground until that moment when he stood tall and handsome a few yards away—this tom put on a show. We first spotted him when he was 100 steps out and walking toward us, his head high. Dwain clucked, and the tom went into a strut, taking short steps, his wings low and his tail fanned out high and colorful.

He came up on Bill's side of the swamp and stepped into an opening in the low brush. This time Bill had his over-and-under cocked and primed. The load of No. 6s in the top barrel of his 12-gauge Winchester Model 101 put the bird down, so the backup load of 2s wasn't needed.

Dwain and I were on our feet simultaneously, sprinting to see what kind of prize Bill had. We found him wearing a wide grin and holding up what our guide judged was a 16-pound tom. I had to chuckle at Bill's reaction.

"Thank goodness," Bill said. "Now I can sleep tomorrow morning. But did you see that second bird fly off when I shot?"

"Sure did," Dwain replied with a grimace. "It was coming from a different angle. If that bird had let out a single peep to tell us he was around, we could have stayed put and let him come in. Turkeys hear thunder and other loud noises in the woods, so a shotgun blast doesn't scare one much."

Then our guide glanced in the direction that the gobbler had flown and said to me, "He went into a little triangular patch of shin oak bordering on that open wheatfield. There's a wide deep area of shinnery beyond the wheat, and he'll head for that. He won't cross the open field, though. He'll go around, either through the woods or along the edge. Find a spot where you can see both sides of the wooded strip bordering the wheat. Then settle down and call. You might have a chance at him."

I made a circle and moved into position behind a big tree, where I could stand and see both sides of the strip. I waited a few minutes and then gave a low call on my mouth yelper. No answer.

I figured that the bird was too far away to hear the softer call, so I took the cedar box out of my shoulder bag and sounded the high-pitched notes of a hen. The gobbler replied almost before my call had died away. After five minutes, I yelped again. When the tom gobbled in answer, he seemed definitely closer.

I dropped the box into my shoulder bag and waited. The bird came on, gobbling frequently, but I could not see him and didn't know whether he was strutting. My first glimpse was of the top of his wattled head above the low brush. Since I was out of his sight behind the tree, I slid my gun into position. When his head showed again through the brush 25 yards away, I was ready.

My tom was a twin of the turkey Bill had just bagged. They were not the trophies we'd hoped for, but Dwain had another hunter booked for the next day and time was running out. Anyway, come Thanksgiving, 16 pounds of wild gobbler would taste a lot better than 16 pounds of anything else.

Those are the moments that make it all worthwhile. They compensate for the sleepless hours, the sand spurs and briers, the mosquitoes and ticks and chiggers, the muscles aching from endless immobile contact with hard and sometimes wet earth. Such times bring you back season after season, morning after morning, to take part in an experience that, for anyone other than a gobbler hunter, might add up to nothing but solid misery.

Did we sleep the next morning? Of course not. Fifteen minutes after I'd downed my bird, the rain begain to pelt down again, and for the rest of the day we had virtually no light for taking pictures. So the next morning, dutifully at 3:00 A.M., we went out with Dwain and his new hunter, just to get some fill-in pictures, especially a shot of a couple of hunters slogging through beautiful Cedar Creek canyon.

In twenty minutes the clouds moved in again, and the rest of the day was just as dark as the one before.

That's turkey hunting too.

7

Fall Turkey Hunting
Is Different

One of the best lessons in fall turkey hunting I ever learned was with Earl Groves and Ben Rogers Lee in western Alabama. In a way, it was typical of many such hunts I've had since. This experience, however, brought out such a wealth of information on fall habitat, signs, turkey habits, calls, and what a hunter might expect in the autumn months that I feel it should be presented as a chapter in this book.

Ben Lee and I were sitting together in the dawn woods. I know that turkey hunting is generally a lone game, but in this instance I wanted to know exactly how a master craftsman went about getting his gobbler in the fall.

Ben didn't move a finger or bat an eye.

"He's right over there—in that direction," he suddenly whispered out of the side of his mouth. "Just beyond the contour of the ridge. Hear him?"

The guy had ears like a bobcat.

"Slide around a little toward me. Put your gun up, and point it to the left of that big pine. He's moving in this direction."

As far as my senses could detect, Ben was just having a wishful dream. The only sounds that registered with me were made by a pair of crows quarreling over something beyond a beaver pond at the base of the ridge. My partner clucked out a couple of coarse, but soft, notes from the diaphragm call in the roof of his mouth. The gobbler out in front of us replied, and this time his inquisitive *Kowlk! Kowlk!* was loud enough to penetrate even my hardening ear pans.

"Don't move," Ben cautioned under his breath.

That's one thing he didn't have to tell me. I'd been close to gobblers and failed before because I'd twisted my head around half an inch to get a better look.

"He's coming on," Ben breathed. "To the left of that pine."

He and I both were inhaling gulps of air as though we'd just run a foot race up the hill. In spite of the gobbler working its way toward us through

67

the autumn woods, in spite of the beauty and drama of the morning, I suddenly felt a brand-new touch of kinship with this guy. He was human. Even he didn't know how many gobblers he had called in for himself and other hunters, and yet here he was panting just like me or any other ordinary citizen. We both knew that when we stopped doing that, we'd give up turkey hunting.

We were in West Alabama on Chilatchee Creek, north of the village of Alberta. The land here, just west of William (Bill) Donnelly Reservoir on the Alabama River, is a wild mosaic of hills and creek swamps, of forest and farm and winding roads that seem to lead nowhere. It contains a high population of wild game, including quail, deer, and turkeys in abundance.

This section of Alabama has a turkey season in the fall as well as one in the spring. The evening before the fall opening, we had moved into a cabin on Earl Groves's farm and set up camp in preparation for a try at the big birds at daylight.

I was with an all-star cast. Earl Groves is a manufacturer, with his home plant in North Carolina, but his heart lives out of doors in such places as duck blinds and turkey woods. He devotes most of his Alabama place to the gobblers and hens and has built several sizable flocks in the magnificent upland hardwood forest that sprawls in a series of ridges and valleys on the back side of his property. Earl is like an Indian in the woods. He misses very little of what goes on around him.

Ben Rogers Lee, in his early thirties, is already a legend in the turkey-hunting world. He has done most of his hunting in the South and East and has won about all there is to win in turkey-calling contests, including a world championship. Since he was seven years old, Ben has lived with the wild-turkey flocks and can speak the turkey language better than I talk Crackerese. Ben comes in as a heavyweight at about 230 pounds, but he goes through the woods with the speed, endurance, and stealth of a panther.

From these two men I hoped to verify the basics of hunting gobblers in the fall, which in some respects bears little resemblance to spring turkey hunting.

The other two members of our party were Lea Lawrence, known to the readers of many magazines through his hunting, fishing, and outdoor stories; and Ralph McDonald, a noted wildlife artist whose paintings are greatly in demand by collectors of fine art. One of the prized paintings in my library-workshop is Ralph's canvas of a magnificent gobbler striding along the edge of a lowland hardwood forest.

That first night in camp, much of our conversation had centered on the basics of fall turkey hunting. When I first became acquainted with the big birds more than half a century ago, I had done all of my hunting in the fall and winter. Then, decades ago, I had shifted my affections to gobbler hunting in the spring. This was my first fall hunt in many years.

The way I picked brains that night should have been embarrassing to me, but those two mentors seemed to enjoy talking about fall gobblers as much as I enjoyed listening.

The first thing I wanted to know was the basic difference between spring and fall hunting.

"We'll start out," Ben said, "by saying that the greatest challenge of all hunting—and this includes all game species—is bagging an old gobbler in the fall season."

"In the spring," Earl said, "the driving force in a gobbler's life is sex. Then the hunting comes down to a test of skill between you and him. You must convince him you're a hen, and with his strut and gobble he tries to impress on you that he's the boss and it's your duty to come to him. Since you can't make such a trip, you have to sell him on reversing the usual procedure and coming to find you.

"In the fall, though, it's a different story. Instead of one bird, you've got a whole bunch to deal with. Then you must take advantage of the gregarious nature of turkeys. They stay together in flocks, so one is unlikely to leave his flock and come to your lone call. About the only way you can get one of the birds within range is to bust up a flock and then sit right there and wait. When they begin to call to get together again, you join in the conversation until one comes looking for you."

"How long before they start getting together again?" I asked.

"That depends," Ben put in. "Where they haven't been molested, young gobblers and hens may start calling within ten or fifteen minutes. Usually wise old gobblers stay separated for hours before they try to find one another. Where they were heavily hunted, I've flushed old long-beards at ten or eleven in the morning and waited the rest of the day without ever hearing them say anything, except perhaps a cluck or two. Maybe they go to roost in separate locations and don't regroup until the next day."

"The best hour of the day to flush a flock of turkeys is just before or just after they fly up to roost," Earl said. "If you hear them fly up, they are usually close enough for you to get to them pretty quick. Run under them, making as much commotion as possible, even shooting your gun, but not at a turkey since there's less than one chance out of ten in killing a bird this way. All this commotion will scare hell out of them, and they'll fly off in all directions.

"The individual turkeys don't have time to reassemble before dark and often roost in separate parts of the forest. Apparently one of the first things a lone bird thinks of at flying-down time in the fall is joining the other members of its flock. This is the best time of day to call one to you."

"If you don't hear them go to roost," I said, "how do you go about finding a flock to flush during the day?"

Earl grinned.

"Ben and I will show you in the next few days, plus some other things that make fall and spring hunting two different ball games. We could sit up all night talking about it. Right now I suggest we crawl into the sack. Ben and I scattered a drove of gobblers late in the afternoon. We want to be on that spot before daylight, and that's not too far off."

He never spoke truer words. I crawled into my sleeping bag and closed my eyes. The next instant, it seemed, someone was building a pot of coffee in the kitchen.

An hour later I was following Earl through the predawn blackness. We skirted the rim of an old field and cut into an even blacker tunnel that I had to guess was a woods road. A few minutes later we stepped out of the road and felt our way downhill for a hundred yards. Earl pointed to the base of a large tree, and I assumed this was the spot where he wanted me to park my fanny. Then he disappeared in the darkness to my right.

Since I had no idea whether I might be sitting under a tree full of turkeys, I dared not make the motions necessary to build a blind, which normally I would if I knew more about the setup. But this was Earl's party, and I had no intention of spoiling it.

The night before, Ben had given me a face mask he had developed and was marketing along with calls and other turkey-hunting equipment of his own design. This mask fitted snugly around the top of my head, under my cap. Made of camouflage netting, the mask has built-in openings for the eyes, and these were constructed in such a way that I could fit my glasses over the outside of the mask.

Gradually, light seeped into the hillside woods. I strained my ears to hear the purr of a thrasher. In Southern latitudes this is usually the first sound of the day, and a signal for the awakening chorus of dawn. Soon after that, the turkeys begin to talk to one another in low tones before they leave the roost.

A cardinal added its voice. This was followed by the sleepy *churrr* of a squirrel down in the hollow, and the forest came to life. The first indication that turkeys were near was the barely audible cluck of a hen. The night before, our two mentors had told us that normally in November the flocks were composed either of old gobblers, or were mixed (hens and young toms). Later in the season, the hens and jakes split up into separate groups. So I had to surmise that Earl and Ben had scattered a mixed group.

A second hen called before Earl answered with a low cluck. This brought the raspy note of a gobbler, farther up on the hill, causing me to wonder about this strange assortment of sizes and sexes.

Somewhere I heard a turkey fly down, and then another bird left its perch and flew into the top of a pine tree about 50 yards down the hill from where I sat. The foliage in the top of the pine was too thick and the morning not yet quite bright enough for me to identify the bird as a hen or gobbler. Some minutes later it moved to another limb in the pine, and I guessed the bird was looking for a hen where it had heard Earl cluck. The next move in this normal sequence was for the bird to fly to the ground between Earl and me, where one of us would get a shot. But after five minutes the turkey left the tree and flew off in another direction.

I was still puzzling over this when Earl, who had been lower and to my right when he called, came down the hill behind me.

"Guess I made a goof," he said. "I saw that bird light in the tree in front of you. I couldn't quite make out what it was. I took my eyes off it for a minute and heard the bird fly. When I looked back, I couldn't see it any more, so I figured it was gone. I heard some turkeys go into a little feed patch I planted up on the hill. I got up to go around them and try to run them toward you. When I moved, a big gobbler flew out of that pine and went the other way."

"It appears," I commented, "that you've got all kinds of turkeys in that flock."

"It was actually two flocks," Earl said. "We scattered some big gobblers and were saving them for you, but they must have gotten together again before night. Then the hens and young toms moved in and roosted close to them. I guess our best bet is to find and scatter another bunch."

Thus began three of the most fascinating days I'd had in a long time, revolving as they did around gobbler hunting in the fall.

That first day Earl and I covered a sizable percentage of his property on the north side of Chilatchee Creek. It was heavily wooded upland of mature hardwood and pine trees, sprawled over ridges and hollows with little creeks streaking through them.

If I hadn't already known Earl was a veteran turkey hunter, I'd have been convinced of it after one hour with him in the woods. He moved slowly and cautiously, not missing a trick as far as I could see. We talked in sign language, whispering only when words were necessary. Turkeys have sharp ears as well as telescopic eyes.

"Usually turkeys range different territory in the fall," Earl had told me earlier. "Where you find them at any time of year depends on the abundance of food and on safety. Since the turkey is a gallinaceous bird, most of his food is taken from or close to the ground. His diet includes a great variety of plant and animal matter but leans heavily towards vegetables. In the spring, his dinner includes grasses, insects, worms and snails—and he has also been known to make a meal of quail eggs, baby quail, or young snakes. Often you'll find him in a swamp or some other lowland spot where such food is most plentiful.

"In the fall, the turkey is likely to range where he can find late fruits, acorns, beechnuts, blackgum, wild cherry, grape, and other seeds. But he won't pass up other foods either. He has been known to swallow hickory nuts whole and grind them down in his gizzard."

Earl and I came upon a group of oak trees where the ground was almost bare and torn to bits.

"The acorns," he whispered, "fall out of a tree to the ground around its base. The gobbler feeds on them. He finds worms and grubs there, too. He'll keep the young birds beat off that spot. You'll find their scratches around almost anywhere, but it's paper plate stuff."

Where you see sign such as this, you know turkeys are in the area.

The large round droppings under the tree were those of old gobblers. Neither these nor the scratchings were fresh.

We'd had a chance to compare these droppings with those of the hens and young birds, which leave slender curlicues. These are generally little and long, shaped like a horseshoe. Those left by a young gobbler are about .4 of an inch in diameter; those of the old bird about .6 of an inch.

One of the best signs are the tracks. The older a gobbler grows, the bigger and thicker his toes become, though his track may not get any bigger. It may even be smaller because he walks more on his toes than on the balls of his feet. Young gobblers have long, keen toes.

Usually the best place to find turkey tracks is where the ground is bare and soft. Such places are likely to be recently cultivated fields, sandbars, the muddy borders of sloughs, or the edges of old roads, especially when they are sandy or muddy. Look in these places, and walk the roads. If the tracks are old, keep searching for fresh ones. Unless a gobbler is unduly molested, he usually doesn't travel too far.

Examine the ground under groups of large tall trees. You may find droppings and loose feathers that indicate roost sites. Turkeys have preferred roosting places. They won't come back every night, but they will use these places frequently.

"It helps a lot," said Ben, "to know their habits. A lot of big gobblers often establish a pattern, like following an old logging road or cattle trail, or maybe they'll feed in planted fields at certain times of the day. If you can figure out his routine, sometimes all you have to do is sit and wait.

"I think most turkeys feed in circles," he continued. "When I was a lot younger, I remember one flock that I hunted all the time. Every Thursday I could count on their being at the same oak tree. I wouldn't see them at this spot any other day during the week.

"Now turkeys up North may travel 3 or 4 miles, and one that carried a telemeter was recorded as going as far away as 7 miles. Down here they have so much food that they may not move much more than a mile. And young turkeys that are undisturbed often don't range more than half a mile during a whole season.

"But no matter how far they travel or what kind of fall routine they follow, you've still got to find where they're using. That's why scouting out an area in advance is one requisite of fall hunting."

After you find fresh scratching, tracks, or droppings and know the turkeys are in the vicinity, what's the next move?

I pointed out to my mentors that, long years ago, I hunted fall turkeys in the swamps of both the Savannah and the Altamaha rivers in southern Georgia. When we found signs where a bunch of turkeys had been feeding and these were fresh enough, we'd make a big circle and try to get ahead of them. Then we'd sit down in a blind and call, hoping the flock would consider the swamp safe where the calls were being made and feed in that direction, even though it meant varying their route a little.

"Sometimes they'll do just that," Earl agreed. "One, perhaps more curious than the rest, may break off from the others and walk over to investigate. And often when he does this, the others will feed along behind him."

Ben said that when he finds very fresh scratchings, he works along behind them, stopping every 150 to 200 yards to call and hope for an answering cluck to tell him where the birds are. He stays in that spot for fifteen or twenty minutes before he moves on.

"If I can find some real fresh scratchings," said Ben, "I know the birds have been there and I'll work that general area. When I first find the sign, I pick out a good spot, sit down, and give a long, lost yelp. Then I listen. If I can just get one to answer, and he's far enough away, I ease in that direction and call again. If I can get close enough to hear the birds talking among themselves and decide which way they are moving, then I try to get around and ahead of them and wait until they're close enough so that I can scatter the bunch."

"Sometimes," put in Earl, "you can hear the scratching and tell by that which way they are moving. I like to fall hunt on a dry, still day. A windy day is the worst for any kind of hunting. A wet day is excellent for getting around the woods, but you can't hear turkeys scratching, so you can't as easily tell which way they are going when the leaves are soaked."

Twice during the day we watched hens and jakes feed by at a distance. We didn't bother them. We were after old long-beards. Not until late afternoon did we see any of the big gobblers.

Just before flying-up time, Earl cut through the woods to peep into a rye patch at the end of a woods road. The turkeys grazing there saw him first—which turkeys more than often do—and ran out of the patch into the trees. Earl charged across the rye field in an attempt to flush them, but they disappeared into the brush.

"I never did hear them fly," he said, "so I guess they're roosting somewhere close. You and Ben may be able to find them in the morning."

I spent the second day with Ben Lee in a drizzle of rain. Before daylight we built a blind around the base of an ancient oak several hundred yards below the patch where Earl had spooked but not flushed the gobblers.

"It's difficult to work them as a flock," Ben commented, "but we'll give it a try."

The soaked forest was slow in waking up, and the gobblers lingered on the roost beyond the normal flying-down time. From the conversation they carried on with one another and with Ben, he counted five gobblers in the trees along a small branch below where we sat.

"We didn't come far enough downhill," he whispered.

The turkeys came off the roost and grouped below us. They continued to chat with my hunting partner and for half an hour remained in the same location, as if undecided which direction they wanted to feed.

"They're going the other way," Ben finally said. "Let's move. You circle right and try to get above them. I'll go to the left. If you see the birds, run toward them and shoot into the air so they'll scatter. If you hear me hoot like an owl, come to me without wasting any time."

I worked my way through a thicket toward the head of the little branch, but I hadn't gone a hundred yards before I heard Ben shoot. Moments later he hooted, and I ran toward him through a tangle of cat briers. My rain suit was thin fishing gear, and the spines on those briers literally tore it off me.

"I was hoping the gobblers would flush back over you when I shot," Ben said when I reached him. "But they flew that way. We'll follow, sit down for a while, yelp, and hope to get one on his way back to where I ran them up."

We made ourselves comfortable and listened for an hour before Ben made his first call. It was answered immediately by the raspy yelp of an old gobbler. My systolic pressure jumped a few notches, but Ben turned his head toward me and grinned.

"That ain't anybody but old Earl. He's up on the hill yonder. He may be working something. We'll wait a while and see."

Another hour went by with both men calling periodically, but without any response from a gobbler. Then we walked up the slope to where Earl and Lea Lawrence had made a stand.

"We had hens all around us," Earl said, "and a couple of young toms that came almost within range. Ralph is up on the hill above us. Those old gobblers you flushed didn't scatter. They flew together across the beaver pond at the base of this ridge."

Ben and I hunted the remainder of the afternoon in the rain. For me it was a rewarding day, for I continued to gather more information on hunting in the fall than I'd ever known, even back in those decades when I'd been a dedicated chaser after gobblers during the autumn and winter months.

One of the most fascinating differences between fall and spring hunting is in the calls and calling techniques. You don't make the same notes in fall hunting to call up a gobbler that you make in the spring. When the early flowers are underfoot and the tree buds are bursting, when romance is in the gentle wind and warming shafts of sunlight, a gobbler's ear is keen for the dulcet notes of a hen. Those are what you must give him if you expect to get his attention. In the spring, it's love he's after. In the fall, companionship comes to the fore. The lone tom now seeks out other males.

"The old philosophy," said Ben, "that a turkey yelps just three times or five times, or however many, is just a bunch of bull. Not a one of them's got a college education, and they can't count."

After the day with Ben and a session back in camp that evening with both Ben and Earl, my tape recorder working overtime all the while, I was ready to step up to a podium somewhere and accept my Master of Woodsmanship Degree in the art of turkey calling. Here are some of the more relevant highlights, then, left mostly in the words of the fine men who passed on their knowledge and storehouse of stories to me:

In the spring, you yelp with a fast rhythm and cadence. In the fall it's more drawn out, just now and then like he was calling in a barrel somewhere and is uninterested. If you heard an old dog way off—*Yowlk—yowlk—yowlk*—well, that's how an old gobbler sounds.

Old gobblers don't do a lot of calling. They do a little coarse clucking, and occasionally in the fall they'll give a short gobble that is not full volume. Often an old bird will sort of work it in with his yelps, like *cut-cut-cut-obble, cut-cut-cut.*

The best policy in fall hunting is that you should start making the same sounds the turkeys make. Do this, and you're gonna be in with them. No matter if it's young turkeys—when you hear one start *kee-keeing*, then you start *kee-keeing.* If they *cluck,* you *cluck.* If they yelp coarse, you yelp coarse. Those are the best calls you can count on in the fall.

In the South, turkeys don't gobble much in the fall. Now, up North, they gobble like crazy. We think the pure strain of wild turkey does less gobbling. And that's in the spring and fall.

(At this point I asked Ben to name some of the fall calls he likes best.)
I'd say (Ben explained) that one fall call is the lost call of a hen. I don't like to go through this call without adding a little something to it, like a sort of cackle built into the yelps. If you try it, don't be afraid of making a mistake. Turkeys make mistakes. Just blend the off note in with your calling and forget about it. The philosophy of "Aw, hell, I let my caller slip—I might as well get up and go home" is a crock. If you let it slip and then stop, it's a detectable mistake. The turkeys and everybody else will recognize it. But if you blend it in so that it's just one more sound a turkey makes, it's normal and natural.

A fellow doesn't have to be good on a turkey call to kill gobblers, but it's hard to overestimate the importance of the rhythm.

One morning I went turkey hunting with a fellow down by the side of a growed-up pasture. There were cedar flats with openings in them, and it was an ideal place for the birds to fly to out of their roost trees.

Just as we got about halfway down the pasture and found a cross fence with lighter-wood posts and rusty barbed wire, a turkey gobbled over across the patch. He sounded about 250 yards away. We had to get past that fence to be near enough to set ourselves up in business. When my partner pushed down a strand of barbed wire for me to crawl through, it went *kyalk!* That damn turkey just gobbled its head off. I said, "Do that again, three or four times." So he kept his foot on the fence and pumped it up and down. The wire moving through the staple went *kyalk-kyalk-kyalk-kyalk!*

That turkey double-gobbled, twice, one right on top of the other. We sat down within ten steps of that fence, under a leaning cedar tree, and the gobbler walked just as straight to us as he could come. I never clucked, yelped, or made another sound.

The rusty barbed wire in that staple made a yelp just like a hen, or at least the gobbler thought it did. It wasn't a good yelp, but it must have sounded to him just like something he wanted.

In the fall I like to do the cluck and then run it down, like: *Cluck. Yawk-yawk-yawk-yawk-yawk-yawk-yawk-yawk-yawk-yawk-yawk*, getting a little higher in pitch all the time, then hit it with a couple of *putt-putts*, then *yawk-yawk-yawk-yawk* again. All that is, is a lost call. You just run it up and break it off, with whatever rhythm you need. It's the worst sounding thing in the world. You might think it's a feisty dog barking—real coarse. But you listen to the rhythm of it, and when he does it again, the rhythm is going to fall the same way. To be a good turkey caller, no matter what kind of call it is, you can be successful if you get that rhythm down.

I like the *kee-kee* run, but this generally is for calling young turkeys. Now for an old gobbler, I like the coarse cluck, and three or four deep yelps. On occasions you'll hear an old turkey *kee-kee*, but it's so darned low that most people won't know what it is. It's really not a *kee-kee* but more a deeper whistle. I've never heard it but a few times in my life. But when I did, I repeated it—and looked at a turkey.

One of my partners heard it and would have sworn it was a hen. But he gave it right back, and a 19½-pound gobbler walked up. Old turkeys do whistle, but it's rare.

Now what I like to do in the spring is a whine—*cut-burrrr, cut-cut-burrrr, cut-cut-burrr-burrr*. When an old gobbler makes it, it's real shrill, high-pitched, and he sounds like he wants to gobble.

There's also the cackle. (Here Ben gave us a demonstration of the cackle. There is no way to put it into words. It's a different, broken rhythm and cadence, which might possibly be described in musical notes, but I doubt even that.)

Most callers call too loud. There's no way to estimate how good a turkey can hear, but it can hear so much better than any of us that it's unbelievable. He can pinpoint the tree you are sitting beside and knows exactly where you are. Most people yelp so loud that he walks up to within 65 or 70 yards and stands there and starts looking, and says *Cutt?* sort of sharp, as if to say, "Well? Where are you?"

When he does that, say something. If you know how to reply, real low, *putt, putt,* he'll just keep on walking in. If you don't know much about turkeys, you may think, when he makes that sharp *Cutt?* that he's scared, but he ain't. And if you can make any kind of soft call at all, he'll come on to you. But if you yelp real loud, that turkey is gonna walk up just so far, and stand there, and look, and look, and look. And if he don't see a hen, he'll walk off again in almost any direction. If I'm using a diaphragm call and am in such a situation that I can sort of turn my head without him catching me at it, I yelp away from him—or I put a box between my legs and sort of muffle the sound. That keeps him coming.

Every experienced turkey hunter will carry more than one call into the woods. Mr. M. L. Lynch, who manufactured the famous Lynch box, always had several calls with him. He figured that if a turkey had been called up once with a box, he remembered it. If you changed over to a slate call, or wingbone, or almost any other type unfamiliar to him, he wouldn't be so spooky.

One of the most unusual turkey sounds has been aptly described as the "wildcat" call. It is made only by an old gobbler that has been separated from his companions. It is a weird, high-pitched whine that doesn't sound at all like a turkey, but more like a wild animal.

You are more likely to hear this in the fall, after you have busted up a flock of old gobblers late in the day or when for any other reason they become separated and go to roost in separate locations. It's a sort of CB system of communication between the birds, one that helps keep them in touch while they are apart.

You'll hear the wildcat call late in the evening and sometimes early the next morning. Often you can promote it by making this sound on your own diaphragm call, or wingbone, or whatever. It is not a call for bringing in a bird. If you can get an answer, it merely establishes the location of a roosting gobbler out of touch with his buddies. Your next step is to get as close as possible to the tom, and woo him with more orthodox notes.

Late the next afternoon we five separated to listen for birds flying up to roost. I went down a winding woods road to where we had flushed the big gobblers earlier in the day. Earl and Lea had also scattered a bunch of hens and young toms in the same area.

I sat out the last hour of daylight, calling occasionally, but getting no response. Having considered flying time over, I got up to leave my spot when I heard the heavy *flop-flop-flop* of wings across a low hollow. I strained my ears at the gathering dusk until I knew roosting time had to be over. Hearing that lone bird was an indication some of the turkeys, at least, were still separated from the flock.

When we got in that night, we found that Ralph McDonald—who had studied, photographed, and pictured on canvas some graphic poses of the wild turkey, but had never yet bagged one—was the first of our party to bring in a big bird.

Ralph had chosen to watch over the corner of a field that bordered the hills and hollows dropping off into the creek bottom. The corner was planted to rye, and tracks and droppings showed that it was a favorite feeding place of both turkeys and deer. Wanting to be prepared for any eventuality, Ralph had packed in both a rifle and shotgun and sat under a large oak at the edge of the field. He pulled some brush up in front of him, leaned against the tree, and went to sleep.

When some instinct woke him, he opened his eyes on eight turkeys about 100 yards away out in the field. They were picking and walking toward him.

"My heart," Ralph said, "was pounding at my throat like it was trying to get out. I kept swallowing, trying to keep it down."

When the birds fed behind a little rise out in the field, Ralph put his gun up. Then it suddenly occurred to him that he hadn't put his face mask on. Earlier, Earl had impressed on us all how important it was to be entirely camouflaged.

"For some strange reason," Ralph said, "I got to thinking about polar bears and how they hunt seals. They put a white paw over their black nose to hide it. So I asked myself, 'Now, what would a polar bear do in a situation such as this?' I had on camouflaged gloves, so I put one hand up to hide my face, leaving the fingers spread so I could see through them."

The birds came over the little rise and walked straight toward Ralph. Four were young gobblers.

"By then," Ralph said, "my heart had left my throat and was trying to get out through my ear drums. But I kept saying to myself, 'You gotta be cool—you gotta be cool.' So I took two or three deep breaths, like I do when I get up to speak. This sort of calmed me down. I picked out what I thought was the biggest gobbler and put my sights on his head. They kept walking and were within about 30 or 35 yards. Then they stopped and began to stare at me. I figured the time had come—so I pulled the trigger."

All of this led up to the third morning, which dawned bright, rainless, and cold. Ralph and Earl had gone off to another part of Earl's forest. Ben, Lea, and I went back to the hollow where I'd heard the turkey fly up the afternoon before. Lea stationed himself at the lower end of the cove, and Ben and I went up the side of the ridge, where we took the time to snip off a few branches and place them around a tree trunk to set up our stand.

Ben's young ears heard the low, awakening cluck of a turkey before mine did.

"Damn!" he said under his breath.

He must have sensed my unasked question.

"A jake turkey," he whispered. "I was hoping for one of the old boys."

His answering cluck was so low that had I been 30 feet away, I'm sure I would not have heard it. But the gobbler did, and he came right back with a *kowk, kowk* loud enough to reach my ears.

"He's on the ground," Ben said after a few minutes, "and just over the contour of the ridge. Better get your gun up."

We sat through a breathless five minutes while the gobbler came on slowly. Then Ben said under his breath, "He sees us. Take him."

I don't know what happened. I had to swing my gun barrel about 6 inches to put the sights on his head. He went down, but it was not a killing shot. The gobbler bounced and was in the air, winging to our right. Ben and I fired so close together that it sounded like a single shot, and the bird collapsed no more than 30 yards away.

In those three days, Ralph, Lea, and I each settled for a young gobbler instead of the old long-beards we had hoped for. More important, though, was the post-graduate course in fall turkey hunting given me by two of the most knowledgeable and delightful woodsmen I had ever met in so many seasons of going after gobblers.

8

Where, How, and Why to Build Blinds

Although it happened too many years ago, when I was still in the kindergarten of whatever education I might have in wild-turkey hunting, I've never forgotten a single mortifying moment.

Lurton (Count) Blassingame, a hunting partner over many years, was on a fall turkey hunt with me near Blakely in the southwest corner of the Cracker State. Unlike the flat Coastal Plain that makes up a sizable part of Georgia, from the fall line to the salt-water marshes, a series of rolling hills extend down the western boundary, all the way into the panhandle of northern Florida.

Claude Howell's plantation, where we were housed in a hunting cabin, lay along the Chattahoochee River and included a section of river swamp bordered by a number of cultivated fields. With its abundant food and cover, the area was natural turkey range. And the birds were there.

Late in the afternoon, we blundered into a flock on its way to roost, and we scattered turkeys in all directions. Before daylight the next morning, we were back on the edge of the swamp, where we'd flushed the birds. Lurton sat down on a hillside that sloped off into the swamp, and I walked on down a cattle trail for another hundred yards. There I found several old treetops piled together from an earlier logging operation.

This spot was what I considered a natural blind. I slithered right down into the middle of it like a snake and made myself comfortable. When daylight came and the scattered turkeys began yelping to one another, I got in on the act. My yelping must have been at least adequate, and this advantage—plus the fact that turkeys usually reassemble at the point where they are flushed—brought the flock together all around me.

Not until that moment did it occur to me that I had made a most grievous error. I had so completely submerged myself in that jam of treetops that not a turkey, as sharp as its eyes were, could see me—but neither could I see a

81

turkey. From the clucks and yelps I heard I figured some of the flock must be within 15 or 20 feet of my burial place. The way things stood, I'd have had about the same chance at them rolled up in a tarpaulin.

Finally, I decided that my only solution was to bust out of those treetops like a jack-in-the-box and maybe get one of those big birds going away. Well, it didn't work quite like that. When I tried to come swiftly to my feet, my gun caught under a limb. I jerked it free and once more started my ascent. Then my coat pocket snagged on the stub of a log, jerking me sideways. I fell against brittle brush and once more lunged upward. This time I broke so many dead limbs I must have sounded like a bulldozer plowing through.

The only glimpse I had was of one turkey flying through the swamp trees 100 yards away. I aimed my gun in that direction and exasperatedly pulled the trigger. Count saved our day by downing a young gobbler that ran up the hill toward him.

That experience should have taught me at least one lesson about blinds—but, of course, it didn't. A number of times since, I have buried myself in vegetation so thick that a gobbler and I couldn't have eye-balled each other from five steps away.

I remember one time I was with Jimmie Shirley in western Alabama. Jimmie had been working with an old gobbler so long that he knew the bird's daily routine. It was never far from the same roosting area. After daylight, it would fly off its perch into a flat that extended along a little creek. For a while the gobbler would strut and gobble there. If no hens showed, he'd work his way up a brushy draw to an oak ridge.

"That," Jimmie said, "is either a smart old buck turkey or one that lives a charmed life."

We were on the spot just at first light. Jimmie showed me the route the tom turkey usually took. Then Jimmie went on up the slope to another gobbler he'd heard a few days before.

When the light was bright enough for me to study my surroundings, I saw that the only cover within a hundred yards of the gobbler's routine route was a small patch of head-high canes. I had no idea how far away the bird might be on the roost. So, with as little motion as possible, I crawled into the thicket. It was only about 30 feet wide, and I intended to worm my way through to the side that faced the swamp and the drain leading to it.

I was only halfway through the canes when the turkey gobbled on its roost. I made my first mistake right then. Instead of scrambling on through the cane patch to the edge, I couldn't resist making a series of soft yelps to tell him where I was. I expected him to remain in his roost tree and gobble at least another time or two before he flew down. Instead, he pitched out of the tree. From the sound of the wings, I figured he had hit the ground only a few yards away from where I lay on my belly.

I was caught flat-footed—or even worse, flat-chested—on the ground. I was in a mass of canes that grew so close together it was impossible for me to move in any direction without shaking their tops like a water buffalo.

Unusual motion of the brush around a gobbler is always a dead giveaway to him that he is not alone. I had no choice but to lie there.

I could see very little of the open swale in front of me, and I really didn't know whether the bird out there was a hen or gobbler until I heard an unmistakable *va-r-o-o-r-r-m!*—the sound a gobbler makes when he forces the air from his lungs at the end of his strut.

The tom turkey moved, and through the tangle I got a glimpse of him as he went into another strut. He wasn't more than 15 yards away. Here I made Mistake No. 2. His fan was toward me, and I figured that while his head was drawn down against his breast I could lift the gun to my shoulder. I'd aim it through the canes and—still in a prone position—I'd take his head off when he lifted it again.

Mother of misguided souls! I should have known better. No matter what position he's in, a wild gobbler that's been under the gun never loses his awareness of what's going on around him. When I moved that gun toward my shoulder, he came out of his strut as though I'd shone a spotlight in his eyes. I got one fleeting look at him, standing erect, head high. That was all. He simply vanished.

Many years and many gobblers later, experience has taught me I should have remained motionless on my face until that wily old buck turkey had moved on up the draw. Then I should have crawled to the edge of the thicket, set myself up, and made an attempt to call him back.

Once I sat behind a huge clump of treetops left from a logging operation and called. A gobbler came in on the other side of the treetops. He couldn't see through the mass of limbs and branches. Neither could I. Both of us lingered there for an hour, trading sweet talk. I waited for him to show on one side or the other. He never did. Finally he went off to where he could hear and see a live hen calling to him from the base of a nearby hill.

As far as I can remember, the only time I ever killed a gobbler when I was too well-hidden happened on Brooks Holleman's Turkey Farm in south-central Alabama. Brooks calls it a "turkey farm," but it's the wildest jumble of wooded hills, creek bottoms, cedar thickets, pasture, and old fields in which a hunter could ever get involved with turkeys. By protection, planting feed patches, and harvesting wisely Brooks has built an excellent population of a pure strain of wild turkeys. They were hunted so much that every gobbler there could have been eligible for a bachelor's degree in the art of survival.

Shortly after daylight, I was following a narrow ditch across one end of an open field when a tom gobbled from his roost in the trees on a slope behind me. He didn't sound too far away, and I knew there wasn't time to get back across the open meadow to his stretch of woods. So I simply jumped into the ditch and crouched down in cold, liquid mud. (What a turkey hunter won't go through!)

From this uncomfortable position, I yelped. The gobbler answered. No bushes grew along the ditch, and the field around it was so open that I didn't dare lift my head above the rim of the ditch. I didn't hear the turkey fly, so apparently he pitched out of his tree and sailed. The next time he gobbled, he was so close he raised the hackles on the nape of my neck. But I couldn't quite pinpoint his direction. I heard him strut and then get quiet, and I knew he must be looking and listening. Then he clucked. His sharp *Klop! Klop! Klop!* carried a puzzled note, like "O.K. Where are you?"—as if he wondered why in all that open expanse he couldn't see the hen that had called to him.

I didn't know how far away he was, but he sure sounded close. There wasn't but one thing to do before he decided that something was wrong, and I did it. I stood up in the ditch, knocking the safety off my gun. He was only yards away, and my sudden appearance so startled him he jumped a foot off the ground with the most unusual turkey squawk I ever heard. Then his feet hit the ground, and this time he took off as though he had every intention of making a trans-Atlantic flight. I led his big white head by only a few inches and toppled him on the meadow.

Normally, being too well-hidden is unwise. Just as bad is not being well-hidden enough. Some very good turkey hunters that I know camouflage themselves well, sit with their backs to a large tree, and depend on being absolutely still. Ben Rogers Lee, whom I discussed in the previous chapter, is one of these hunters.

"In spring hunting," Ben says, "I get as close as I can to a gobbling bird just after daylight, and I don't have time to build a blind. In the fall, I move a lot, either following fresh scratches or trying to get ahead of a drove to flush them. Occasionally when I sit down, I do put up some bushes to break my outline. This is usually after I scatter the turkeys and must wait awhile for them to get together again."

Without realizing it, Ben supported my theory of complete camouflage when he said, "A turkey walking through the woods can see a sardine can at 200 yards. He'll stop and start looking because it's not supposed to be there. He won't walk a step closer. He'll do the same if he spots a reflection on your gun barrel, your face, or anything else strange. These woods are his living room, remember. If you walk into your house and there's a new couch, you're gonna notice it. That bird'll damn sure notice anything different out there in his woods."

Many of my old mountain neighbors in the southern Blue Ridge neither tried to camouflage themselves nor built a blind when they turkey-hunted. They depended altogether on immobility. Being constantly in the sun and wind had darkened their complexions, and the clothes they wore blended well into the mountain background.

George Shuler, my hunting partner for the last forty of his ninety-year span, declared it was a waste of time to "put on them strange-lookin' britches and coat and paint my face like a wild Indian to go turkey hunting. I jest back up agin a tree and set down."

George's face was the color of mahogany, and his clothes could have passed for old sacking. He could sit down and disappear even while you were looking at him.

Build your blind in such a way that you are not buried in vegetation. The idea is for you to be invisible to the sharp eyes of gobblers but still well able to see out.

Phil Stone, one of my contemporaries, went along with George's philosophy on no blinds. Phil's handicap was that his face looked more like human flesh than it did the bark of a walnut tree and his clothes could still pass for clothes. When Phil sat with his back to a tree, there was no way he could take on the appearance of an old stump.

One time Phil almost became converted to camouflage. He and I were hunting on Tennessee's Ocoee Wildlife Management Area in a region known as the Dutch Settlement. Back in 1850 a group of twenty settlers from the Netherlands, Germany, France, and Italy purchased a huge tract of land in the Sylco Mountains and moved in. The settlement endured about half a century before some of its founders passed on and the land once more reverted to wilderness.

This region was one of the top spots for big gobblers. The game-management men had planted several rye patches there, and the tracks and droppings showed that these patches were favorite feeding places for turkeys as well as deer. One morning Phil and I had it all to ourselves.

I made my blind on the brushy tip of a peninsula that ran out into the field, and Phil went to the far corner. There he stopped on an old terrace 5 or 6 feet higher than the field and a narrow alder swamp running along a small stream that skirted the rye patch. A huge poplar tree grew out of the terrace, and my partner sat and leaned against it. He was in the open, with not a sprig of brush to hide him.

Shortly after daylight, a turkey in one of the tall white pines across the creek gobbled. I clucked, but apparently the big bird was too far away to hear. Then I yelped, and he came right back. He gobbled several times on the roost, then flew down beyond Phil's end of the field.

My partner had said he would leave the calling to me. I hadn't heard a peep out of him, but it seemed to be a good setup, and I was elated. If the tom came to investigate my call, he'd have to pass in front of Phil—within range of his shot pattern, I hoped.

The turkey came on. I couldn't see him, but he'd pause now and then to gobble. I knew he was getting nearer. Then suddenly he was silent. My cluck couldn't get an answer. Neither could a series of low yelps. When this happens, a tom is either spooked and going in the other direction or else is on his way in. I waited, every sense alert. After about ten minutes, the turkey gobbled again. I figured he was about 200 yards away, up on the point of the ridge. Two minutes later he gobbled again from farther up the hill.

Phil left his stand and walked to where I sat.

"You'll never believe it." he said.

He'd first seen the gobbler in the alder swamp, about 35 yards away. The bird was working toward the green field. Afraid that his shot string might break up in the alder thicket and only wound the bird, Phil had held his fire, waiting for the tom to step into the rye patch. The gobbler moved slowly through the swamp, stopping here and there to scratch and peck. Less than 10 feet from the edge, suddenly he came to a halt, straightened up, and held his head high for a long half-minute.

Then, almost casually, he went back to picking. The gobbler made a swipe with his big foot and backed up a step to peck at something on the ground. He scratched again and backed up another step. Phil simply sat there, fascinated, as he watched the tom back out of that alder thicket.

There's no doubt in my mind that the old turkey—probably shot at by hunters on many other occasions—was smart enough, after he saw Phil, to know that if he flew or ran while he was so close, he'd get a load of pellets in his tonkus. So he simply backed away from danger. I'd guess, though, that if my hunting companion had raised his gun or made some other quick movement, the bird wouldn't have retreated so gracefully.

At the edge of the alders and beyond range of Phil's gun, the big tom suddenly turned and streaked for the crest of the ridge, where I heard him gobble. Phil could hear him running through the dead, dry leaves.

After that, Phil was convinced that perhaps camouflage wouldn't have been such a bad idea.

My head works slow, and thus it took me a long time to learn that when I ranged the woods—pausing occasionally to cluck or call and hope for an answer—I should always stop near cover into which I could blend myself if I happened to get an answer. Whether in the spring or fall, or whether I traveled on the ridge or in a swamp, I had often been caught so completely out in the open that my lack of woodsmanship must have been embarrassing even to the turkeys.

Often a good way to find the birds at any time of day both spring and fall is by moving as slowly and cautiously as possible through the woods, stopping every hundred or so yards to call. My first note is always a cluck. If a turkey is real close and has not seen me, it will often answer immediately. If I've had no response in about five minutes, I make several soft yelps with whatever call I'm using. Then I wait another five minutes. I'll yelp louder then and listen. On a spring morning, my last call is a gobble. This often gets a reply late in the morning, after the tom turkeys are supposed to be out of their romantic mood and have gone back to feeding.

If I happen to get a response to any of these notes, there's always a chance of stopping right where I am and bringing a curious bird to investigate. I've killed some gobblers by ranging the woods and calling. And I've lost some that answered unexpectedly and so close by while I stood in the open that I had no chance to reach a natural blind where I could sit down, be hidden, and finish the job.

After a while it began to dawn on me that I'd improve my odds if I stopped near a thicket, brush clump, stump, old log, rock outcropping, or any other such natural blind where I could crouch or sit and immediately blend into the surroundings.

Natural blinds are usually a matter of emergency. Man-made blinds fashioned out of natural materials are normally much better. When I have time, and I usually do, I prefer to pick out a suitable spot where I'll be well concealed but can still see any movement for at least 50 yards around me. If the elevation is a little higher than the area in which I expect a gobbler to appear, the extra height gives me a better view.

It's a good idea to take every advantage of the terrain. Once, in Tennessee, after I'd heard a gobbler below me on the same ridge I hunted, I almost set up my blind on top of a contour where the land dropped off sharply to a

When you stop to call in open woods, be sure you're near some sort of natural blind. Then if a gobbler answers you, it's easy to merge into your surroundings, as this hunter has done.

broad flat. The visibility from the contour was a 100 yards or more through open forest. I reasoned that if I were perched on the crest of that contour, blind or no blind, any turkey coming up the slope would have a better chance of seeing me before I saw him. So I changed sites. I backed up the slope about 30 yards above the dropoff and set up quarters around the base of a large tree. This decision proved to be a wise one. The tom that answered my call came on up the ridge. He gobbled while he was still out of sight just under the contour of the hill. I had time, before he appeared, to put my gun in position. When he walked over that rise, he was well within range and I was ready.

Just at daylight, one morning in Mississippi, a tom gobbled on the roost. It was so early that I had time to assess the situation. A little creek with sloping eight-foot banks separated us. On the gobbler's side of the creek, the woods around his roost tree and the brush under it were so thick that the average human eye could not have penetrated more than 20 or 30 feet into them. On my side of the creek, the forest was open, with only scattered brush. I quickly built my blind around the base of an oak about 25 yards from the creek.

When I clucked, the bird gobbled once more on the roost and only once when he hit the ground. I couldn't get another peep out of him. I sat for thirty minutes and was beginning to wonder if I'd called too much, too little or what. Then a tremendous gobbler seemed to materialize right before my eyes. How I had missed seeing him when he came up that sloping creek bank was beyond my comprehension—but he was 20 feet closer and out in the open. He was so close, in fact, that I didn't dare bat an eye.

He went into a strut so silently that he seemed to be an apparition. Then he straightened up and took a couple of steps toward my blind. That gobbler was so much in the open I couldn't move. If he kept coming, I'd eventually have to flush and kill him on the wing before he walked right into my lap. Suddenly he turned at right angles and went behind a large tree. When his eyes were well out of sight, I put up my gun. When he stepped out from behind the tree trunk, I turned him over.

I am sure that it was a combination of luck and experience that caused me to place that blind in exactly the right spot. In the next two hours, I had a chance to test the site further while I waited for my companion to finish his morning hunt and pick me up in his truck. I remained in the blind and continued to call. Two more lone gobblers, at thirty-minute intervals, came looking for me. But I let them go. I already had my bird.

By now you must have realized I'm a firm believer in blinds for turkey hunting. I've had too much experience both with and without them not to be. Blinds are made in a variety of ways and using a variety of materials. Doc Hines spends days before each gobbler season dragging together logs, stumps, old tree tops, and brush to build a number of permanent blinds in various places where he has found much evidence that turkeys were using in the vicinity. He locates his blinds in strategic spots, near known roosting areas, on ridges, around flats, and near feed plots where birds have been seen or heard. Doc constructs his preseason blinds in such a manner that he can sit comfortably and have plenty of room to swing his gun over a wide angle. He kills turkeys from them, too.

"I figure," Doc says, "that if I can hear an old gobbler, he's close enough to hear me. Instead of trying to go where he is, I let him come looking for me. It may take longer that way, but it saves me from chasing all over the mountainside, like I used to. And I bag about as many birds as I always have."

In spite of Doc's preparations, the blind for turkey hunting is almost always a spur-of-the-moment arrangement. A man after gobblers never knows when, where, or how quickly he'll have to set up such a place of concealment. You must know by now that I don't quite go along with the man who simply sits where he is or else backs up against a tree. Regardless of how well camouflaged your body is, including your hands and face, having enough brush to hide you completely or at least to break your outline is always a better idea than sticking out in the open like a bandaged thumb.

Constructing a blind on the ground, no matter what species you are after, follows the same general procedure. After decades of experience, plus a few thousand suggestions and ideas from various of my turkey-hunting partners, I have developed a pattern that allows me to build a blind effectively and efficiently.

To the compass, waterproof matchbox, extra calls, knife, and such I always carry in my shoulder bag, I have added a small pair of hand-pruning shears. With these I can neatly clip small bushes and low limbs from shrubbery and small trees, and arrange them quickly, noiselessly, and with very little motion in a semicircle around the base of the tree I choose. Formerly I did this cutting with a pocketknife. This took longer and caused too much commotion. Using a knife, I usually had to bend the bushes and limbs to make a quick, clean cut.

With hand shears, I can make an angling cut. Then the butt ends of my brush are more easily pushed into the ground. If bushes are already growing where I intend making my blind, I cut only enough to fill the gaps through which a keen eye might spot me. No one ever knows the direction from which a gobbler might approach, so I hide my flanks as well as the way I'm facing.

I make the inner circle of the blind large enough for me to swing my gun in any direction without hitting and shaking one of the artificially placed bushes. At times vegetation growing naturally inside my circle of brush interferes with the movement of my gun, or its top will shake if I happen to touch it, thereby alerting every creature in the woods. Hand pruners are priceless for snipping away such sprigs quickly and noiselessly. Inside that blind you need plenty of room to operate without giving your presence away.

Very little vegetation is required to build a blind, and hunters of any kind of game are usually spread widely over a territory. So cutting a few bushes or lower tree limbs can't conceivably denude a forest. Yet in this land of the shackled and the taxed, there are a few places where cutting limbs or brush

When you must build a blind in a hurry, you appreciate the advantage of small pruning shears over a knife.

for any purpose is prohibited. Obviously, carrying an armload of brush until you need a temporary blind would be rather inconvenient. Some hunters solve this problem by packing along a length of camouflage netting, which can later be draped around the vegetation to serve as a blind. This cloth— usually a yard high—is thin, weighs practically nothing, and can be folded and carried in the game pocket of a hunting coat.

Earl Groves made an interesting observation on this camouflage netting. He says that a turkey does not have good depth perception and that when he looks at the flat surface of the netting, that is as far as his vision goes. Behind the netting, you are practically invisible.

Doc Hines verified this belief. He was behind a wall of netting when several hens walked by, no more than 15 or 20 feet away. On an impulse, Doc waved his hand from behind the netting. The hens paid absolutely no attention, even when he took off his camouflage gloves and made violent motions with his white hands.

As you may well imagine, Doc is a disciple of the camouflage-netting cult.

Ray Redmond, with whom I hunted on the Westervelt Reserve of the Gulf

States Paper Company in western Alabama, carried a blind made of such material. Ray added a smart touch of his own. Every 2 feet along the 10-foot length of netting, he attached a slender 4-foot metal rod. These could easily be pushed into the ground to make an instant blind in a semicircle around the base of a tree.

Indirectly, Ray's blind once cost me a gobbler. Still, any blame for this mishap would have to be mine. I allowed my attention to momentarily stray, something you can't do in gobbler hunting. But the trouble did evolve from a rather peculiar set of circumstances.

One morning Ray and I scouted a lot of country before we heard a gobbler. We had stopped on a dirt road to yelp and listen, as we'd done a hundred times already that morning. This time the yelp was answered immediately by a gobbler down in the hollow. We collapsed off the road into a ditch on the side of the hollow.

"I'll watch the woods," I whispered. "You take him if he comes out in the road below us."

Since the bird would see us instantly if it stepped into the road, Ray unfurled his camouflage netting and quickly set it up by pushing the metal pins into the ground. I lay against the 4-foot bank of the roadside ditch, with my gun pointed toward a narrow opening down through the woods. If the turkey stepped into that little aisle, I had him dead to rights.

A movement caught the corner of my vision, and I took my eyes off the woods for a minute to watch Ray. The wind was whipping at a corner of his netting, and the movement of his hand in holding it had attracted my attention.

When I looked back into the woods, there was the gobbler. He had passed the opening on which I had my gun trained and was in the brush on the other side. He was no more than 10 steps away—I paced it off later.

I didn't have to move the tip of my gun barrel more than a couple of inches to put the front sight on his head. The barrel moved, and he jerked his head down just as I pulled the trigger. At that distance the shot column couldn't have been any larger than my fist, and it must have gone over his head by at least a foot.

The terrified tom took to the air like a jet. He swung in an arc that carried him across the road about 45 yards from where I'd jumped to my feet. My second pattern of pellets got a few feathers, but that was all.

If I could have foreseen this comedy of errors, I'd have sold Ray a ticket to the show. As long as he lived, Ray never again mentioned the incident, but every time he saw me, he'd bust out laughing, even before we shook hands. Gobbler hunters have a strange sense of humor.

A blind on the ground can be comfortable or uncomfortable, depending not only on the spot itself but also on what preparations you make before you sit down. I can remember a number of times when I worked a reluctant gobbler that remained within sight but would not come within range for a long period. I had to sit still, and the blind gradually turned into a torture chamber. Rocks and roots that I hadn't noticed when I sat down eventually began probing at my posterior with fiendish delight as though they were alive.

I've been through this routine so many times that I now always try to make the place as comfortable as possible before sitting down. If the ground slopes away from the base of the tree, I scratch it level with my hands. Unless I do this, every time I shift position even a little, I'll slide downhill. I remove all rocks and sticks, which otherwise will eventually annoy me, even if they do not actually pain me. And I stay away from roots that project above the surface. With my heels, I dig holes that keep the soles of my boots from slipping whenever I draw my knees up under me. This is a comfortable position when I lean against a tree trunk, and my knees serve as a prop for my elbows if I must hold my gun in a shooting position against my shoulder for any length of time.

I also take along a light cushion to make my position against the tree trunk even more tenable. Camouflage cushions are manufactured by a number of companies that make equipment for turkey hunters. Before these appeared on the market, I carried an air pillow. This I could fold flat to carry in the game pocket of my hunting coat. Then I'd blow it up to the desired firmness when I was ready to sit down.

All of this preparation may sound like "softy" stuff, but a guy can pay more attention to his hunting if he's not beset with aches and pains.

There is, of course, no law that says you must *sit* in a blind. I've killed more game birds and animals in this position, but I've also bagged turkeys—as well as deer, ducks, and doves—while I was well concealed but on my feet.

I remember one Rio Grande gobbler that Dwain Bland and I flushed off a roost in Oklahoma. The bird flew toward the end of an open field that bordered the creek swamp around his roost tree. We waited about twenty minutes before we called. The tom answered. After a few minutes, he gobbled from a different location.

"Moving down the edge of that field," Dwain whispered. "If you can get below him and yelp, he'll probably come right to you."

I ran up the swamp for a 100 yards, then turned up a slight rise to the rim of the field. My intention was to sit down in the heavy copse that bordered the open area. But about 20 feet from the field, I came upon a shoulder-high fence. The strands of barbed wire were so tight and close together that there was no way to get past the fence without climbing over. Still, if I did that, the turkey would surely see me. And the brush was so thick that if I sat down at the fence, no part of the field would be visible. So I stood quietly beside a large pine tree at the fence.

I yelped, and the gobbler answered immediately. He was closer than I'd realized. Partially hidden by the tree trunk, I propped my gun on the top strand of wire and waited. The bird appeared, walking slowly, watching. When he was well within range, I put my sights where I was sure he'd become another statistic.

Another time on Wolf Creek in south-central Alabama, I paused in a cedar thicket to cluck. A tom answered under the brow of a hill, so close I had no choice but to put the gun to my shoulder and wait. I was well hidden by the cedar limbs between us. The ground was clean under them. If I had sat down, I would have been on a level with the turkey's eye and clearly exposed. As it was, all he would see were my feet and lower legs.

Standing that way, I held the gun in position for a full ten minutes, which seemed like an hour. My gun barrel was beginning to waver from the strain when the bird at last put its head up over the contour.

I've stood in log jams, honeysuckle thickets, head-high ditches, and brush, waiting for gobblers to work within range. Not all paid off, but the percentage in such situations has been in my favor.

A blind is really an interesting place to be, not only for the help it gives you in hunting turkeys, deer, and other game but also for what you see going on around you while you're sitting still. This is especially true when gobbling hours are over and you're waiting and hoping for a curious bird to appear.

In Alabama during a recent season, I sat for half an afternoon and watched a pair of chickadees dig a hole for a nest in a dead stub no more than 6 feet from where I leaned against a tree. I hadn't even noticed the stub when I sat down. Occasionally one of the birds would come a little closer, to study me with its bright eyes. Apparently assured that I was harmless, it would go back to work on the nest again.

In my blinds I've entertained crows, foxes, snakes, bobcats, and other creatures who came around to investigate calls that I'd made for the ears of a gobbler. In addition to enhancing your hunting, a blind can prove a delightful place for any outdoorsman.

9

Camouflage, Clothing, and Equipment

I settled back against a big red oak, confident I had chosen the perfect spot for my blind. It was atop a relatively flat saddle between two high ridges. My position afforded a good view of the saddle and also of the two bottoms that dropped off on either side. The gobbler I was after strutted and gobbled some 150 yards away on the ridge facing me.

Confidence can be either the worst or most wonderful trait for a turkey hunter to have. This time I was dead certain, and I guess a smile toyed around my lips as I added the last branch or two to my blind. The way I saw things, it was only a matter of time until that old tom would come a-courting and slip across that saddle into easy gun range.

I adjusted the camouflage pad under my bottom until it felt completely comfortable. Experience had taught me years ago that I might have to retain my position for one, two, even three hours before a gobbler finally moved into range. Even the smallest twig can assume gigantic proportions when it prods against your unprotected bottom for several hours. And, in fact, discomfort can provoke even the most experienced hunter into moving too soon.

These movements invariably come at the critical moment and usually manage to ruin the hunt.

I prefer to raise my knees when I am seated against the trunk of a tree. My legs, if they are out-stretched, have a tendency to "go to sleep." My raised right knee makes an excellent rest for the shotgun when I am sure a shot is not too long away. If you misjudge, you may be called upon to hold your gun at your shoulder a long time without moving, which is difficult and usually impossible unless the gun also rests atop your knee.

Always make certain to avoid cramping positions. Never cross your legs.

This time I got down to the business at hand, which—as always—was to convince the old tom that the love of his life waited breathlessly just across the way. We communicated for almost two hours, promising each other wild and wonderful things. As I recall, it was a soft cackle tailing off into a few delicate clucks that finally won his heart and made him commit himself.

When he hushed completely, I knew he was on his way. Slowly I brought my Model 12 up to rest on my right knee. The soft drone of his strut told me he was approaching from slightly to my right.

Moments later, I glimpsed him. It was only a glimpse, but enough to assure me this was a trophy bird. Five minutes later he reappeared, and this time the fiery red of his head had faded to a cold blue. He was on the move, and the shot was only seconds away.

Range to that big pine—20 yards. When he moved behind the trunk I would bring my gun to bear. When he stepped clear of the pine I would claim him.

As he neared the tree I could feel my heart pounding in my neck and temples. I had an almost irrepressible urge to try a snap shot. But no—I must wait for the turkey's head to pass behind the trunk in order to move my shotgun's muzzle those last few inches.

The gobbler's long and heavy beard bobbed slightly with each step he made, and his wattles looked as big as hickory nuts.

Then, just as he reached the trunk of the pine, his head jerked upright.

Phutt! and he disappeared behind the pine and streaked away, deftly managing to keep the trunk between us. Fifty yards out, he rose and flew for the next county.

I sat there stunned. My position had been perfect. I hadn't blinked an eyelash. My blind was excellent—and still that bird had spotted me! I sat there and tried to determine what had spooked my prize. I looked for a shining watchband or a glint of sun on gun metal. Perhaps some natural object simply looked unnatural.

And then I noticed. When my knees were drawn up, my trousers revealed an inch of white athletic sock at the top of each boot. My gobbler had spotted that band of white.

Since that day, I've worn green socks when I'm hunting turkeys. And if my collar is open, you will note I also wear green G.I. T-shirts. Both socks and T-shirts are available at very economical prices at most army-surplus stores.

The importance of proper clothing, camouflage, and equipment to the turkey hunter cannot be overemphasized. Unlike deer and most other big game (and I certainly class the wild turkey as big game), turkeys can detect color. They possess minute nerve cells in their eyes called cones, which register light of various wavelengths. These are in turn interpreted as color.

The vision of a wild turkey is often the subject of much conversation in turkey camp. Many hunters put it on a par with that of wild sheep.

A number of years ago I discussed this subject with an old-time turkey hunter in Kemper County, Mississippi. I think he put it rather well when he drawled, "Most of the whitetail deer I've watched thought ever' man they saw was a stump. But most turkeys I've studied seem to suspect ever' stump is a man—with a shotgun. Deer look, but turkeys see."

To take a wild turkey in the classic manner—that is, by calling him into range and bagging him with a shotgun—mastery in the art of camouflage is essential. It has been said that movement spooks 90 percent of the gobblers. True. But isn't it logical to assume that the better your camouflage, the less likely movement is detected?

What I am referring to here is total camouflage. Simply going out and buying a suit of camouflage clothing is not enough. The pattern of camouflage must be compatible with the landscape you will hunt. Often this color pattern of the forest changes drastically in the course of a single season, especially during the spring. For example, camouflage that has strong greens as its primary colors is most unnatural and quite obvious in the early spring, when trees sport very little green foliage. Camouflage patterns that have brown, tan, gray, and black are better suited for early-spring and late-fall hunts. In most places, dark greens are good choices during the last days of spring gobbling season.

Depending upon the woods I hunt, I will sometimes wear a shirt or jacket of one camouflage pattern and trousers of another, to reduce still further my apparent mass and break my outline. My hat and gloves will be of yet another pattern, if possible.

Nowadays most camouflage garments are of lightweight material, totally unsuited for cold-weather hunting. Cold snaps often occur during the early spring, even in the Deep South. During the fall turkey seasons, cold fronts are usually pushing through one after another. Since the use of hunter-orange material has become so widespread, and in many states is now mandatory in hunting clothes, it has become increasingly difficult to find good cold-weather outfits in camouflage patterns. Still, a number of the more elite mail-order houses offer top-quality duds, though prices may run fairly high.

Many turkey hunters of modest means meet the problem by purchasing extra-large lightweight camouflage outfits and wearing them over their normal cold-weather clothing. Coveralls are especially good for this purpose—but first make certain they are roomy enough not to restrict movement. Some manufacturers make zip-up jackets out of camouflage netting. These can be effectively worn over any type or weight of clothing.

Some avid turkey hunters create their own camouflage patterns, which are suited to their special needs. They buy cans of inexpensive spray paint and rework their store-bought outfits. Khaki or green cloth makes a good basic color. Clothing can then be custom-tailored for camouflage effect.

I've hunted turkeys in the Rockies during early-spring seasons when the woods were still marked by snowbanks here and there. White coveralls and a bed sheet would have served very nicely as camouflage in these hills.

As with all types of cold-weather hunting, the turkey hunter is better off

Even when you're standing in the open woods, you'll be hard to spot if you're dressed to blend with your surroundings.

wearing his clothing in layers so that body heat may be controlled under various conditions. A long hike in down clothing can steam you up quickly. It is nice to be able to peel off a layer and then put it on again when you start to cool down.

Comfort is a primary factor to successful turkey hunting, for the successful hunter must remain motionless. This is difficult enough to do under ideal circumstances. It's impossible when you are cold and shivering.

If you instruct a novice turkey hunter to sit still, he invariably thinks you mean to sit without speaking. Only an experienced hunter or guide is aware of just how many bodily movements are unconsciously made by beginners to the sport.

In my experience, most body movements are set off by the ears and not the eyes. A twig snaps to the left of the blind. Immediately the novice hunter's head whips around. If you watch closely, you will be amazed at the speed with which most people move their heads. A mosquito buzzes near the tyro's ear—and his hand unconsciously swats at the sound.

For these reasons, it is imperative that both face and hands be completely camouflaged. In my opinion this advice applies to beginners and old-timers alike.

I believe that the best of all choices for facial camouflage is grease—or cream, if you will. Most of these creams are offered in tubes like toothpaste and are easily carried. Most suppliers offer green, brown, and black camouflage cream. It is water-soluble and is easily washed away with a little soap and water after the hunt. Some brands contain insect repellent, a decided plus. I prefer the commercial brands over the army-surplus sticks, whose grease is much harder to remove.

With the camouflage creams, you can be as artistic as you please. But it seems to me that big swaths of contrasting color blend better with foliage than do small checks of color. Don't neglect your neck and your ears. If you wear spectacles—especially those with shiny wire frames—be sure to coat these with color as well.

If you had rather not use camogreases, then try a mask of camouflage net similar to the masks worn by the desperadoes of the Old West. These are very effective and have served me well over the years. Make your mask large enough to cover your ears and long enough to hide your neck.

Camouflage headnets are available commercially. They fit over your entire head. These are best worn under a hat, which helps to keep them properly aligned. Unless holes are cut out of the face and removed from the headnet, eyeglass wearers may find that breath (which is trapped behind the net) tends to condense on the lenses.

One headnet now available has plastic spectacle frames with no lenses. These frames are large enough to fit over regular glasses if need be. Plenty of air is admitted to help prevent condensation. Also, since it is secured to the frame, the headnet tends to move with your head. Old headnets (which impaired vision occasionally) were difficult to coordinate with head movements.

The human face seems to shine and all but glow in the woods. Over the years, I have used a wide assortment of things to hide my face. Among these have been actor's make-up, burnt cork, mud, clay, and the juices of various berries, some of which proved damned near impossible to wash off. Luckily, they wore off with the passage of time.

I have always considered head gear of primary importance. Personally, I prefer a camouflage cap with a large visor. Since I must hunt in spectacles, the large bill helps shield my glasses from rain, snow, dew, and other types of moisture. It also helps keep dust and dirt off my glasses and the lenses clean and sharp.

But even if I did not wear glasses, I would still wear a cap with a large bill. When I pull the bill down low on my forehead, my camouflaged face is fully shadowed and thus even more obscure to the keen eye of a sharp-spurred old tom. More important still, the bill is a defense against getting poked in the eye by a sharp twig or branch as I move across country to a gobbling turkey. It is often essential to move far in a short time. These walks are always at a good clip and may even become a jog if time is growing short. Since the vast majority of gobbles are heard very early or late in the day, light conditions are usually poor. The bill of my cap has protected my eyes many times as I hurried to an early-morning conference with His Highness.

Over the years, I have lost a number of my pin feathers on top, so I require a cap with more insulation than you might find comfortable. As a rule, though, choose the lightest cap you can get by with. This is especially true if you wear glasses. Turkey hunting often requires spirited exercise, which generates a good deal of heat about the head. This heat will strike the cool surfaces of your lenses and condense as mist or fog. Glasses that fog up can be a real problem in any season. As you already know, I've had that experience.

I recall one extended hike I made several years back. I was hunting in almost mountainous terrain. It was late in the season, but a cool snap had convinced me to wear my long johns and a down-insulated cap that morning. When the tom gobbled, he must have been a mile away. By the time I had moved into a respectable calling distance of 150 yards, the gobbler had already flown down from his roost tree. I made a lick and a promise at building a blind, and then I hurriedly sat down. I gave a short series of calls and that old tom double-gobbled from less than 100 yards away.

I remember thinking that it was going to be an easy morning. I called again, and he responded from just beyond gun range. It was then that I noticed my glasses were fogging rapidly. I took a chance on moving and quickly flipped up the bill of my cap to allow more heat to escape from my head, but the tactic did little good.

Moments later, my tom thundered again. He sounded as though he was almost standing on my foot, but I couldn't see him. I was afraid to tip my head forward or move a muscle. Soon the tom double-gobbled as he continued searching for the hen he was certain was close at hand. I tried to direct my breath upward with my lower lip in an effort to defog my lenses, but that did no good. Finally, I could stand it no longer. I tipped my head forward and peered over the top of my useless spectacles.

From a scant 20 yards and slightly to my left came a low *pert!* and my bird vanished behind a large huckleberry bush.

Hats and caps are available now with a netlike material in the crown. These are fine for dispersing heat while still offering the protection of a bill or brim.

Remember to look for a camouflage pattern different from the one on your jacket and trousers.

Various types of camouflage gloves are available. Those most often seen are made of a thin netting and are cut large enough to fit the Jolly Green Giant. I find these difficult to keep properly aligned on my hands. They offer no protection from brush or weather. I've torn several pairs off my hands when I tried to walk through the woods.

My personal preference for warm-weather use is a snug-fitting glove of cotton or nylon. In cold weather, olive-drab woolen glove-liners, sold for a couple of bucks or so in Army surplus stores, do nicely. I try to buy camouflage patterns, but I'll settle for most dark colors if need be.

Some hunters I know use camogreases on their hands rather than wearing gloves. If the camogreases contain insect repellents, fine. Otherwise, your hands must be protected by repellent of some type. Since the hands will be exposed and must remain motionless, they are favorite targets for blood-sucking mosquitoes, gnats, no-see-ums, and such—all of which can turn a supposedly exciting and rewarding outdoor adventure into one of the most miserable interludes of your life. Don't forget, too, that many repellents will damage the finish on gun stocks, causing them to soften and gum. Read labels carefully.

Certainly one of the most important pieces of equipment for every turkey hunter is footwear. A well-worn and comfortable pair of boots can carry you a great distance in the course of a day. An ill-fitting pair, particularly those that are too small, can deal you more misery than just about anything else but a bad toothache.

I have a good friend who is an ardent gobbler chaser and an excellent hunter. He has great respect for the hearing of the wild turkey. He also believes the hunter should approach as near the bird as possible before settling down and beginning to call. For these reasons, he often goes into the woods wearing tennis shoes—sneakers, if you will. To be sure, they are dyed a respectable shade of dark green. This fellow moves through the woods like a wraith, and he credits a number of his kills to those tennis shoes.

Could be. But not for me! I wasn't on a turkey hunt, but the only time I have ever been bitten by a poisonous snake was on a warm spring day when I strolled along a wooded trail near my Georgia home. I wore low shoes, and a copperhead I hadn't seen struck me about ankle-high. I'm thankful that the bite wasn't too serious. I soon recovered with no complications.

I don't worry about snakes when I am hunting turkeys, but I don't entirely forget about them either. The boots I prefer all lace up well above the ankles. If I am hunting an area known to be infested to an unusual degree by poisonous snakes, I will wear snake-proof boots, which offer protection over the calves of my legs. I also pay particular attention to where I put my bottom. As the old joke says, a bite there and a man soon finds out who his real friends are.

For sections of the country where water is often encountered during the course of the day, boots with rubber bottoms and leather tops are an excellent choice. These boots are nearly waterproof and will handle shallow marshy areas, small creek branches, and the like and still keep your feet warm and dry. They also have felt-lined insoles, which can be removed at night and dried.

Where water is not too much of a problem, I like leather boots best. If the country is rocky and some climbing may be required, I prefer boots with Vibram soles.

This may sound like nit-picking, but I pay particular attention to the color of my boots, especially the soles. Once several years ago, two pals and I were hunting turkeys along a high ridge in Mississippi's Homochitto National Forest. When we met for lunch, one of my buddies remarked that he had seen me slipping along a ridge next to the one he walked. We were all wearing similar camouflage outfits, so I asked him how he was certain it was me.

"It had to be you," he grinned. "Them yellow boots of yours with those white soles were the first thing I spied."

If my pal could see my boots, so could a watchful gobbler. Since then, when it comes to boots, I stick with green or dark brown.

As any hunter who has a few winters behind him knows, it is impossible to stay put if your feet are cold. You've just got to get moving and stomp some life back into those frozen clod-busters at the end of your legs.

Insulated rubber pacs are surely one of the wonders of modern civilization. When it comes to keeping feet warm, these pacs work. Some call for felt innersoles, others take wool socks, and still others work best with only light cotton socks. But regardless of the manufacturer's recommendations, you should try them out and experiment to discover what works best for you.

It is also a good idea to take along an extra pair of socks. It is surprising how a fluffy, dry pair of socks can revive tired feet around about midday. I prefer very thick socks with cushioned soles.

Weather conditions have a strong effect upon the gobbling activities of wild turkeys. Wildlife specialists seem to agree that the best mornings for gobbling are those that dawn clear and bright after a heavy dew and have little or no wind.

I agree, since these are also the mornings when I feel like gobbling myself to see what I can drum up. But this doesn't mean that turkeys are silent during other kinds of weather. In fact, an old tom, when his ardor rises, is apt to sound off regardless of the weather or anything else.

So do not discount rainy days. Perhaps you should force your worn-out body to leave that warm sack and take to the woods once again. Take along a rainsuit, but choose it wisely. To me, black slicker suits stick out in the woods like sore thumbs. I know there is much in the woods that is black, but a man in a slicker is still patently obvious to my eyes. And I am sure a turkey sees it even better than I do.

Find camouflage rain gear, preferably a two-piece suit. Raincoats and ponchos have always caused my trouser legs to get soaked sooner or later. Also, it is a good rule of thumb to buy the best rain gear that you can afford. Good stuff will keep you dry and will last for a number of years. Cheap rain gear usually does a poor job of keeping out the rain and, what's more, is good for only a part of one season.

I recall one spring day in South Mississippi when Bruce Brady and I stood watching for dawn to come. Thunder groaned and complained in the distance, and clouds tumbled above us. Just at dawn, lightning flashed, a clap of thunder pealed forth, and a turkey gobbled down in the bottom. Bruce insisted I try for him.

That tom gobbled every time it thundered and every time I called. I killed him when the first drops of rain began to patter down. He was a huge old bird with a 12-inch beard. A short time later, and before we had made it back to Bruce's truck, a deluge fell and a tornado flattened a barn a short distance away. A camouflage rainsuit proved mighty welcome that morning.

Innovations in camouflage techniques are innumerable and limited only by the imagination of the hunter. One of the most common practices is to add a little native flora to the hunter's costume. I recall that on one hunt my partner Sonny Stoddard attached to his cap a small forked branch with leaves. The idea worked well enough, and Sonny succeeded in getting his gobbler into gun range without being spotted. However, when he dropped his cheek to the comb of his stock to make the shot, his branch fell forward across his gun and momentarily hid both the sight and the turkey. The bird got away.

Attaching any sort of brush to yourself isn't necessary, provided you have set up a good blind and are otherwise camouflaged. In fact, I find that attached flora only increases the bulk I try to hide. Any movement you might make is exaggerated by the waving about of leafy branches.

You should strive to eliminate all bright and shiny objects from your apparel and equipment. Chrome buckles and buttons on jackets, vests, and straps can be spray-painted a darker color, or they can be taped so as not to reflect light.

The one item of equipment most likely to reveal your presence is also the most vital: your gun. Guns are a great source of reflected light. However, the camouflage grease that is applied to face and hands can also be rubbed onto barrels and stocks. But be sure before applying it that any insect repellent in the grease will not damage the stock finish. Camouflage tape, such as that used by bowhunters to reduce the glare of their bows, can also be used on guns.

In this discussion of camouflage, we have taken a good look at the basic equipment used by most turkey hunters. There is, however, a substantial amount of other paraphernalia considered essential by some hunters. A host of such items is useful and can be thought of as optional. Over the years, though, I have noted that my turkey war bag gets progressively lighter as the season wears along. After many middle-of-the-night breakfasts and nights with little sleep, I find by season's end that my bag contains only a minimum of items.

To carry all my essential stuff, and my accessories as well, I use a shoulder bag. It is made of heavy canvas and has a stout strap. Seems to me I bought it for just a couple of bucks in an army-surplus store years ago. It is olive drab and still serves my purposes well.

In this bag I carry a selection of calls, including boxes, slates, turpins, wingbones, and a plastic case full of mouth callers. If the weather looks threatening, I also toss in some lightweight rain gear.

The bag also holds an extra pair of eyeglasses and occasionally a small pair of binoculars. I take along a small 35mm camera, too.

I am never without that small, inexpensive pair of pruning shears I mentioned earlier with which to clip enough branches to make a blind in half the time it would take with a knife. This speed is important if you must move several times while working a turkey.

I learned long ago that moss doesn't always grow on the north side of trees and that not all rivers flow southward. The sky is sometimes cloudy, too, so I always take along a compass in my bag. My compass is a good one—one that I can and do trust. If I am in unfamiliar country, I always include a topographic map of the area if I can lay my hands on one. Though I enjoy a night in the woods, I prefer not to have it come about unexpectedly.

I have a small flashlight in my bag, too, which helps get me into the woods before dawn and out after dark. Disposable flashlights are now available. They throw a bright enough beam, they are small—about the size of a pack of cigarettes—and they last for a year. They cost only a couple of bucks and are a bargain at that price.

If I need a fire, I have the makings in my bag. I carry a small cylindrical waterproof match container half-filled with kitchen matches and half with birthday-cake candles. The candles last longer than a match and the dripping wax can be used to ignite damp twigs and branches, if need be. This is an emergency store. For general use I carry an inexpensive butane lighter with an adjustable flame.

A pair of leather boot laces can be used in a variety of ways, as can a length of nylon cord. A piece of polyethylene folds into a small package and can be

This hunting jacket has a built-in seat that you can lower as protection against damp or hard ground before you sit down.

easily fashioned into a one-man tent or ground cloth if a shelter is required in an emergency.

Other items I sometimes include are insect repellent, a snake-bite kit, toilet paper, a knife, extra shells, and a small roll of packaging tape, which can be used for an endless number of things.

I have mentioned that I prefer a shoulder bag. Other turkey hunters like small backpacks. Some hunters I know use small packs that strap around the waist and ride at the small of the back or on the hips. All are acceptable. Just pick the one that best suits you.

Folding aluminum stools that have small canvas bags attached are used by some hunters. Sitting on a stool is certainly more comfortable than sitting on the ground. That's the good news. The bad news is that a stool puts you well above ground level, so you need a much higher blind. This requirement can pose a problem when time is short and blind-making materials are scarce. Furthermore, level ground may not be readily at hand for the legs of the stool.

Regular camouflage vests are often convenient for carrying the turkey hunter's goods. And since only a few shotgun shells are needed, the pockets can be used for carrying other equipment as well. At least one firm I know—McMillan's in Carthage, Mississippi—makes a camouflage vest with a hinged seat (padded with foam rubber) on the back. The seat remains up and out of the way for walking, but it swings down to form a comfortable seat when the hunter gets ready to take his stand. Ben Lee of Coffeeville, Alabama, makes a single cushion, lightweight and easily carried by its strap over one's shoulder.

Many hunters use no bags or packs of any type and sometimes make disparaging remarks about my "purse" and its contents. Let them. Many's the morning I've impatiently waited for one of these same guys while he groped about the house in the dark searching first for this piece of equipment here and that bit of equipment there, all the while trying not to wake up "the old lady and the kids."

I check my gear when I return from a hunt, and it stays in my bag. That way it's ready and waiting for the next hunt when I pull my boots on.

10

More Misses Than Kills

Turkey hunters have a combination of qualities that sets them apart from all other kinds of hunters.

They love the deep woods and distant places, but that in itself is not rare. After all, a great many other people seek out the solitudes of the earth.

Turkey hunters prefer to hunt alone, for their mania is a lone game in which the gunner matches his skills and woodsmanship with one of the sharpest creatures in all outdoors. But hunters of many other species go the lone route, too. The man after an old gobbler is first of all different in that he feels a decided sense of accomplishment whoever wins the bout. If he loses, he knows there'll always be another time. In addition, he is the only hunter I know who brags as much about his quarry when it rubs his nose in the dirt as he does about himself when he brings a cagey old tom out of the woods.

Now here's an odd fact. The man who hunts alone has no witnesses, except for maybe a jaybird or a crow or some other wild creature. So only the man himself can reveal what goes on in the woods. He can pull such a stupid blunder that he wants to kick himself over half an acre of ground. By so doing, he misses an opportunity at his gobbler. No one else need ever know the story of his big goof. But do you think he'll keep quiet about it? Not on your life! Around the campfire or cabin stove that night, he tells it just as eagerly as if he'd jumped off the top of a cliff and caught a gobbler on the wing. He's as likely to brag about how some old tom outwitted him as he is to relate a story highlighting his skill and success. To my mind, this quality separates the turkey hunter from every other type of hunter I know.

A gobbler hunter can do at least a hundred things wrong for every precisely correct move he must usually make in order to be successful. (Naturally there are exceptions, such as I will describe in a later chapter.)

I've made my share of wrong moves, as has every turkey hunter. I still make them, and I'm sure I always will.

Most of what I have learned about gobbler hunting over the years came out of an accumulation of such oafish blunders. It took me, for instance, a long time to learn how to walk through the woods. There were times I just couldn't understand why I couldn't get close to a gobbling bird when I was over a sharp contour and knew I was out of sight. I could get only so near—but no nearer. He'd shut up and go away, though the lay of land was such that I knew he hadn't seen me. I finally found out why by watching another fellow.

For years I'd been trying to help Phil Stone kill a gobbler. This just didn't seem to be in the cards for him. He'd come close, but that was all. Once when we were coming over a mountain road to camp after the morning hunt, two huge gobblers strolled calmly across the road in front of our car and stopped on the other side, no more than 20 feet away. Phil's gun was in its case. Mine was on the back seat. I reached for it and handed it to Phil along with a couple of shells.

"Step out, now, and bushwhack one," I said.

"I'll take one any way I can get it," he panted.

When Phil opened the door, the gobblers walked away, up the hill, but still remained close enough to kill with a slingshot. Phil dropped the two shells I had handed him and had to scramble in the leaves for them. Then, watching the turkeys, he tried to shove them backward into the magazine. He was digging at the shells with his fingers when they popped out onto the ground again. By the time Phil got both shells into his gun, the turkeys had walked on slowly, out of range. He shot at them anyway. Both birds pitched off the slope and flew directly over our heads, no more than 50 feet high. Phil watched them go and never did a thing about the second shell in his gun.

But that wasn't the lesson I learned. It came about one morning when I'd had a gobbler answer 150 yards below us on the crest of a ridge. He sounded anxious, and I'd have bet my boots in a cactus patch that we would put that bird in the bag.

"O.K.," I said to Phil. "Now you crouch low and slip down to that old log that will let you cover the little knoll right in front of you. When the gobbler walks up over that, he'll be within range."

Phil did a good job of crouching and getting himself unseen to the log. To help himself sit down, he caught a slender sapling. Its bunched leaves, 20 feet off the ground, shook as violently as if they had been hit by a tiny tempest. All the remainder of the forest around us was motionless.

The tom stopped in the middle of his gobble. When, after much calling, we heard him again, he was on the next ridge and sounded half a mile away.

That scene hit me like a thunderbolt. As long as I could remember, I'd been going up and down slopes, holding on to small trees for support, and shaking their topmost branches—seemingly for the benefit of tom turkeys that had no other way of spotting me. Now, even if I'm falling off the side of a mountain, I'll never grab another bush in turkey woods.

Some of the mistakes by which a hunter fails to bring a gobbler out of the woods are so obvious that you either want to laugh or cry at your own stupidity. Others are not. You think you've put every piece of the pattern in place. But for some reason completely unknown to you that gobbler walks off and leaves you as though you were a discarded relative. It makes you want to get up, run after him, tap him on the shoulder, and say, "Listen, good buddy, I don't want to harm or even annoy you in any way. Just tell me what I did wrong."

Movement is the most common mistake of both tyro and pro, though the tyro is likely to be the one most guilty of this. I can't talk enough about movement at the wrong time in turkey hunting. Over a lifetime, it has cost me more gobblers than any other pestilence I know. I can remember any number of times when the inquiring cluck of a turkey sounded so far away I knew I had time to get my gun in position, or turn my head, or shift my weight. And yet, thanks to my moving, I'd never see the bird or hear it again.

It also took me years to learn that one of the big birds standing just outside your blind may often cluck in such a low voice that you might think the sound came from the next swamp or the next ridge. Whenever you hear a bird cluck, your best bet is to freeze immediately into a camouflaged statue.

Early in the game of calling up gobblers, I did learn one lesson about movement that has been of immense value. I was on one point of a ridge and the gobbler was on the other, about 150 yards away. For two hours I called and he gobbled, but not always in the same spot. He'd walk off down the ridge and sound as though he were almost out of hearing. Then, after a while, he'd return to that piece of real estate where I'd first heard him.

This tom made these round trips twice; the third time I thought to myself, "Well, I'll just outfox you." So I got up and circled under the contour of the ridge to where I'd be close enough to pot him when he came back to his original gobbling ground.

I called, but he didn't answer. I sat there half an hour or more, clucking, yelping low, yelping loud, but without hearing the slightest peep out of the gobbler. I could only assume that he had seen me move, and betaken himself to safer terrain. I was on the verge of leaving to find another turkey when this tom gobbled again—right from the very spot where I had sat and talked with him for two hours. I can only guess that while I stalked him on one side of the ridge, he was stalking me on the other. This was my first lesson in the general truism that when a tom quits gobbling, he's either spooked or on his way to find you.

I say "general truism." Some of my turkey-hunting friends have told me how they've successfully pulled off this stunt of intercepting a bird as I tried to do—but they are real pros at the business and usually know when, how, and where this can be done. Normally a bird will come to that spot where he first heard you. Unless you know exactly what you're doing, it's best to wait him out.

Some gobblers seem to live charmed lives. I remember one old tom from years ago. I'd have bet my Sunday teeth that he would die of old age. I'll still bet them that he did, though it's a different set of teeth now. Some good turkey hunters were after him—guys who knew what they were doing—and every now and then someone would manage to get him under the gun. Whoever was watching over that bird, though, caused the strangest things to happen to any human who got too close to it. That "whoever" must certainly have enjoyed himself hugely as long as that turkey drew breath.

For instance, one fellow had the gobbler within 50 feet—and his gun only snapped. If you've experienced it, you know that's just about the loudest sound you can hear in the woods. The turkey stepped behind a tree and took off afoot as though it were training for the Olympics. The poor guy was so amazed he didn't even think to fire his second barrel. Instead he opened his gun to see if he had forgotten to load it. The shell in the first barrel was there. It had a little dent in the primer, made by the firing pin. He drew back his hand to throw the shell into the swamp, but, on second thought, just as a matter of curiosity put it back into his gun and aimed at a pine limb overhead. On the second try, this same shell blew the limb clear off the tree. The poor guy never went back for another attempt at that gobbler.

"The critter's blessed by the devil," he said. "Who knows? The next time I might end up shooting myself!"

Another fellow did almost just that. He actually shot at the turkey one time, but it was beyond the range of his regular 12-gauge load. He considered carrying a rifle on his next trip, but he finally settled for a 10-gauge magnum.

I was hunting in the same swamp that morning, almost a mile away, when the gun went off. It sounded as if someone had blown up an ammunition dump.

My curiosity finally overwhelmed me. I hadn't heard a turkey anyway, so I made my way up the swamp, looking for bodies on the ground—human or otherwise.

I found my friend sitting on a log, his face with a long gash in it, as though somebody had gone at him with a hand ax. That was proof enough of the strange tale he told.

Just after daylight, he said, he had walked across the creek on a log and was pussyfooting along when he heard a hen cluck. He crouched behind a tree with his gun to his shoulder and braced against the trunk while he looked. Finally he spotted the hen sitting on a limb. He examined all the trees around her for other roosting turkeys. A movement on the ground caught his eye, and the big gobbler stepped out from behind the trunk of a large tree, no more than 30 yards away. It was well within range, so he put the bead where it should have been and pulled the trigger.

Both barrels of his double went off. The force from the double load of 10-gauge magnums kicked the gun upward, knocking it out of his hand. It slammed against the side of his face, conking him flat, and then spun over his head. The gun finally landed in an upright position, its barrels downward into the soft swamp mud.

A turkey hunter dies hard. This one rubbed his eyes, sat up, and glanced again toward the turkeys. They were in the same place, apparently so flabbergasted by the explosion and the antics of something that did not at all resemble their idea of a human that they stood as though transfixed. This hunter, with blood still streaming down his face, retrieved his gun, poked the mud out of the barrels with a stick, and grimly put in two more shells. But this time, when he looked up, the turkeys must have finally recovered from their shock, for they were gone.

Today that hunter sports a scar on his cheek. I've never asked him, but every morning when he looks in the mirror to shave, I'm sure he must remember that encounter.

My one experience with this same charmed gobbler wasn't quite so dramatic. When he gobbled, I built a quick blind out of sight of his roost tree and pulled my camouflage mask down over my face. I'd cut two eye-holes in the netting.

I heard the turkey fly down, and I heard him strut. This was another time my hot breath inside the mask began to fog up my glasses. I continued to sit still, muttering curses under my breath, hoping the white film on my eyepieces would go away. It only got thicker. When that tom gobbled again, he was so close he rattled my ear pans. I'm sure I could have sprung on him like a bobcat and caught him with my hands, but I sat there as completely blind as if some neighbor had temporarily borrowed my eyes.

Under the stress of the moment, I made a wrong move—as I usually do. If I hadn't felt so frustrated, I'd have sat motionless and let the tom walk away, then cleaned my glasses and called him back. Instead, I moved my gloved fingers with what I thought was the slowness of the minute hand on a clock. My thought was to wipe one eyepiece clean of the fog. The tom turkey gave forth with a *phutt! phutt!* right in my ear and by that I knew he'd seen the movement. I snatched off glasses, mask, and cap, but by that time he was gone as completely as if he had never been there at all and I was just waking from some bad dream. If nothing else, that should prove even further my point about always wearing the proper kind of camouflage.

In the life of every turkey hunter there comes a time when he is sure he knows everything there is to know about shooting gobblers. This delusion usually comes after he's downed his first turkey—or perhaps his second or third, if he's a man of rare intelligence. This dream state is especially likely if his successes have all come easily.

But after that—it may be the next season or even years later—the wise hunter begins to realize that the more he learns about turkey hunting, the less he knows.

Apparently some of the more ignorant and stubborn outdoorsmen, like me, never do learn. Time and again, in my fifty years of chasing wild toms, I've come to the honest conviction that I knew all the answers—which, of course, is the ultimate folly.

This deceptive state happened to me again only a few springs ago. Every move I made seemed to be a winning one. I always sat down in the right spot at the right time. My turkey calling was seductive—or the turkeys thought so. Young toms came readily. The long-beards strutted and gobbled out of range awhile, but they too eventually came in, fairly drooling over the prospects of what they thought to be an eager hen. It was a beautiful season. By the time it ended I was certain I had at last mastered the art of taking a tom turkey whenever and wherever I wanted one.

At least, though, I had one grain of sense. As smug as I felt, I didn't brag about it—not to strangers, anyway.

So when the next spring crept in with its first young blush of pastel greens and bejeweled dogwoods in the forest, I had never felt more confident.

"I'll fill the freezer with turkeys this year," I boasted to my wife. "You won't have just one gobbler and have to choose between roasting it for Thanksgiving or Christmas. I'll get you enough wild turkeys for Easter, Mother's Day—even the Fourth of July!"

"Whose turkey farm do you plan to invade?" Kayte asked. She's listened to such wild predictions for many years now, and refuses to be impressed.

Probably you're already ahead of me. Need I even say it? I hadn't had a worse spring-turkey season in twenty years. No matter where I went, what I did, or how, I just couldn't get a gobbler within range. But I discovered some facts I had never learned in all my previous years of turkey hunting. And finally, with the season about runnng out, I did contrive to use one bizarre discovery to bag a gobbler.

Gobbler hunting is a precision game with little room for error. You may get by with a false note in your call, if you follow it immediately with a cluck or yelp that rings true. The turkeys themselves often make weird calls. You may even shift your weight in the blind, from one sitting cheek to the other, as long as a keen-eyed bird is not out there. But few mistakes are allowed by a wise old gobbler.

Circumstances do crop up that you cannot foresee. These, plus some goofs that I thought I was experienced enough to avoid, completely deflated my swollen ego that spring. The one bright spot was that my failures taught me some valuable lessons.

The first series of impressive goofs I made was in Butler County, Alabama, where I had gone to hunt with Tom Shanks and Roscoe Reams. The swamps along Muscle Creek, which runs through Ed Poole's place, and the surrounding wooded hillsides make up some of the best turkey territory. In previous springs I had taken my share of gobblers there.

This time, I seemed to do everything wrong. After three hours one afternoon in a blind without hearing a turkey sound, I laid my gun beside me and leaned back against a big pine to relax my paralyzed muscles. That, of course, was when a gobbler chose to make an inquiring *cluck-cluck* from only a few yards away.

He'd see me if I moved, so I sat perfectly still. He came in sight through the brush, circling to go beyond a large tree 30 feet away. Once he stepped behind that tree trunk I'd have plenty of time to snatch my gun and put the sights where his head would be when he walked into the open again.

It didn't work that way. A few steps before the gobbler reached the tree, he turned and came directly toward me. I must have been pretty well camouflaged, for he walked within 10 feet. We were eyeball to eyeball a few seconds while I sat stupidly, as though I expected him to walk into the blind and lie down in front of me.

The gobbler moved first. With a startled *phutt,* he ducked into the brush. I caught up the gun and staggered to my feet on legs rubbery from long inactivity. By the time I got stabilized, the big bird was 75 yards away, flying behind a thick clump of limbs.

The next morning I was in a blind just as the sun came up. I'd heard no gobbler, and I was waiting for Tom and Roscoe to come back from a little creek valley where they'd gone before daylight. Now and then I'd yelped my call. I was even a bit surprised when I finally got a response from a young gobbler so late in the morning.

I remained immobile while the tom worked closer. I'd had no glimpse of him and was sure he hadn't seen me. But suddenly he gave a startled *yowk* and flapped his wings a couple of times. Then he *phutt-phutt-phutted* down the hill as he scooted away.

I was still feeling puzzled when Roscoe and Tom came back. They stopped at the edge of my thicket and Tom laughed.

"Boy! Not even a jaybird would come near you like that."

"What's wrong?" I asked.

"Come over here where I'm standing."

We changed places. He sat in the blind and held my gun as I had done when the tom walked up. The broad receiver surface caught the sunlight and reflected it into my face like a mirror. It's a wonder that tom turkey hadn't fainted from sheer fright.

The bluing had worn off the shotgun's receiver so gradually over the years that I hadn't noticed. Back in camp, we covered that part of the gun with black electrician's tape. After the season, I had my gunsmith "brown" the gun, a process akin to bluing but one that provides better camouflage. In fact, it's preferred by many turkey hunters and waterfowl hunters.

Another of my mistakes that season I made on an afternoon hunt, when there was a threat of rain and more than a threat of mosquitoes. Life on the edge of the creek swamp where I sat was at low ebb. Roscoe and Bill McKinnon, a young hunter he had in tow, had gone up the swamp and were somewhere beyond me. I built a blind, sat down, and called for a couple of hours without attracting the attention of any critter except more mosquitoes, who had apparently sent out word to friends and relations how they'd found some fresh meat that was smeared with a delicious new sauce called mosquito repellent.

Thus far, there had been not the slightest indication of a turkey's pres-

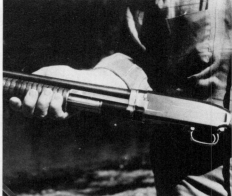

Left: Few things will spook a gobbler as quickly as the reflection from bright metal such as the surface of this shotgun's receiver.

Right: A few strips of electrician's tape may not give a very esthetic appearance, but it quickly and economically eliminates reflection from a gun's receiver.

ence; so, to relieve the monotony of parking on my can for two hours, I dug out my pipe and tobacco. In addition to feeling the need for a smoke, I wanted to discourage the miniature hawks with their rapier bills.

I didn't throw all caution to the wind, however. Instead of striking a match to my pipe tobacco, I used my cigarette lighter, so that I could better cup the flame in my hands and hide it from the sharp eyes of the forest. Ever so quietly (I thought) I shut the lighter and slipped it back into my pocket.

I didn't know it then, but Roscoe and Bill had stationed themselves up the swamp and across a large meadow from me. They had been watching a flock of gobblers work around the edge of the field toward where I'd built my blind. Roscoe had located me by the occasional calls I was making.

The half-dozen gobblers he was watching were in no hurry, feeding as they moved silently, without exchanging a cluck or a putt among them. Roscoe later reported that they were no more than 60 yards from where I sat and were headed for the corner of the field I could see from my blind, one well within range of my magnum shells. But because of the dense brush bordering the rim of the field, I had not seen the flock.

"As though someone had pulled a switch," Roscoe told me later, "the entire flock stopped feeding, stood for a moment with their heads up, then turned and trotted back the way they had come and ducked into the woods."

When anything unusual happens, almost any turkey hunter will glance at his watch; so, when I began to compare times with Roscoe, we both decided that what had spooked those birds was the click I made closing my cigarette lighter. Any old gobbler chaser who reads this will shake his head disbelievingly because I also violated one of the turkey hunter's cardinal rules: no smoking on a stand. When he does, I'll point out that (dammit!) no one *forced*

Left: For a better-looking and longer-lasting job of cutting reflection, it's hard to beat the process of having the gun "browned," a process akin to the more familiar job of having it blued.

Right: Here's the result of applying one type of camouflage covering to a turkey gun.

me to tell this one on myself. But I've done it because it should be revealed as one of the most inexcusable goofs any self-respecting hunter can make.

Roscoe related a similar incident. He was working a big gobbler that his hunting partner had not seen or heard. His partner lit a cigarette and snapped the lighter shut. The gobbler simply evaporated.

There's no doubt that one of the worst errors any turkey hunter can pull is to talk above a low whisper—if it is necessary to communicate with his companion. The human voice penetrates into the silence for an amazing distance. And as far as seeing game is concerned, that sound is one of the deadliest a man can make. Wild creatures are accustomed to loud reports such as the clap of thunder or the breaking of tree limbs. So even the report of a gun doesn't worry them too much. But the human voice is as identifiable to them as their language is to us. On the morning of a hunt, my Alabama friend Brooks Holleman won't let his hunters talk out loud, even at the predawn breakfast table.

I had a good example of what the sound of the human voice does to turkeys when, on the expedition with Tom and Roscoe, I went out for the morning with Perry Luckie, one of the best hunters in the region. Perry had been in the middle of turkeys all of his seventy-four years and could bag one for the table whenever he felt like it. With so many birds around, he never had to be exceptionally cautious. He just didn't see the need for having to talk in whispers.

Perry had an old gobbler spotted and we went out to the spot before daylight. I built our blinds in such a way that he could watch a narrow swamp below our hillside and I could oversee a small open meadow above us. We were seated about a dozen feet apart.

Turkey hunting from time to time demands a certain amount of ingenuity from its practitioners. Roscoe Reams was confronted with the problem of how to cross a creek to get closer to where a turkey was gobbling. Roscoe pulled a plastic trash bag over each foot, grabbed the tops of the bags, and took off across the creek.

Just after good daylight, a large gobbler stepped into the edge of the clearing above me, but out of range. Perry, with a chest cold, was trying to stifle a cough, so I put a finger to my lips to warn him.

In a normal, conversational voice, he asked, "What? Did you hear anything?"

The gobbler immediately vanished. I continued to call, however, and in a dozen or more minutes, a hen and a young tom came clucking to the wingbone and paraded around the edge of the clearing. At times they were close enough to touch with a long fishing pole. I passed them up, hoping the old gobbler might come back to check out all the turkey conversation we were making. Unfortunately, he never did.

After more unsuccessful tries in a couple of other states, I finally called my friend Tom Rodgers in South Carolina. It wasn't entirely desperation that led me to make a date with Tom to look over some of his turkey territory. After all, I'd had turkey-less years before. I must have figured that if I were going to carry failure with me to the end of the season, I might just as well relax and enjoy it. Tom is a delightful companion in the woods and around a campfire.

I admit I may have had an ulterior motive. Tom, in addition to being surrounded by an excellent turkey crop, is one of the best gobbler hunters I know. With him, I thought I might break my jinx.

It's Tom Rodgers's business to know more about wild turkeys than almost anyone else. He is executive vice president of the National Wild Turkey Federation, a nonprofit organization that has gathered membership of 25,000 to 35,000, with clubs in most of the turkey-hunting states. The federation is growing almost faster than Tom and his staff can keep up with it. The group's attractive and informative magazine, *Turkey Call*, features many top writers.

The federation is building towards a goal of hunter education that stresses safety, proper procedure, and sportsmanship. One aim is to seek more public hunting territory and eventually establish a system of wild-turkey refuges across the United States. To finance and publicize this program, the organization puts out an annual Wild Turkey Stamp, along with a limited edition of prints of the original painting from which the stamp is made.

Tom Rodgers grew up in the wild turkey woods of North Virginia and can't remember when he wasn't trying to call and shoot one of the big birds in season. After college, he became highly successful in the insurance business, but his first love remained turkeys and gobbler hunting. With other kindred souls, Tom organized the National Wild Turkey Federation, and stepped out of his insurance career to guide the new organization, whose headquarters were eventually moved from Virginia to Edgefield, South Carolina, in some of the South's finest turkey range.

The unfriendly gremlins who had parked on my hunting coattails all spring seemed to have decided to stay on for the ride. The week before I was to meet Tom, I had won a bout with near-pneumonia, and this wear and tear on my system in no way improved my chances to get a gobbler. The sickness left me weaker than an unhatched chick and with a cough so persistent you'd think I hadn't been properly warned by the Surgeon General.

I know I shouldn't have imposed myself on either Tom or his turkeys, but this was one trip I didn't intend to miss.

Tom thought some of the best turkey territory lay along the East Fork of the Little River in Fairfield County. The swamps there are exceptionally wide for Upper Piedmont creek bottoms. The hills are big and rolling and covered with pine and hardwood forest, except for a few tracts of several thousand acres each that have been completely denuded of all vegetation, bulldozed to barren soil, and planted with seedling pines. In these tracts the topsoil seemed to be washing away with every rain.

Tom and I rode through one of these desolate areas that had once been fine turkey woods. Now all we saw were gaping gullied hillsides with no sign of life. It made a fellow want to shed a tear over the callous and unenlightened forest policies of these big land-holding pulp-and-paper corporations. Clear-cut logging was also under way in the lower basin of the creek we'd formerly hunted, where trees and brush were now so thick a rabbit would have had difficulty pushing through.

"I suppose it's only a question of time," Tom said, "until turkeys in this part of the range won't have even a corner to hide in."

Tom and Jerry Allen, one of his close associates in the federation, and I had been invited by Henry Johnson, a banker and farmer in nearby Winnsboro, to stay at his huge two-story country mansion that dates back to slave days. Henry has restored it to its pre-Civil War magnificence.

On the first afternoon, we scouted along the parallel branches of the East Fork, with Jerry exploring one creek while Tom and I went to the other. Tom and I separated, and I followed the stream up through the swamp. The tracks and other sign I found along the creek sandbars and in the muddy flats indicated that the swamp had its share of big birds.

I sat out the last couple of hours of daylight on a small knoll overlooking the swamp, yelping my wingbone occasionally. At dusk I listened for the turkeys to fly into the roost trees. Though I neither saw nor heard a hen or gobbler, I knew they were there.

One thing did disturb me. After my bout with the flu, I still coughed occasionally. I seemed unable to prevent it, no matter how many coughdrops I sucked.

The next morning Jerry went back to his creek branch where he had seen a gobbler. Tom and I retraced our steps and were in the high hills a good half-hour before first light.

"The gobblers are likely to roost in the big trees on the hillsides around the swamp," Tom whispered. "When they fly down, they'll go to the swamp, where they're picking on lush grass in the open spots. If you hear a gobbler, try to get between him and the swamp before you call."

Over many years, I'd learned that any tom was more easily called if you were in front of his path. In the mountains, you were more likely to entice a gobbler when he was working his way up a ridge. Here he would be going downhill.

I suggested that we separate and could tell Tom wasn't at all displeased. For a day and a night he had listened to me bark like a Walker hound worrying a treed coon.

We parked Tom's four-wheel-drive a good half-mile from the swamp. He went down an old logging road, and I took a course at a right angle to the road. I crossed a couple of hollows to the next hill, where I could listen to a section of swamp beyond Tom's hearing.

Shortly after daylight, a buck turkey on the adjoining hillside gobbled lustily to greet the dawn—and any hens that might be within earshot. From the ring of his voice, I knew he was still in his roost tree. I swung down the slope into a deep hollow that put me out of sight behind a contour of the hill. Then I circled to a point between the roost tree and the swamp.

I quickly set up a blind that faced toward where the gobbler would come downhill on his way to the flat land along the creek. I had only one misgiving. The night before, as we sat around the table talking turkey, both my partners shared a thought they'd put through their mental computers over a couple of seasons. It came after I had asked the perennial question: "Why does a turkey always approach the backside of a man in a blind?"

Of course I was expecting a smart answer like the one Brooks Holleman, my long-time hunting partner in Alabama, once gave me: "Because the hunter's facing the wrong way."

"Jerry and I have made a study of that," Tom told me seriously. "No hunter can see too well looking into the sun, so he normally sits with the sun to his back. A gobbler has the same idea. The instant you call, he pinpoints the sound. When he comes to your call, he maneuvers to get the sun behind him. Like you, he sees better that way. He may come from one side or the other, but neither of us can ever remember a gobbler that approached with the sun in his eyes."

As long as I had been hunting turkeys, this notion had never occurred to me. Even that morning, in the excitement of building a blind, I didn't think of it. The brightening skies were at my back.

The night before, we had also discussed a point I did know but otherwise would have ignored.

"At least some of these gobblers," Tom said, "have been hunted enough to be spooky. Often when they're that way, the less you call the better. All the gobbler has to know, anyway, is your location. He'll find you."

"How much calling?" I asked.

"Usually one or two clucks are enough. If he answers with a gobble, you can sit back, wait, and watch for that movement or sound of footsteps in the leaves. Often a bird with plenty of hunter experience will come to a cluck while a series of yelps might send him off looking for a hen on the other side of the swamp."

Apparently my gobbler had flown down while I was circling to make my blind. When I gave the inquiring cluck of a hen, he answered immediately with a double gobble from the hillside 100 or more yards above. His voice was so lusty and excited that I might have expected him to come charging down if I hadn't known tom turkeys better. I pictured him in his strut and little dance, trying to attract the hen. I figured how long it would be before he'd gobble again.

He was almost on schedule. I needed a lot of will power to keep myself from sending back the seductive yelps of a hen. For twenty minutes or more I waited while the dawn chorus of the other birds swelled. Not another sound did I hear from that tom on the hill. Maybe he had attracted a real hen, had lost interest, or was on his way to investigate my cluck.

The suspense was palpable. After a few minutes, some instinct told me to gamble. Cautiously I tried another cluck. My turkey answered without hesitation. He was down from where he had first gobbled and to my left, making me wonder whether he was bypassing me or just circling.

I knew I had to sit motionless and wait. If this were a cagey old bird, any sound or movement now would send him streaking for the swamp. At such a time, the minutes seem to drag into hours. The roots under a man's rump,

Jerry Allen proudly displays the bird he called in when he, Tom Rodgers, and Elliott hunted in South Carolina.

scarcely noticeable when he first sits down, prod into his anatomy. His legs tingle, hurt, and gradually begin to go dead. He'd swap his soul for a chance to shift his weight for even a smidgen of relief. He dares not move.

After an interminable period, I heard a stick crack behind me. I had been immobile before. Now I froze. Seconds later a *tawk-tawk-tawk!* told me that a long-beard stood somewhere behind my tree and was looking for me. Eventually he would walk around the tree to where I might get a shot.

I'm sure he would have done so, except for one thing. The post-pneumonia tickle that had been building up in my gullet was ready to blow the top of my head off. I tightened my throat and held my breath. My face surely must have turned as red as an old gobbler's looking for a fight. I held my breath until I darn near strangled. Then I exploded. That gobbler didn't stay around to identify the eruption. With a roar of wings, he took off. My blurred eyes got only a glimpse of him flying through the tops of the tallest trees.

Tom and Jerry saved the day by bringing in two magnificent gobblers, from opposite sides of the series of big ridges separating the two creeks. Each had a graphic story to match his trophy. All I could contribute was my sad account.

My run of bad luck had held steady up to that point, but after a lifetime of experience I was still learning new things about turkey hunting. From that South Carolina experience, I developed another wrinkle. The cough stayed with me to the end of the season, but I finally got my gobbler, even with it.

I was telling my story to Bob Card of Cleveland, Tennessee, with whom I hunt gobblers each year in the Ocoee.

"I had exactly the same experience," he said. "I guess there's not much we can do about it."

"It may be," I said, "that we could cover up our coughs by gobbling the Lynch box at the same time."

Bob and I were sitting back to back near an opening in the Ocoee Management Area. A couple of times a gobbler out on the end of the ridge had replied to our yelps and then shut up. We'd been there half an hour, failing to rouse another note out of the turkey. Bob leaned around the tree and whispered, "I feel a cough coming on."

"Me too," I said. "Hold it a minute while I get my box out."

Bob Card and the author got this gobbler on the Ocoee by coughing and rattling their gobbling box at the same time.

When I had the call in my hands, I whispered: "Ready?"

"Let 'er rip," he said.

I gave the wood the best and loudest gobble I was capable of to hide our spasms of coughing.

A few seconds later, a big tom *yowked* from just under the crest of the hill. We sat immobile, and he came on in.

"I only wish," I said, as we stared at the lifeless colorful bird, "that I'd been smart enough to try this on that big gobbler in South Carolina."

"Maybe he'll be there next year," Bob said.

That kind of optimism just about sums up the philosophy of us turkey hunters.

11

Calls: How to Make and Use Them

Not long ago I had a telephone call from a hunter in Salt Lake City. He told me about his difficulty in locating gobblers in the La Sal Mountains of southeastern Utah. He couldn't find any sign, he said. But what had him upset above all else was a man he met along the road who bragged about wiping out a whole flock with a .22 rifle the winter before. When he heard that, my caller said he and his hunting partner gave up the hunt in disgust and went home.

What the Utah hunter told me was a reminder that there are no end of ways to kill a wild turkey—legal and illegal, sporting and unsporting. Some hunters have a strict set of ethics; others couldn't care less as long as they kill what they're after.

Almost every region has its hunter who is always the first back to town with a gobbler to show off. This happens to the same guy, year after year. He's got lots of folks fooled. Thanks to his stories of how he called in a reluctant old bird that had been hunted hard for the past four years by everybody else in town, he gets the reputation of being the best turkey hunter around. The truth may be that the bird was skilleted straight off its roost limb. The satisfaction of pride often makes some people forget ethics.

On the other hand, there's an army of hunters in these United States who figure that the only satisfactory method of killing a wild turkey is to call it to the gun. They might conceivably bushwack one or take a shot after a long stalk. But for the ultimate in turkey hunting, they want the bird to come to the call.

Facts bear me out. Some states conducted surveys of methods used by successful hunters. The findings were that the hunter who uses a call has a much greater chance for success than one who doesn't. Not long ago a young fellow I'd never met came by the house one evening and asked if he could have a moment of my time. He had never hunted wild gobblers, and he wanted to learn. He was so sincere that I gave him a short course on calling

123

and loaned him a box call. I had shown him how to make a series of four to six yelps on the box, and I'd marked the part of the striking surface so that he'd not lose track of it. Then I pounded the rhythm into his head as best I could.

Two weeks later, the Sunday paper had a picture of him holding an immense gobbler. The caption on the photo mentioned the gobbler's weight and spur length, and details of the young man's hunt. Sure enough, the next evening he was knocking at my door. What a story he had! The gobbler had come to him in the middle of the afternoon on a heavily hunted public area. He was the only hunter in a camp area of twenty people who'd bagged his bird. Who knows how many turkey calls will be sold, scratched on, and carried for many years because that boy came into camp packing such a fine trophy?

I can only guess how many devices, instruments, or whatever you might call them there are that will imitate the possible noises from a turkey's throat. Hundreds, I'm sure. Some folks can copy a turkey with their mouths. This ability is a real asset. You always have it with you. About the only thing that could foul up such a call would be a bad cold, a sore throat, or getting "dry mouth" from being too excited.

Besides the human voice, other natural calls you'll see being used are blades of grass, certain leaves, and short sections of cane. One of the best-known is the cat brier (several species), which has leaves that are tender and yet tough enough to stand the pressure of your blowing against them. The new, young leaves are best for making calls. Then there is the slender cane that, when cut into sections between the nodes, is hollow and open. By sucking on this exactly as you would on a wingbone, you can make excellent turkey yelps and clucks. How good depends on the size of the hole running through the cane. I like the opening to be slightly larger than three-sixteenths of an inch in diameter. A fine call may be made by gluing together two or three larger sections to this small calling section.

And when you consider man-made calls, there is no end to the possibilities. The common varieties are the box, the slate, the mouth "diaphragm," and the trumpet yelper. I've seen scads of what I think of as "snuffcan calls," which are made of everything from discarded 35mm film cans to actual snuffcans, with a wide assortment of plastic pipes, wooden tubes, or what-have-you as well. A thin sheet of rubber is stretched across one of the open ends. By holding this edge to your mouth, you may imitate any number of turkey sounds. Some people can make the notes just by holding the rubber between their fingers and blowing across it. An experienced caller can also gobble with a snuffcan, though I haven't seen such a call that could be heard over a goodly distance.

At one time the American Tobacco Company sold snuff in a shallow cardboard box. An empty one could be used as a call by drawing the blade of a sharp pocketknife across its raw cardboard edge. There was no way you could make a loud call with this rig, but the soft yelps fooled many a turkey.

This layout shows various types of turkey calls that are in popular use. The accompanying sketch and caption indicate which is which.

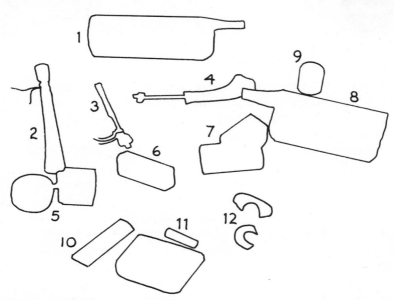

Here's the key to identifying the turkey calls in the accompanying photo: (1) Lynch call and gobbling box. (2) Turpin call, also known as Tom Turpin yelper. (3 & 4) two types of wingbone calls. (5, 6, & 7) three types of slate calls. (8) hen call, which makes only clucks and yelps of hen—no gobbling. (9) snuffbox call. (10) Rhodes turkey call. (11) chalk used on most slate, box, and wood calls. (12) diaphragm yelpers.

Among the simplest and lowest-cost of calls is the type shown here by George Shuler. It's made from a cardboard snuffbox.

Smoking pipes have filled in for calling a gobbler to the gun. A sucking, kissing action, plus a good ear for turkey sounds and some practice, are all that is necessary. Then, too, there's no better excuse you can give yourself for buying a new pipe.

Did you ever hear of using a fiddle for a turkey call? One of my mountaineer friends who goes for bluegrass music swears he called up a gobbler with his fiddle and that his buddy killed it. I believe almost anything I hear about turkey hunting. At one time in the Blue Ridge, there was a call known as a Virginia Banjo. It was built with a small round front and back much like a real banjo. It was scraped with a hunk of thin slate, no different from some sounding boxes. The Virginia Banjo had a long forked handle and could be used when the hunter wanted to imitate the sounds of turkeys scratching in the leaves.

There has probably been a far greater number of box-type calls than of all other man-made types combined. You'll run into boxes so big that you might stumble over one of them in the woods. By contrast, I've seen boxes made by the Apaches that can easily fit in the palm of your hand. Box calls have been made from almost every kind of wood that grows: four-sided, three-sided, deep, shallow, and narrow. Some have a chalk scraper, others a slate scraper. Some even have a sounding board attached. One type of box can be scraped on a gun stock to make an imitation of a turkey yelp.

Possibly the No. 1 box call in popularity is the big box. Among many of the older turkey hunters, this is known as a Gibson box, after the man who first made it in Missouri. Basically this call is a large hollowed-out block of wood some 9 or 10 inches long, a couple of inches deep, and an inch or so wide. Attached to it at one end and covering the hollow area is the paddle, or striker, which is around a foot long and has a curved lower side. This lower side, after being chalked or sanded, is stroked across the box's thin edges (or sounding boards, as some people know them) to make the proper sounds. Numerous woods such as willow and mahogany make fine Gibson calls. The best box calls I've heard, though, were made from either cedar or poplar.

Gibson boxes are usually too large to fit an average pocket comfortably. Dwain Bland, who calls them shufflin' boxes, thinks this bulkiness favors the people who manufacture and sell these calls. One turkey-hunting buddy of his stretched out for a nap, then walked off and left his call under the tree where it had fallen out of his pocket. Another time, Dwain and Ed LaForce, a turkey-hunting crony, were stretched out atop a high hill in far western Oklahoma, glassing the country below them. Dwain noticed Ed's box on the ground between them, but he thought Ed had purposely laid it there and made no comment. Hours later, and fifty miles away, LaForce missed his box. Only then did they realize it had fallen from his pocket. At the day's end, Ed made the long drive back, plus a long hike, to retrieve the box. By then it was thoroughly soaked from an afternoon storm. A night in a warm (not hot) electric oven had it ready for use the following day, none the worse for wear. I lost one of the best gobbling boxes I ever owned when it slid out of my pocket at one of the stops I made while hunting through a section of western Alabama.

Then, too, a Gibson box is likely to squeak while you are walking or from any sudden jar such as when you jump across a small creek. You can prevent such unwanted sounds by placing a rag or a rubber band between the paddle and the box's sounding edges. You can also fasten a long strip of cloth to the box to wrap it up after every calling session. I myself use several rubber bands to hold the lid down tightly while I walk.

Perhaps the greatest advantage of a Gibson box is its carrying range. Notes made on one of these can be heard for considerable distances. It's good for gobbling, too. You gobble by shaking the lid back and forth across the sides. You should attain fair accuracy after a bit of practice. The call has all the other notes needed to hunt turkeys in both seasons except the *kee-kee* run of the young turkey. At least I've never mastered that one on a Gibson.

Excellent commercial Gibson-type boxes are manufactured by the M. L. Lynch people of Liberty, Mississippi; Penn's Woods Products of Delmont, Pennsylvania; and the Mason Athletic Company of Gastonia, North Carolina. I am sure there are others.

Left: Here's how to hold the Lynch box when you want it to produce yelps.

Right: But when you want the Lynch box to imitate gobbling, hold it by the back end, as shown, and shake it.

The smaller boxes usually employ a scraper of sorts. The scraper is not attached to the box itself but is held by hand. Either the box is stroked over the scraper, or the other way around. While these smaller boxes are easier to carry and to keep dry in wet weather, they don't have the range of the large boxes. This limitation is not necessarily a detriment in mountainous or wooded terrain, but it becomes a serious fault in the more open ranges of the West, where gobblers must often be called from great distances. The soft notes that would be easily heard by an Eastern gobbler for 100 to 200 yards in rolling piney woods country would be a waste of time in trying to toll up a strutting Merriam's gobbler a half-mile off along some high mountain meadow in the West.

Fortunately for me, I was using one of the big Lynch boxes in the high country of the Apache Indian Reservation in New Mexico when Bill Rae and I called a big gobbler from more than half a mile away, while a high wind blew through the forest.

Finding the box that is "just right" for you is often a matter of hit-and-miss. Few store owners will permit a person to go through their entire inventory, just for the sake of selling one call. Besides, as each year goes by, more and more turkey calls are packaged in ways to prevent any manhandling of the merchandise. And the dealer wants them to stay wrapped. This factor is somewhat of a handicap to the hunter trying to find a call that suits him, especially since today there are scads of turkey calls on the market that would make better kindling.

Suppose you do find a box call that suits your taste. Your next task is to tune it up. By this, I mean: to learn what it will do. Changing the set of the lid, or even switching the chalk you rub on its surface, could bring about some startling changes in tone quality.

Dwain tells me that he never uses white chalk on a large Gibson box he cherishes—only blue carpenter's chalk. And except when he's afield he keeps this chalk in a desk drawer year-round, because chalk draws moisture. Blue chalk is somehow worse when it comes to this than is white.

An old call made by Lou Stephenson of Pennsylvania includes a small vial of rosin for use on its striking surfaces. The box sold by Roy Rhodes, up Pennsylvania way, has white chalk sent with it, as does the box made by William Hanenkrat of Virginia. John Grayson, also a Virginian, sells a box with a striker that ingeniously holds a round stick of hard yellowish chalk.

Dwain argues that red cedar lacks the quality needed for making the large Gibson box but works fine for the smaller, narrower boxes. The best box I ever owned was a Lynch call made of cedar. But Dwain thinks that poplar, willow, walnut, and mahogany are proven turkey-box woods. Actually, the thinness of the sounding boards and the materials of the striker are what determine how the call will sound. For turkey hunters who make their own calls, the long patient procedures involved in finding out what woods will work best do have their payoff when a call is made that brings in the big gobblers. Most important, it adds that little something extra to a hunt when you call in a boss gobbler with a call you've made yourself.

With a box, you often need a small piece of fine sandpaper as well as chalk. After several series of calls you may notice a shiny area on the striking surface of the scratch or paddle. If this area is not sanded lightly, it will cause the notes to squeak or screech. By keeping the wood surfaces that come into contact with each other sanded and chalked, you avoid that problem. Above all else, box calls, like slates, must be kept dry. Letting the wood get damp, or getting a few drops of water on the sounding edges, is worse than leaving it at home. It won't work again until it's dried out. Because of this vulnerability, hunters always carry two or three types of calls.

The main drawback to a box call is that it ordinarily requires the use of both hands. Another is the motions you have to make when stroking the box. Those can give away your location. One thing I've noticed is that the folks who are really proficient with a box call always look at the call while making the notes. If you operate this way, mistakes are much less likely to happen. But you can't watch the call and the territory at the same time, and it is extremely important to see the gobbler the instant he comes into view.

Even so, I've had little difficulty calling in gobblers with a box call. By drawing my knees up toward my chest while I'm sitting with my back against a tree trunk, I pretty well hide the call from the turkey's view, and I can ordinarily make the calls without visible movement. The gun is best held across the lap, where it's close to the hand when the box is laid down.

A box call in the hands of a veteran turkey man is a deadly invitation to a waiting turkey. It will make the calls common to just about all turkeys in both the fall and spring seasons—some of them so well you'll swear a turkey is near. Many a time I've listened to a hunter close by sounding off with a box, only to learn it wasn't a box at all, but an old hen belting them out. Most boxes, and most hen turkeys, can imitate each other to a T.

The remaining group of friction-type calls are of the slate-and-peg variety. Easy to make, they are perhaps also the easiest to learn. One of my finest slates was made by the late Bill Tannehill of Virginia. It is still sold under his name. This slate is mounted on a small boxlike sounding chamber, which helps to give it amplification. The peg, or striker (sticker, as some hunters know it), is inserted into a hollow block, which also increases the range. What you do is hold the slate portion cupped in one hand, slightly away from your chest, and then write in longhand the letter *e* several times while holding the peg at a slight angle to the slate surface. You thereby make an excellent rendition of turkey language. Clucks are as simple as holding the peg to the surface and then jerking it away swiftly. What I like about the slate call is that with a little practice—just an hour or two—a novice hunter can call a turkey to his gun. Heaven only knows how many turkeys are pretty sorry callers themselves. A bobble now and then won't mean a thing to a listening turkey unless he's an old reprobate that's been hanging around for years. Young turkeys, especially, make all sorts of crazy noises—some that don't sound anything like what should come out of a turkey's throat.

Just as with a box call, slates must be "gotten used to," if you're to become a real expert caller. Each has its own personality: where on the surface the best notes can be made, how hard to press in making the calls, what calls it will make, and what calls it won't. Besides carrying a couple of small squares of light sandpaper, when you're toting a slate you'd best carry along some matches, too. As with the box, after several series of calls you will notice the slate surface getting shiny. These spots should be lightly sanded so they won't screech. Why the matches? Two reasons. The first: for charring the end of the peg. Now, some pegs don't have to be charred. But others—like those made of mountain laurel, birch, or cedar—sometimes sound better if they are lightly charred, and then slightly sanded to take away some of the burned surface.

The No. 1 dread of folks who depend on the slate for most of their turkey calling is that the slate surface will get damp, or worse yet that it will get a drop or two of water on it. Then's when a couple of dry matches look awfully good.

Many years back I was laid up in a patch of oaks one spring morning. It had rained the night before, heavily enough to put me in mind of the storm preceding the Mount Ararat incident. The slightest brushing against any shrub brought a deluge off the greenery. Why I was in such a fix, I'll never know. But there I was in that mess with nothing workable on me but a slate call—the one made by Tannehill. A big boss turkey was bellering down the country a ways, so I fished out the call. You guessed it. I didn't get it sanded before a few drops fell smack on the slate surface. But like any good Boy Scout, I'd come prepared. Digging into my pockets, I came out with the matches. In jig time I had the call dried out.

I prefer to look at a slate when using one. Otherwise I may make so many bad notes that even the dumbest turkey would catch on. I hadn't looked up when the old boy answered my first series. My second calling a moment later got an even quicker reply, and it was closer.

I am positive that from the first call to the last took no longer than three minutes. I'd no sooner laid the call aside when he walked into view at less than 20 yards. A moment later, after making sure he was dead for keeps, I walked back to retrieve my call. It was shiny wet.

Making a slate call is easy, and that's probably who so many are homemade. If you can't find a thin hunk of blackboard slate anywhere else, drop in the five-and-ten store. In the toy department they often have small blackboards for children. If it's real slate, buy one of these.

Then find a dry corncob and break it in two. Keep the better half. From a dead cedar branch, whittle out a striker peg about the size of a small pencil. Insert one end of the peg into the soft, pithy part of the cob. I char the end of the cedar stick, and then lightly sand away the black soot that remains from this burning. I've even seen large nails stuck into a cob for use as the peg, though I've never tried this type of rig.

By experimenting with slates of various thicknesses and breadths, you'll finally come to one that will make the sounds you want. Putting together any kind of turkey call takes no end of tinkering and puttering and about as much patience as you'll need for turkey hunting. Consider this making of calls as a kind of warm-up for the big event.

Missouri has some brown slate that makes excellent calls. But it is considered a "soft" slate—not as durable as the black or gray varieties. A slate call of

This version of the slate call has a striker that's held in a corn cob for balance.

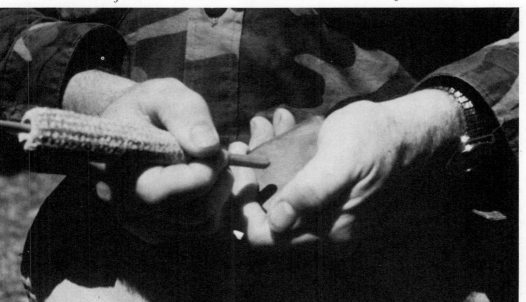

whichever type, when properly tuned, can make turkey music that will fool the best of them. Though I never heard a decent gobble on a slate, it will sound all the other notes made by a drove of turkeys, including the purr of both young and old turkeys in the fall and winter months.

Perhaps what makes the slate so deadly is its ability to copy the calling of the lost young turkey—known as the *kee-kee* run. This call is made by holding the slate loosely while you make the first two or three loops, or yelps, and then, as you draw the following loops across the surface of the slate, tightening the hand that holds the slate. The tightening causes the pitch of the note to rise up the musical scale sharply. The result should sound somewhat like *clauck, clauck, kee, kee, kee, kee.*

This calling of a lost and frightened young turkey should impart a sense of loneliness, a whining call for help, a wanting to find company. The best method for learning how these and other turkey notes should sound is to get your carcass into the woods at every opportunity and listen to how the turkeys themselves make them. Scatter a gang of young turkeys in the fall, and then hide close by. Listen as they call back together. Practice those notes right on the spot. On some slates, the *kee* sounds are more easily copied by making the strokes more up and down, as in the penmanship strokes ("push-pull, push-pull") many of us practiced in our early school days. These strokes, if drawn on a blackboard with chalk, would look like this: /////. When making *e* or *m* strokes on the surface of the slate, it is best to have your arms and wrists free of any hindrance, exactly as in penmanship or in freehand writing, so that your hand may rotate in an unobstructed manner. Proper rhythm can then be maintained.

Did you ever try to keep time with a band's beat with just your big toe? It's nowhere near as easy as using your entire foot. The same principle applies when keeping rhythm on a box or slate call: the greater the movement in your arm, the better the calling. This isn't exactly true, of course, when you try the whines, putts, and purring sounds. These are perfected by practicing exactness. That means you should stroke the slate in precisely the same spot each time.

Whether a slate turkey call is made of store-bought fine materials or is homemade, it is simple to learn, remember, and use. Not much pocket space is needed to carry one. And if you have learned the slate you're toting, it can be relied on to perform in the same manner time after time.

One variation of the slate is known as a "coconut shell" call. A hollowed out section of coconut shell is used to hold the striker, which is a small peg driven into a hole drilled in the end of the shell. A similar version of the slate call is a hollowed and cleaned section of cowhorn. Both shell and horn help amplify the sound. As with any slate, the length and size of the peg affect the sound of the notes. So does the size, shape, and thickness of the slate. Patient experimenting eventually leads to your making a slate call that will bring in the best of turkeys. On the commercial market, excellent slate calls are offered by Tannehill, the Lynch Company, and the Penn's Woods people.

An entirely different type of call might be classified as the breath-operated group. These include the diaphragm call that fits against the roof of your mouth. There are many advantages in being able to use the diaphragm call. Among these are:

• Your hands are always free.

• The call takes so little room that you could pack a hundred or more in your pockets, though you'll never need that many.

• You don't have to worry about getting them wet or broken.

• With practice it will make any call a turkey can make—better, louder, and longer, if that's possible.

In Chapter 12 on how to call up a gobbler, I mention a tactic known as "calling or hunting your backtrail." This came about as a result of years of experience with a mouth call. It seems normal to stroll along a little-used woods road, yelping now and then, much as a hen will often do as she wanders along in the early hours, or as one or two turkeys in a drove will do during the fall and winter months. If you stop, make the call, and listen for a few minutes before continuing down the trail, you can cover a great amount of territory and yet call it in a turkeylike fashion. No doubt you'll sometimes walk off from turkeys. But in a way that's better than calling from a few "dry" stands or remaining on only one all day.

Since you'll probably return along your backtrail anyway, this first trip allows you to look at the country around you and gives you the opportunity to find a prime area. A mouth call leaves your hands free for quick action while you range the forest.

Possibly the prime asset in knowing to perfection how to use a mouth call (or "horseshoe call," as some hunters know them) is the ability to change from one note to another, or to quickly copy the notes of an answering turkey. This ability is particularly valuable in the fall turkey season.

One real trick with the mouth call is to use it with another type of call. For instance, yelping may be started on a hand-held box or slate. Then while those yelps are being made, the yowks or gobbles of an adult can be "cut right in," creating the illusion of a gobbler being with the hen. Both gobblers and hens come to such parties. Or you may cut in on the hen yelps with the half-gobbles of a year-old jake gobbler. At times this combination will create jealousy in an adult gobbler or will even bring in other young gobblers.

Diaphragm calls come in several sizes. The call's size and the thickness of the rubber allow for great variance in the sounds that can be made. Diaphragm calls with the lead backbone can be adjusted to fit the roof of your mouth and then "tuned" by tightening or loosening the rubber by working the ends of the miniature lead "horseshoe." In effect, a hunter can carry in his pocket almost as many "turkeys" as he wants to imitate.

Probably nothing sounds more like a drove of fall or winter turkeys than do two or three hunters who are experts at using diaphragm calls. The hunters sit within 20 to 50 yards of one another, near where a drove has recently been scattered. *Kee-kee* runs can be copied to perfection, along with lost yelping and clucks. And if the birds commence calling back and forth in such a fashion, the half-gobbling of the six-month-old jake can be copied. On occasion, when a young bird "hangs up" and won't come on in, your ability to copy its very notes may turn the trick and bring the young turkey within gunshot. Anyone adept with the mouth call will have little trouble imitating such turkeys.

Perhaps the oldest known of all turkey calls, besides the human voice, is the wingbone, or trumpet call. It's often referred to as a Turpin yelper, after Tom Turpin, an old-time turkey hunter from Memphis, Tennessee, who made them so popular. It's said that the Indians first called turkeys with bone instruments. Supposedly these were much like the ones we use today and the notes were made with a kissing, sucking action while the call was held along the lower lip. The white man's first modification was to insert a section of bone into a section or two of cane. Later, an excellent call was made by inserting the short calling section of bone into a long trumpetlike bell made of walnut or other lathe-turned wood. Other calls had a length of bone attached to a cowhorn by a long piece of small rubber tubing. The commercial trumpet yelpers on today's market utilize hard rubber or plastic for the section through which the notes are made, but these calls still use wooden barrels for the longer amplifying section.

I've had a good many letters over the years from budding turkey hunters who've asked how to make a wingbone call. This is no great chore, unless you consider getting the bones a chore. What you need to make a true wingbone call are the bones from the wing of a wild turkey: the large bone from the first joint nearest the body, and the two smaller bones from the outer wing section adjoining it.

The very best bones are those from an adult hen. A young hen's bones are often too small, and a young gobbler's wingbones may prove too large. A young gobbler tipping the scales at 8 or 9 pounds will do, but the bones of a long-beard turkey are out.

Eat the turkey. When you get down to the wings, gnaw the meat off those too, but save the bones. Boil and scrub them clean. Dwain Bland says you might add a tiny touch of dish soap during the boiling to give them a "better taste." As for me, I've never tried it.

With a three-cornered file, cut a line around each end where the bone levels out from the knoblike sockets. When the lines are deep enough you can break the socket ends off cleanly, leaving a small straight length of bone that only needs to have the marrow cleaned out to be ready for use. Hot water and a small wire will do for the marrow. I find a pipe cleaner very effective in cleaning out the bone.

Select three sections of bone that will sleeve one into the other about like the sections of a fishing rod, and—when they're thoroughly dry—cement them tightly together. You'll have a call with a larger amplifying end and a small end through which to call. A flat slice section of small bottle cork can be drilled, slipped over this small end, and glued in place, once you've learned exactly where on the tip it should be placed to fit your lips. The cork acts as a buffer against which to set your lips, and it also gives a "firmness" to your calling.

Instead of blowing through the wingbone call, you make the sound by sucking air through it. The yelps of a hen turkey are made simply with a kissing action. Clucks are a smacking action that pulls air quickly through the call.

Few types of calls require as much practice as does a wingbone or any variation of the trumpet calls. One person might begin making noises right at the beginning, but the next may not get any kind of sound from the instrument until after many dry-mouth attempts. From then on, it's practice, practice, practice. A bone in the hands of a master caller is as deadly to a turkey flock as the gun across his lap.

My first experience with this type of call involved a Turpin yelper. I practiced with that instrument until I drove all the dogs, cats, and two-legged citizens in the neighborhood to the verge of insanity. My own family threatened to leave home. But I got it down to perfection—or thought I had.

Putting it through its serious paces in East Georgia on a fine spring morning was another matter. Three turkeys had gobbled close to me, each from a different direction. Mentally I was already putting at least one of them in the pot.

One was so close I didn't have time to make a blind. So I sat down with my back to a large tree and lifted the Turpin to my lips to make sweet, dulcet notes. Not a sound of any kind could I get out of that tube. I puckered, kissed, sucked, and gulped. But I might as well have had a solid pine stick against my lips.

If I'd sat still, one of the gobblers might have strolled by, but I guess that by then I was a little frantic. I started digging for my Lynch box in the folds of my garments, and I'm sure the birds must have seen my motions. Anyway, they went in the other direction.

Later in the day I asked my companion, an old veteran, what I'd done wrong.

"The excitement made your mouth dry," he said with a grin. "To get the proper tones, the inside of your mouth should be moist."

"How do you do that?"

"Work your saliva around. To get it started, chew something like a sassafras twig."

The same thing happened once more during that season, so the next time I practically browsed down a whole sweetgum thicket.

I've heard some people attempt gobbling sounds with a trumpet-type yelper, but it never was what I considered passable. So if you want to truly gobble, get out one of your boxes or something similar that'll turn the trick. A wingbone has its uses, but I don't think gobbling is one of them.

If you are downright serious in wanting to learn to call turkeys at any

Here's the old professor trying to look invisible and attract the right kind of attention by sounding off on a Turpin call.

season, one of the best ways is to go live with them in the woods for a spell. About two or three years might be long enough. A lifetime is better.

An old hunting book in my library puts it this way: "The right kind of calling is what works best for the time being." This is excellent advice, provided you know what'll work best. If you don't, then it's not the right kind of calling. From the same old book: "You will never *read* exactly how to turn the trick when using a caller." No truer statement has ever been printed.

Dwain Bland's story of how he started hunting turkeys contains some interesting lessons for the novice hunter. What follows is in Dwain's own colorful words:

"In those early days, you couldn't find a printed word on the subject, as the turkey hunting of 'the good ole days' had been lost in time and today's crop hadn't fully come about. Sporting magazines apparently wouldn't print stories about the sport because not too many people were hunting turkeys. At least, none up in the East, where the editors lived, so they figured there was no such thing as turkey hunting anywhere.

"A friend of mine, on learning I was wanting to hunt turkeys, called to offer me the loan of a turkey call—a small box that had been given to him by somebody in the family. He had no idea who had come by it in the first place, and he damned sure had no idea how it was used. I was welcome to it, he said. The call was still in the cardboard box from the store.

"At home later, I was elated to find a set of instructions, and I set about learning 'how to call and kill a majestic wild turkey gobbler.' I practiced half the night. Had I called up a gobbler bright and early the next day, I'd maybe have thought there wasn't much to turkey hunting, and given it up then and there. But this wasn't the case.

"About the middle of the morning, I spied a turkey crossing an open flat below the heavy clump of woods where I'd been hunting. What surprised me was that the bird hadn't seen me. Until then I thought a turkey could see clean through a tree—trunk, leaves, branches, and all. Such were the stories I'd heard about their eyesight. The turkey wasn't heading towards me, but he wasn't going off in the opposite direction either. About then I remembered the box.

"I'd sanded and chalked it earlier, after calling from a place I thought should hold a turkey or two, but none had showed, so I was ready. Making what I considered several yelps, I looked up to see what the turkey thought of them.

"He didn't. The notes had scarcely cleared the call's edges, I swear, before the bird lit out in a hard run, not towards me, but for the far woods. He never slacked. As far as I know, he could still be running. I learned Lesson No. 2: A turkey can run like hell. So at that time Lesson No. 1 to me was: Don't call unless you have turkeys to spare."

If there's no way to get into the woods to listen to the real McCoy, your next best bet is to listen to tame turkeys. In rural America, there are few places farther away than an hour's drive from some farmer who doesn't have at least a couple of turkeys in his barnyard. Turkey farms—where the birds are raised for the commercial market—are scattered all over the United States. A tame turkey has the same vocabulary as the wild kind. By listening to the tame variety, you can learn what you'd hear in the wild. The main difference is that tame turkeys sometimes talk incessantly. A wild one rarely does. You hear the same notes. Just remember that the wild bird is not so profuse with them. But the timing, or rhythm, is virtually the same.

If you can't make it to the turkey woods or find a tame flock, then your best bet is to look up a successful old turkey hunter and cajole him into making some calls while you listen. If none of these courses is available, the only thing to do is to buy one or more of the instruction records on the market. These are sold both as disc records and in the popular cassette form. Recordings can be found that have, in addition to calls and instructions by some expert caller, the sounds of live turkeys recorded right in the woods. Now I don't say all these experts are expert turkey killers. The key words here are expert turkey callers. It is possible that some of them haven't killed enough turkeys to make one good bowl of soup. But they are good callers—or so the judges at the calling contests say.

Still, my pick of all the above methods is to go into the woods and listen to *live* wild-turkey music. I do this every chance I get. You should too.

For fall hunting you'll want to find a drove and scatter it to the four winds if you can. Then hole up nearby and listen as the turkeys call to come together again. Get your call out, and join in if you want. Just don't let them see you—or they'll run off to less crowded parts. In this manner you will not only learn what turkeys sound like but also what works best in calling them to you. There may be sounds that to your ear won't be precisely what you consider most desirable to get the bird to come to you and yet will turn the trick. This gets back to an idea you'll hear quite often: turkeys are often sorry callers, too. Calling is often all right to another turkey, no matter how bad it may sound to you.

Few old turkey chasers will turn down a new hunter who asks for advice on how to call. The only problem here might be how much time either the instructor or pupil has to spare. There will be no end of stories after each series of calls—to prove a point, or to explain why this call is more desirable than that one. A smart rookie listens well. Such stories help build him into a successful hunter.

A turkey's vocabulary is doggone near unlimited. You learn this truth if you listen to a drove throughout a whole day. But for practical calling purposes, the language boils down to only a handful of notes. The best known of these is the hen yelp, as used in the mating season. A hen yelp is coarse and quick. You might say it sounds like a string of clucks, but without the sharpness. The basic thing to remember about hen yelps is the rhythm. This may surprise you, but the second hand on your watch will often record as many as three or four yelps *in one second*. This tells you something about each yelp; it is short and follows instantly the yelp preceding it.

There has been no end of literature published that admonishes the reader to call thusly: make two or three yelps, wait five to ten minutes, then make another series of two or three yelps. After doing this three or four times, do not call for twenty or thirty minutes. If no turkey has come to you at the end of this time, then move several hundred yards away and repeat the procedure. Somewhere in these instructions there's usually a warning to the hunter to "refrain from excessive calling."

This strategy may work in some places, but more often I have found that a hen turkey can be extremely vocal, making a series of yelps that will contain thirty or more individual notes. Therefore, my advice is: Don't get into a habit of making *the same number* of notes time after time. A turkey seldom does. As my friend Ben Rogers Lee points out, no turkey ever went to college and learned to count.

The hen yelp is made for a purpose. It's the female turkey's way of calling out to the gobbler, who will gobble back an answer. Just after flying down from the roost tree, shortly after first daylight, he'll gobble again to tell her where he stands at stud. When a man tries to convince a springtime gobbler to come to him, he should realize he's going against all the rules of nature. The hen is supposed to go to the gobbler, and the gobbler knows this. He gobbles and struts, in a favored location. The hens attend him there and a short while later wander off to feed. Then he must tag along, trying to strut when he gets a chance. But much of the time he simply has to settle for being puffed up, with his tail partly spread and cocked off toward the treetops. When the hens pause for a few seconds to feed, he'll once again go into full blossom. Then, seconds later, he'll be hustling to catch up.

A fair number of today's hunters can properly imitate a gobble, but a good many can't. The gobble tells the hens where to find the male turkey for mating. It is also the male's way of letting other males know who is boss hereabouts, and anybody who doesn't think so will get his wattles pecked. So it's an advantage for the hunter to be able to gobble. Other male turkeys will answer a gobble, and some will come to it, either for company or for a fight. Gobbling can and does call in many gobblers each year. Imitating the half-gobble of a young gobbler during the fall season is also easy to do, and once in a while it will bring another jake to the hunter.

One other call that has worked for me in the spring season is the lost call of a young gobbler. Some people may be too choosy to shoot a young gobbler in the spring hunt, but I can remember days a hundred miles from home when a jake looked to me like the granddaddy of them all.

One April morning a friend and I, hunting together, had laid up where we could keep watch over a small rye field. The field was shaped like an hour glass, and we could keep good lookout on both of the bigger hunks of pasture from the middle where the field narrowed to less than shotgun range. Turkeys passing from one area to the other had to come within shooting distance or else cut through the woods. Habitually they walked the narrow gap.

A couple of hours after we'd gone on stand, two jakes came into the upper field, feeding along slowly as they worked toward us. Not wishing to louse up a good chance, I whispered that the show was all my partner's and that he should shoot when he was ready. I didn't want him to be concerned about which bird he should attempt to kill. He took his time, but for some unexplained reason he missed. Both birds flushed high and wild, one going off at an angle from the other bird's course. Watching them as far as terrain would permit, I hurried off in the direction they had gone. All the way I heard uncomplimentary remarks about the ancestry of all the turkey clan. My partner's carrying on would have made a gentle man faint.

Turkey hunting was something new to him, so he had no idea of my plan when I put him on stand and then took up my position 100 yards back of him on the same ridge, but slightly higher. I couldn't see my partner from my blind. One of the gobblers had sailed into the valley below us, the other behind us, where he was probably too far away to hear my calling. I chalked my big "shufflin' box," as Dwain calls it, and then began to make two or three yelps every now and then—the slower plaintive yelps of a young lost gobbler.

This routine went on perhaps twenty minutes before my partner's big-gauge gun boomed out. One time. Trotting down to where I'd left him, I finally made him out, standing 30 yards farther off, looking down at a turkey that was thrashing its last. When I walked up, I could see it was a fine young gobbler.

"Well, looks like you got him,"I said.

My partner was so short of breath he could hardly talk as he glanced around at me.

"Hell's fire," he said. "I didn't even know the damned thing was around till he come busting across that little clearing. Running like hell right at me. I damned near didn't have time to get the gun up."

This incident proved that young gobblers separated from each other will often have the same urge to get together during the spring months as they have in the fall. They'll sometimes come to a hen's yelping or to an adult's gobble. So, if you're not too particular, a long ways from home, and turkey-less, a jake may look mighty good.

Dick Bland, Dwain's brother and a crackerjack turkey hunter, said if he had his druthers, he'd choose the *kee-kee* run over all the rest of the turkey's vocabulary for calling up and killing turkeys. He thinks no other call approaches it for early-fall hunting. Not only do young turkeys come to such calling—old hens and adult gobblers will, too.

Understanding what the *kee-kee* run is in a turkey's life will explain its effectiveness. As soon as a young poult turkey can utter a sound, it does so by peeping, much like a baby chick. This soon gives way to a whistle, which is nothing more than a refined peep. Along about October, sometimes earlier, sometimes later, the turkey's voice changes into what is known as yelps. Both the young hens and the young gobblers can make a yelping *caluck* or *keouck* sound and yet still make a peeping sound, which sounds like *kee, kee, kee, kee*. The yelps can either precede the *kees*, follow them, or may be left out altogether. A young gobbler might call from a tree at dawn with a *kee, kee, kee, kee, keouck, keouck.* An average turkey is likely to make a greater number of *kees* than yelps to go with them. Some turkeys make no yelps at all but *kee-kee* continuously. Ordinarily a turkey will stick fairly close to whatever sequence it begins. I try to follow suit with my calling. If my first effort is *keouck, keouck, kee, kee, kee, keouck,* then I make the following calls fairly near that same order. What's more, if you hear a turkey *kee* it's good thinking to imitate his call, which seems to speed up his approach in your direction.

What makes the *kee-kee* run work so well is its appeal to scattered turkeys. Next fall get into the woods a week before season and locate a drove of turkeys. At this time of year, the odds are that this drove will be made up of one or two adult hens and the broods they've raised during the summer— young birds-of-the-year (or "jennies" and "jakes," as some hunters call them). Get as close as possible to these birds. Then run in and scatter them as best you can. The more widely they are scattered, the better will be their calling in getting back together. If season is in and you've got a gun, shoot into the air. Most old-timers believe that if you try to kill a bird under these circumstances, you'll wound it. If they fly off in one direction, follow the bulk of the gang to where you think they went down. Try to call one turkey to you at that point. If the drove scatters to several points of the compass, find a place to hide near where you flushed them. Then call again at that point. If you feel like being technical, you may call this the "scatterpoint."

By now you are probably saying, "The shot scared the hell out of them. Trying to call one back to where they were shot at would be foolish." Forget that idea. Shooting at the scatterpoint only helps scatter them all the more, and that's exactly what you want. Hunt as near the scatterpoint as cover will permit, nowhere else. If you must hunt some distance away, it's best to hunt from a place uphill. The turkeys would rather assemble above the scatter-point than below.

If two or three hunters are in your bunch, the wisest thing you can do is to spread out around the scatterpoint. First one hunter should start *kee-kee*ing, and a little later another should join in. Keep the calls going. And re-member: the *kee-kee* run is the lost call of a badly frightened turkey—so put meaning into your calls. When you make the *kee-kee-kee-kee* run, put in all the pleading and whining you can muster. Make your turkey talk sound like that of a turkey scared witless at being all alone in the great big woods. Don't sit down and wait a half-hour before starting to call. Sit down and get after it *right now.* And keep that call going. Soon as a bird out there hears your calling, he's going to amble your way, looking and listening. Soon as he hears another turkey calling near you (your partner this time), he'll think the drove is assembling, and he might come on the run. I've had them run and fly in, and it wouldn't surprise me too much some day when I'm hunting beside a pond to have one swim in.

Shooting and killing birds from a stand where you're calling with the *kee-kee* run makes little difference, as the birds often continue to call moments after a shot is fired. Young turkeys come best to a *kee-kee* when the leaves are yet on the trees. After the leaves fall, all turkeys get together as much by sight as by sound.

12

How to Call Up
a Gobbler

To "call up" a gobbler means literally that you have called him within shooting distance of a shotgun. I've known some folks who consider themselves experts if they bring a bird as close as 200 or 300 yards, from which point they can commence laying down a stream of rifle fire. They may call themselves turkey hunters. But to a scattergunner, a called-in turkey is inside 40 yards, and he hopes it will be nearer 25.

Regardless of weather, number of hunters, or any of a dozen other factors, there are two kinds of turkey gobblers on almost any spring morning: 1) the loudmouth kind that gobbles incessantly; and 2) the one that might be there but ain't saying nothin'. These silent toms, in the words of Dempsey Cape, are "the ones that play shutmouth."

The bad part about not hearing a gobbler is what it does to your way of thinking. If you're a stranger to the area, the first thing that comes to mind is, "There ain't nothing here." Maybe there isn't. But you can find out by scouting for a fresh sign, or you can check with the truthful local hunters. The only problem there is to find who fits that category.

When you have proof that at least one turkey is in the area, the next thing you think—after failing to get an answer of any kind—is, "Maybe somebody shot him." I know this reaction from my own experience. After I've dealt with an old feathered ridgerunner back in the hills for several mornings running during the season, and then some morning he fails to gobble, I get a little squirmy about his fate.

Heaven knows, with today's hunting pressure, a man can't keep a gobbler all to himself, not on public lands anyway. So if another hunter knows your favorite bird's location, you just have to hope that he's not smart enough to outwit your turkey. The truth is that every turkey hunter likes to think his old bird is too smart for anyone else.

Once I can get a turkey to gobbling again, I sigh with relief that he's still there. That's only one of the many little pleasures of turkey hunting.

143

Not all calling is intended to make sounds that please gobblers. Here Tom Rodgers hoots like an owl in an attempt to arouse gobblers.

Getting a gobbler started can be as simple as slamming a car door before you head into the woods. Sudden noise often brings an instant gobble, as though it comes out before the bird can stop it. Nine times out of ten, he'll gobble only once at such unusual sounds. So get a fix on the first gobble you hear. It may be the last.

Throughout much turkey range, the simulated hoot of an owl is used to start a gobbler. This *who-who-ah-who-wah, ah-who-wah* is easy for a hunter to imitate. Not only will it often get a reluctant tom to sounding off, but also around camp in the evening, it will call up the big barred owl itself. Turkeys will also answer the great horned owl. Such calling is known in turkey-hunting circles as owling. For turkey hunters whose throats won't contract properly to make such sounds, a number of commercial companies offer barrel-type owl calls that do the job.

Your rattling a gobbling box will sometimes stir up a silent gobbler. How many mornings have you heard a bird sound off nearby, and another come right back at him from down in the bottom, then still another on an adjoining ridge? Gobblers do reply to other gobblers, so shaking a gobbling box is always worth a try. A few fortunate hunters can gobble with their mouths. Others can gobble with a mouth diaphragm. I've heard attempts at gobbling with snuffcans as well as with trumpet yelpers, but none of these have the volume of the natural throat or mouth call.

In Mississippi, I once got a gobbler to disclose his whereabouts by throwing a rusty dishpan against the side of an old car body. But when I tried the same thing some time later, he wouldn't have any part of it. Often a turkey gobbles at the most unlikely sounds, some you and I consider ridiculous. It may be irritation or some similar mood. He certainly can't be thinking of a love affair on hearing a rusty dishpan.

Once you make the turkey gobble, if only once or twice, you are ready for your next play to locate near him. Then the question pops up—"How close can I get before I start calling?" There's one stock answer: As near as possible without spooking him. In heavy woods, such as many places in the Deep South, throughout the Northeast, and in much of the Rocky Mountains, you don't dare try to get closer than 100 to 150 yards. The trees might seem to be a solid screen through which you can move to less than a hundred yards, but seldom is the screen of undergrowth that tight.

In the flat open country of the West, "close" is sometimes a quarter of a mile. Where roost trees are scarcer, a roosting bird can often be pinpointed. Then the right kind of stalk may put the hunter within 50 yards of the turkey's limb. How close to get before starting the actual hunt is therefore a problem faced by each individual hunter. A gobble may sound far different to different human ears, so the hunter must decide: 1) the location and distance; 2) whether the gobble was made by an adult or a young gobbler; and 3) if the bird is still on the roost or has flown down.

In mountainous country, it's smart to locate uphill from a gobbler. Build your blind or take your stand where he can come to you in the open. This is especially true if you're hunting the Rio Grande turkey in the flat lands of Texas and Oklahoma. In trying to entice the ladies to his strutting ground, a tom often gobbles less there since he can see the hens more easily.

A turkey gobbling from the uppermost limbs of a big oak along the flank of a mountain can—when conditions are right—be heard as far away as a mile or two. The same is true on the prairie. On the other hand, after the bird has flown down, the same gobbler can't be heard for 300 yards. This difference is largely the result of two conditions: 1) the severity of the roll in the terrain; and 2) the oomph the turkey puts into his gobbles. Either element can cause a quickly approaching hunter to overrun the turkey and spook him into the next county. A number of times I've flushed turkeys out of the confines of a small gap when I was hurrying too far out to the end of a ridge, where I thought they were. Being in the hollow muffled the gobble and made it sound much farther away.

Hearing is one of the turkey hunter's important assets, but—at least for some of us old codgers—time has taken its toll. We can't pinpoint a gobbling turkey the way we did a few decades ago. It must be a smidgen of envy that upsets me when some youngster thirty or forty years my junior stands beside me in the predawn darkness and suddenly says, "Whoo-oo-ee-ee! Did you hear that gobbler?", and my aging ear drums haven't picked up the sound. Keen hearing is an advantage if the bird is a long way off and you want to get there in time to catch him on the roost.

What to do with a gobbling turkey that's still on the roost limb, once you've closed the distance on him, is a matter open to discussion. Numerous hunters just play it safe and wait for the turkey to make the next move— which can be any of several. The old bird might not gobble again. He might leave you wondering what happened to him. Then again he might gobble over and over, continuing to sound off after going to ground, standing and waiting for the hens to come to him.

More often though, he'll fly to ground, gobble maybe a time or two, then remain there all balled up in full strut, drumming and handsome in all his elegance. Hens will come to him; and if you're close, you can hear the wings flopping as he treadles them. An hour or two later, once they've been with him and then sneaked off while he is still caught up in his own importance, he could very well start to gobble again.

Another possibility is that he can fly to the ground, shut up, walk off, and never be seen or heard again. This pattern usually is a real puzzler.

Being one of those nothing-gambled-nothing-gained disciples, I'd just as soon make a play for him while he's still in the tree. I'll make an attempt to get within 100 to 200 yards, locate where he can come to me without having to walk through a thicket or wet underbrush, and then yelp or cluck to him softly, imitating a nearby hen.

If all goes right, you might have what I call "one of those storybook hunts." First you hear the gobbling, get within 100 yards just as day is breaking, and flush all the hens roosting in nearby trees so that the tom's all alone. Then you make those now-and-then yelps that often induce him to fly straight to you, or fly down and walk in.

Killing a storybook gobbler is all but too easy at times. But on other days he hangs up 70 yards out. This averages things out.

Undoubtedly, hen turkeys have caused the loss of thousands of gobblers to the hunter's gun. A hen often goes to a gobbler unseen by the hunter, who keeps calling without results. The poor guy ends up thinking he's no good with his calls, but in reality the competition was just too tough.

Sometimes getting a gobbler separated from the hens is half the game. Many a gobbler has wound up on somebody's meat pole because the hunter tried to get in too close and scattered the whole flock in every direction. Thirty minutes later, it wasn't any trouble to call the gobbler up, because the hens were out of the picture.

When I haven't got all day to fool with the birds, I'll purposely scatter them, hoping that before my time's up the old bird's thoughts of romance will cause him to forget why he's alone. A hard-hunted gobbler doesn't always forget, but such a try is better than no try at all.

How much to call to a tree-bound gobbler is something nobody can answer. Old turkey hunters call only a time or two, to let the bird know where he can find the hen, then cease calling, regardless of how much gobbling the old boy continues to do. The turkey's uncanny ability to pinpoint sound will tell him exactly where the calling came from. And if no seductive hen appears where he can see her, there's a chance that when he flies down he'll go directly and immediately to the area from which your calls came.

Another possibility is that he might fly to ground near the caller, or into the trees directly overhead. Any such action can all but scare you out of a year's growth, though I'm certain every hunter who works a gobbling turkey in the tree always dreams that the next one will do so.

The man who can cluck back quickly to a gobbler who comes down just at the edge of gun range had best get ready for action. The bird will often come straight in without any hesitating. Of course the ideal situation is to get located between a gobbler and a noisy hen. You can spoil the fun if he goes to her; if she comes toward him, you're in a position to run her off. You'll hear talk of chasing off hens that come to the hunter. In my opinion, that's not taking advantage of a good thing. I welcome the hen who joins me and stands there yelping at the top of her voice when I call.

But even this tactic does not always work. While hunting in western Alabama, Bill Rae and Turkey Johnston had a hen fly into the tree immediately over their heads. They'd been talking with a big gobbler and could see him walking back and forth, about 75 yards away.

The hen in the tree started calling and the two hunters shut up, figuring they couldn't have a better decoy. She and the gobbler talked back and forth for fully three-quarters of an hour. Finally he shut up and went the other way. When she left the tree, she flew in the opposite direction.

"Beats anything I ever encountered," Turkey said.

"She was just telling him not to come any closer," I observed.

What kind of calling to do when a gobbler's in a tree depends on the amount of daylight. A hen ordinarily clucks on first going to ground. This is at first good daylight, when she can see to walk about without stumbling onto a waiting wildcat. Such clucking is a continuation of the clucking she did while on the roost branch. Sometimes the clucking is by soft yelps, rarely discernible at a distance.

Ten minutes later she'll change over to yelping. Hen yelps can be noisy, loud, and downright raucous. More than once I've heard another hunter close by yelping with a box, or what I took to be a box, only to discover in time it wasn't a box at all, but a hen belting them out. Back in camp somebody'll say, "Did you hear that old hen cut loose down there along the branch? Sounded jest like a box a-workin'." Perhaps this is one reason I've used a Lynch box for many years. Few devices can so effectively imitate a loud, vociferous hen turkey.

As the day wears on, the hen will cease all calling, except perhaps during the middle of the afternoon while she is still in the process of laying her clutch, and then at such times she calls loud and clear. Seldom do laying hen turkeys call in the late evening just before sundown. Incubating hens never do. Hen clucks are good throughout much of the day, and the hen cackle will often start a gobbler to sounding off. On occasion I've had the privilege of witnessing birds mating and this hen cackle is sometimes uttered when the hen is being pursued by several amorous males.

For the average hunter, there is little need to learn any but the basic calls—which, for the spring season, means the hen mating call—and perhaps to be able to imitate a gobble. Clucks, cackles, whines, and all the other sounds made by a turkey may not be important, though a lot of hunters swear by them. Yet scads of old turkey men use nothing but a hen yelp and have killed their share of adult gobblers. Woodsmanship, patience, and knowing turkey habits did the rest.

A turkey gobbling on the ground and out of sight is why the sport is known as turkey *calling*, instead of turkey killing. It's up to the hunter to bring the gobbler within gunshot.

The first thing to remember about a wild turkey gobbler is that he gobbles for a reason: to tell the hens where he stands at stud, and to wait there *for them to come to him.* His continued gobbling doesn't always mean they haven't come to him. On the contrary, he can be gobbling with them all around him. At the same time, he could be gobbling because they haven't appeared. His not responding to your call can mean that either he's with hens or is waiting for them to come to him. Thousands of times each spring, this situation arises. The hunter does not know whether the gobbler is with hens but surmises he is. Outside of sneaking in for a closer look, which usually results in your getting too close, the only thing left for you to do is play the game: call him to you.

Location is all-important. A gobbler is not going to wade into any tangle or thicket. Locate yourself well back from streams, creeks, sloughs, and other bodies of water, and preferably on the side he's on. Try to be slightly uphill of him, or at least on the same level, and where you can see him once he's within gunshot.

It doesn't do much good to call half the mornng and get him within range of your shotgun if he's going to be out of sight. You're less likely to make this mistake when you hunt home territory. You know the range, how it lays, and its peculiarities. The gypsy turkey hunter who wanders around the country hunting strange woods is the one who can easily get himself into visibility trouble with an approaching gobbler.

Over in Mississippi one April morning, I heard a bird sound off not long after my partner and I had separated at a fork in the trail. The bird was still on the roost limb, so I made my way toward him and took up my calling stand when I figured the distance to him was less than a couple hundred yards. By then the light was good in the piney woods, so I made a soft yelp. The gobbler replied so quickly I knew he'd got the message. A moment later, I could tell by his change to a flatter, not-so-loud gobble that he was on the ground. He answered my next call almost before it was out, and I knew he was coming to me, fast. Then I realized I should have taken a better look at where I had located before I made initial contact. Huckleberry bushes surrounded me, open enough for the gobbler to come through, but he'd probably see me before I could get the gun on him. Having made a tactical blunder, I could only make the best of a bad situation. I knew he had me pinpointed down to the inch, so I made one last call. Then, down on my hands and knees, I scurried 20 yards to a pine that had low, drooping branches. I backed in against its trunk, leveled the gun across my knees toward the spot I'd just vacated, and waited. At my call, he'd gobbled back one time, then another, from what I assumed was some 60 yards.

A white dot was the first thing I saw move, and not 10 feet behind the upturned pine stump on which I'd been leaning. I slowly adjusted the barrel to where the dot was straight down the steel track, but I held fire. The dot moved to the left a foot or two, then back to the right. Then a glimpse of red and blue. A dark form took shape in the huckleberries. I eased down on the trigger, and No. 6 shot sawed away at the green undergrowth.

Running in to where he'd been, I found the old bird in his last throes. His ability to find me, and my knowing it, had cost him his scalp. When I shot, he was inches from where I had made my final call, searching for the hen he knew was close-by. I'd lucked out of a bad spot, a predicament that could have been avoided had I taken but a moment or two to study the terrain before attempting my first call.

If I have a favored location from which to call—and kill—a gobbler, it is on the backside at the top of a slight rise, preferably where the terrain is rough all around. In such a place, the hen's notes sound to the tom as though they are coming from a hen that he can't see until he is within range. For me, hiding in such a spot is no more than being concerned with the upper part of the body, as my lower extremities are behind the solid bulk of the ground's contours.

There's another advantage of such a location. Should the turkey swing around and come in on an unexpected tangent, you have the advantage of being where you can turn with him. Locate out on an open flat and try this with a hard-hunted old reprobate. The first time you wiggle your little finger, he'll shut up and be gone because he can see you.

Where I *don't* locate is out on a parklike flat—you know, in one of those beautiful places where we would like to make our kills. The trees are scattered and big. There's no underbrush to prevent you from seeing his approach. Green grass grows all around, or else leaves cover the forest floor, or maybe pine needles. On a spring morning, it's pure joy to do nothing but just sit in such a place listening to the birds sing and watching squirrels nose among the litter. But it's not much good for gobbler hunting.

Why not? Because of a turkey's ability to locate other turkeys. A smart old gobbler will ease up to where he can see out into a parklike area, which means you are maybe 100 yards from him. He'll stand there surveying the place from where the henlike sounds came. People say wild creatures can't reason, and perhaps the gobbler can't. But he has enough of something to realize that the hen he should see is not in sight. This situation often makes what is known as a circling gobbler. He'd like to meet this girl, but since she's making herself scarce, he'll go around and take a look for her from another angle. Agreed, there are a few turkeys that'll come waltzing out onto such grounds, but in the springtime it'll seldom be one of Turkeyville's seasoned veterans. Now young fall turkeys are different. They'll run across an open park just to get shot by somebody making *kee-kee* sounds. On opening day in spring, though, even they know better.

Try to locate where an approaching gobbler would not be able to see a hen until he came close. In flat country, this is as simple as calling from the backside of a plum thicket or while crouched down in waist-high sand-sage smack dab on top of a sandhill. In Merriam's Country, the shadows of a house-size boulder serve the purpose.

Once we've chosen our location, made our first call, and then sat listening to an excited gobbler, most of us begin to think about putting on some water to undress him for the roast. Excitement boils through our veins. A hundred questions hit us at once. Will he come in? Should I take him from a sitting position, or would I be better off lying out on my belly? Will I loom up like a sore thumb once he tops that last rise? When should I call next? How many times should I call?

Hunters who call not enough, or too much, have probably saved more gobblers than all the other bobbles put together. What's worse is that each turkey is different and there's generally no way of knowing what kind you will be dealing with. But if you happen to be hunting the same gobbler morning after morning, you soon learn the pattern of his behavior. Many of us, though, are not so lucky.

It's best to slight the calling at first. Let the tom gobble as he will while you hang tight through the long periods of silence. You can be assured he knows your location down to a few square feet, so don't fret about whether he can find you when he comes looking. On the other hand, don't make the mistake of calling so little that he loses interest and wanders off.

One morning in the Ozarks of Missouri, I was dealing with a gobbler that refused to come to me. Yet he was gobbling so much I figured every hunter in those hills would soon be keeping us company. I played hard-to-get with him twice that morning. Both times he wandered off, gobbling next far down the ridge toward the spring branch that divided it from the next mountain. With considerable calling, I managed to bring him back up the hill. But there he would hang up as before. Then I tried gobbling at him, thinking if he had a jealous bone in him he'd come a-runnin', but apparently he wasn't that hot. He gobbled at everything I did. One time he was so near that I tried scratching in the leaves, and he gobbled at that. I never came so close to jumping up and having a go at him. I felt certain I could kill him as he flushed, but something deep in my mind kept saying, "yeah, and where are you if you botch it?" I had to leave for home that afternoon, so I knew the next day was out.

Four hours later, the turkey and I were still at a stand-off in an area that covered less than seven or eight acres. I switched calls, from the diaphragm to a wingbone, then to a gobbling box.

The stand-off ended when he came to incessant calling on the diaphragm. By incessant I mean I called time after time: while he gobbled, during his gobbles, and after his gobbles. I wouldn't shut up. He took his time. When I shot him, the sun had moved over and I was lying full in the sunshine, sweating like a politician on Judgment Day.

Getting pinned down out in glaring sunlight is not my favorite position for killing a gobbler. Sun glints too much off polished gun barrels. What saved me here was being in a stretched-out position, which presents an extremely low profile, making it possible to hide behind any ground litter, even grass, and small fallen branches. I've used the belly-down (or prone) position when killing a number of gobblers. I consider it the best position when I'm calling up gobblers where cover is at a premium. The weight of the gun is easily supported throughout long waits, and it is easy to "skootch" around and keep a circling gobbler in line with the gun sight, without the risk of being seen.

The climactic moment for a turkey caller arrives when the turkey comes looking. The first glimpse of a turkey can—and often does—cause a new hunter to forget distance. Even veteran hunters will sometimes misjudge the distance and shoot too soon. This is the one drawback to shooting from a prone position: it robs your eyes of their depth-judging qualities. Unless the turkey is extremely near, your prone position can cause an error in judgment. There's an unspoken rule among old turkey men that goes, "Let 'em come as long as they will." Good advice up to a point. I don't want the bird to come closer than 20 yards. At a range of 20 yards or less, my gun pattern is too small and dense. A wild gobbler closer than 20 yards can easily be missed, as the head is the main target. When a gobbler is bobbing it around the way some of them do, your problem is like trying to shoot a .22 rifle at a cork in a washing machine.

Any old-time turkey hunter will tell you it's uncanny the way a heavy-bellied old gobbler can suddenly materialize in easy gunshot, sometimes balled into full strut, drumming, and dragging his wings in the leaves, and yet you didn't see him coming. There he is. Just like that. And your gun is lying across your lap. Now what?

Don't think you can fast-draw and beat a tom turkey that has been around. Your fast movement will spook him hard, and he'll hightail it over the treetops in a twinkling. Sometimes you'll read that a turkey must run in order to take off. That's so much hogwash. A gobbler can fly straight up as though he'd been shot out of a rocket gun.

When a turkey suddenly shows up inside easy gunshot and catches you off guard, your best move is not to move at all. Play it easy. Study the situation carefully, but as quickly as possible. Where is your gun? Is it in any possible position where you can bring it into play with easy flowing motion? If the bird flushes, can you get some sort of clear shot? What if he chooses to run? Could he step behind a tree trunk or other obstacle and put himself out of sight for even a second or two?

The possibility of your being caught off guard can usually be prevented when you go on stand. Realizing your calls might bring a turkey into shooting distance, you're wise to consider what you will do if the chance presents itself. *Before* it happens.

Unannounced turkeys are old hat to fall turkey callers, but often such shutmouth gobblers come in throughout the spring season, too. They simply sneak in quietly, often on a blind side.

One way to prevent their slipping in from the wrong direction is to be careful in your choice of calling sites. By sitting down with your back to such heavy cover as thickets, rockpiles, and down timber, you lessen the chance that a tom coming in from that direction will see you. By staying alert, you help stave off another large percentage of possible surprises. But there will come a time all the same when a gobbler is standing out front and you're not ready to shoot.

I don't lay my gun on the ground often. But when I do, I always place it alongside my leg, pistol grip where my hand can fall on it almost automatically. Another thing: don't locate with a tree branch hanging in your face or a tree trunk close enough to interfere with your line of swing. A huntable blind should provide uninhibited movement no matter from which direction your game approaches. Make your moves smooth, not jerky, on any turkey that's in the open. He'll stick around a split second longer if you don't jerk and jump. He might even elect to run for it.

Mentioning "unannounced" turkeys reminds me of an incident that hap-

pened one winter afternoon in West Virginia, where hunting hens was legal
in the fall season. I'd been fooling with a bird that kept calling from down
along a noisy mountain stream all morning, but wouldn't come to me. After
lunching from my pack, I slipped down the side of the mountain and
situated myself in the beech trees on the first bench above the creek. No
different from an old hog, I'm always drowsy after lunch. That sun shining
into the bottom made me suspect I'd fall asleep. So I laid the Winchester
alongside my leg, yelped several times real loud, and then leaned back
against the trunk. Dry oak leaves covered the slopes all around me.

I have no idea how long I slept. What woke me were footsteps in the leaves.
Maybe not all old turkey hunters do this, but I wake up just as slowly as I go
to sleep. My eyes come open. I instantly realize I'm turkey hunting, though
sometimes it takes me a moment to decide where. I ease around for a slow
deliberate look, just like the last one I took before dozing off.

This time I awoke slow and easy, but nevertheless alert to the footsteps.
Sounded like a man. Yet turkeys walking through leaves often sound exactly
like humans. Very slowly I turned my head in that direction. Not 20 yards
from me stood an old hen, taking in the scene. She caught on fast.

I swept up my gun with one hand and was on her before she could cover
10 yards. Moments later, she flopped her last. I stood there patting myself on
the back for being such a great turkey hunter. Such changes in the attitude
of a fellow toward himself are common while hunting. Before I'd fallen
asleep I was at the bottom of the ladder, feeling sorry for myself because I
couldn't kill a single bird.

Ideally, as I pointed out earlier, the superior manner in which to handle
your gun is to draw up both legs while you lean back against a tree, and then
place the gun across your knees. This position allows you to hold the gun
there comfortably if the gobbler stops to dawdle for an hour or two on the
way to your stand. Your profile is small. And with the advantage of sitting
upright, you can see a good distance into the woods. Thousands of turkeys
have been killed by hunters who got into this shooting position before the
bird was in sight, and then patiently waited for it to walk within range.

When you're dealing with a circling turkey, it's a simple matter for you to
roll from this sitting position onto your belly while trying to keep the gun in
line with him. That is, provided he's where he can't see you.

Some inventive souls have made a try at taking some of the pain out of
sitting in front of trees by the hour. Manufacturers now offer light, simple
cushions, as well as the drop-seat kind on turkey-shooting vests. Too bad
they don't add crying towels. A boat cushion will also reduce wear and tear
on your butt end.

Later in the morning, after the gobbling has let up or stopped, you might
find one trick worth trying, particularly if you are hunting strange country
and want to hunt into it and retrace your pathway out again. The tactic is
known as "calling or hunting your backtrail," and I have already talked a
little about it in Chapter 11. It can be done while you're on the move, or—if

you prefer—you can go on stand at each location. Hunting your backtrail involves no more than making a series of calls from a location, waiting a period for a possible response, and then (if you don't get an answering gobble or other indication of a turkey in the area) moving on a couple hundred yards and doing it all over again. It works best in thick, hilly cover, where your movements are screened at any distance beyond 100 yards.

It's not while you call during a journey into the area that anything is likely to occur. It's on the trip coming back out along the trail that you're more likely to expect action.

Any springtime turkey range has gobblers that remain silent, or shut-mouth, and upon hearing the calling of a hen, will continue their silence. Such behavior doesn't mean they won't come to calls. I'd hate to think how many turkeys are run off each year by hunters who get up to leave and so spook off an approaching gobbler. Such a turkey, having responded to your calls, often comes to your location after you move on down the trail. He hangs around. And if it's your day, he might be there when you come back, again calling as you move.

I've had best results with this tactic when I was moving at a steady pace, calling as I went. I wouldn't take the time to sit out each stand. I'd just yelp a few times, hoping to get an answering gobble, and then move on to try again. When coming back along the trail an hour later, I might hear the gobble. In many instances, I have killed the gobbler that was waiting and looking for the hen that walked off.

Hunters who can master the diaphragm call have a big advantage using this traveling method. The call can be kept in your mouth throughout the hunt, leaving your hands free for the gun. Always be ready to dive for cover, though—for an answering gobbler can be extremely close when you retrace your tracks to one of those spots. Perhaps such birds gobbled at the initial calling, but were unheard? I doubt it. I think they came to the hen, and—not finding her there—hung around hoping she would call again. When they hear these second calls, they answer to let her know they're on the way. Obviously these gobblers had no intention of waiting for a hen to come to them.

Hunting the shutmouth gobbler later in the day is so monotonous it's hard work. Will he come to the call? That's a sticky question that lingers in the back of your head. Your eyelids get heavy, the dog-ear gnats get thicker, and your morale hits rock bottom. I suppose what makes any of us diehards hunt throughout the long, hot afternoon hours is the memory of long-beards that came to the gun by drifting as silently as swamp mist. That, and gobblers we've stirred into action after things had long been silent.

Year in, year out, the men who hunt from daylight to dark will kill as many gobblers in the afternoon as they will in the forenoon. Though no one has ever explained why, there are certain years when male turkeys of an area gobble considerably stronger after lunch than in other years. A turkey who gobbles at midday is ordinarily easier to call to the gun than at any other time. Looking for a hen gets his guard down to the point that he is a sucker for anything that resembles a hen turkey's yelp. I suppose each spring there is one lusty gobbler somewhere across this land who could be called by merely scratching a tin barn roof with a hayfork.

What kills no end of springtime gobblers is patience. Call it time if you want. Maybe both. Witness this experience of a turkey-hunting sidekick, Tom Preston, in a Mississippi creek bottom one morning. Seems an old bird would strut down the middle of an open field, out where no one could get a shot at him and where he paid no heed to Tom's calling. This routine went on for what seemed like hours. The morning wore on, and the last hen had long since departed the field. Anytime the gobbler seemed to be drifting near a border fence, Tom would slip into bushwack position. But then the bird would go back to midfield, strutting and gobbling all the time.

The open field lay along a small creek. Once, just when Tom thought he could work a bushwack, the gobbler flew across the stream and went into strut on that side. It took my buddy half an hour to get around there. The contest had begun at first daylight. Now the hour was getting on toward noon.

A while later, the gobbler flushed back across the stream and into the first field. Then he worked out into the very center. Not wanting to go all the way around the field to get in the woods—where the turkey would no doubt go when he tired of this game—Tom found a crossing in the brushlined creek and laid up in a blackberry tangle where he could see the bird strutting a 100 yards out.

The calling, as before, drew gobbles but seemingly no other response. Tom Preston had the feeling, however, that the gobbler was moving almost imperceptibly toward the creek. A half-hour later, he pulled the trigger on a 22-pound Dixie gobbler. By all rights, the big bird should never have come to the same calls it had been ignoring all morning. In this case, a combination of patience and time killed that turkey.

Quite often you'll hear a turkey hunter bemoan a previous hunt that ended on a bad note because he failed to act quickly enough, or even to act at all. This failure of "making up your mind" has probably done about as much for turkey conservation as any other hunting fault. Call it promptness of decision, or action, or whatever, but it amounts to knowing what must be done when a turkey stands at the edge of shotgun range, although not quite close enough to kill. Success or failure here often depends on some clever maneuver, quickly made.

Judgment based on past experience is needed most. Many times I've heard a gobbler come in close, easily within gunshot but out of sight. Maybe he was behind me or circling, but somehow I took no action to counter his move. Later, reviewing my actions, I'd ask myself: Why would anybody just sit there and knowingly let a turkey get around to where you can't bring your gun into play? When this dilemma is about to happen to you, remember one thing: It is better to risk cautiously turning with the gobbler (and chance spooking him off) than to let him reach a point where you can't get a shot but will spook him off, anyway.

I was hunting in Alabama one April morning and called up an old piney-woods gobbler. He came in without too much fooling around. Yet when he approached, I found I'd located badly. My ears are not as keen as they once were, so when I hear the drumming noise of a turkey in full strut, he's usually within easy gunshot for my 12-gauge. I could hear the old boy's wings dragging in the leaves. When he gobbled, the sound all but raised the hair on my head—or what's left of it.

That section of Alabama I was hunting in is a jumble of up-and-down hills, all of them roughed up with pockets, coves, knobs, and stumpholes. The gobbler hung around for some time, carrying on just back of a tiny knoll 10 yards or so off to my right. I kept the gun trained on the sound, but the bird never showed. At last he tired and walked away. The last time I heard him gobbling, he was 100 yards off. By Monday morning quarterbacking, I figured I could have perhaps made up for my poor location by charging him when he was so near. Maybe I'd have had a good shot, maybe not. At least I'd have been in action instead of simply lying there and doing nothing. All the same, it's hard to decide sometimes when and where such a maneuver is wise.

In the West, where sagebrush is the predominant shrub, a gobbler will often be lost to the hunter's sight as he weaves in and out of the brush. This is a disturbing fact if the bird gets in close and still can't be seen. You can't afford to dally around, deciding what to do next. He'll get an eyeful of you crouched behind a clump of the stuff and be gone before you even realize he's seen you. So, my only advice here is: Take action. When he gobbles right beside you, stand up and take your chances. You'll either catch a glimpse of him skedaddling through the brush or else he'll come busting up on full flush. It's quick and sporty shooting.

The decision made while a hunter is in the process of calling may be of another variety altogether. I'm thinking about a reluctant gobbler that keeps holding back yet answers your calls time after time. The trouble is that too many hunters continue to call much the same way up to this point.

A turkey that gobbles at 100 yards seems to confuse folks who haven't hunted a lot. This is where man, supposedly blessed with the ability to reason, may be one step ahead of a wild creature. If old tom is not coming in, why isn't he? Are you located badly? Probably bad location is the No. 1 cause. Has he got hens with him? Another very good reason. Is your calling keeping him hung up? More than likely not—or else he'd just shy off and you'd hear no more from him.

But whether or not you can figure out why he's not coming in, what can you do to increase your chances? If you're going to remain at your present stand, your best first effort is to play freeze-out—shut off your calling. Many an old turkey gobbles a couple times and then shuts up and eases in to meet the hen when she fails to show up. Put your call in your pocket, pick up Old

Reliable, and be ready if he comes sneaking by. If he gobbles, don't answer. You'll want to, badly. But fight off the urge and stick to your plan. Of course, he could decide to go off in some other direction. If he does, and you know he's leaving, you'll have to try another tack. Move to where he hung up and go back to calling. Some gobblers I've tried this with came back for a recheck.

Getting around a turkey that has moved off is easier said than done. Turkeys don't seem to cover ground with any speed, but their motion is deceptive. I've run, walked, run, and then run some more—only to have the old rascal pass me by just when I thought I'd outfoxed him. In flat country this attempted outflanking maneuver is complicated by your need to keep out of his sight. In the mountains, the work involved is offset by the terrain that favors your moves. Such moves may be further complicated in "new" unfamiliar country by your possibly ending up on the wrong ridge or bogged down in the next swamp.

Suppose you have successfully maneuvered around a moving, gobbling bird. Now what?

One thing I *don't* do is start the same kind of calling that drove him off. It didn't work then. And though the reason may have been that I wasn't located where he wanted to come to me, there's still no use risking the same calls. Besides, it's no trouble switching over to something different. You gain confidence in the change. You're starting fresh. Tell yourself that. It'll help.

No doubt the best calling you can do at this time, if your earlier efforts were with average hen yelps, is a simple cluck or two. If he gobbles back, just keep quiet. The best thing to do now is stick the caller in your pocket or sit on it. The urge to continue sawing away on it will all but strangle you. Strangle if you must, but don't use the call. He'll gobble maybe another time or two. But when he shuts off, unglue your eyeballs and stay alert.

Now, once again, he might move off. This sort of thing can go on and on all morning, or even all day, until he ceases to gobble and you lose contact. Then the thinking turkey hunter comes into his own. He might not get the shot he's hoping for, but he's not out of the game either.

Another deal, another draw, another chance. It's like a game of chess—thrust, parry, encirclement, withdrawal. You play your best move, he counters, and again you must think in this game how to outwit his wild instincts. Should you be lucky enough to find that your feathered opponent is one of those hard-hunted old mossbacks that's been hanging out for years on some hardwood-cloaked mountain point, then you may have to put on your reserve thinking cap as well. Or go home empty-handed.

13

Shotguns, Rifles, and Ammunition

When it comes to choice of weapons in turkey hunting, I proudly declare myself a shotgun man. More specifically, a Winchester Model 12 man. And from all the time I've spent in turkey woods across the nation, I would say that a sizable segment of hunters share my choice of gun. We might rightly be called the BOSM 12 ST—short for Brotherhood of Old Style Model 12 Shotgun Toters.

It was way back in 1923 that I first investigated the matter and determined the Model 12 was among the best of the turkey guns then on the market. The one I bought had originally a 30-inch full-choke nickel-steel barrel. With 1¼ ounces of No. 6 shot, this barrel would deliver 80 percent of its shot into a 30-inch circle at forty yards, which made it a tight full choke. My "new" barrel is only a little over twenty-five years old, and it does almost as well.

This shotgun, when fully loaded, weighs nearly 9 pounds, which is one reason I equipped it with swivels and a carrying sling. Another reason is that most turkey hunts involve a good bit of hiking and very little shooting. And—although you may not have noticed yet—the older you grow, the more your gun weighs and the steeper the hills become.

A sling is a big help when you're on the move. However, it should be fully detachable so that when you take your seat in a blind, the sling can be removed and put out of the way. If you prefer not to fit your gun with swivels, carrying slings are now available with leather loops on each end. One goes around the barrel of the gun, and the other goes on the butt stock just below the grip. These do a good job and sell for $12 or so.

I cannot remember ever having killed a turkey with a gun other than my Model 12. A number of years ago in the Rockies, I hunted several days with a borrowed gun. My Winchester had been missent by an airline to San Juan instead of Santa Fe. I felt as though I were hunting with a peashooter. Luckily, my gun finally arrived, and I bagged my Merriam's gobbler with it before the hunt was done.

I am partial to my shotgun for several reasons. First, it shoots a full-choke pattern, and this is what turkey hunting requires. I don't mean to imply that shots are customarily long. As I pointed out previously, shots are seldom longer than 40 steps if the hunter does his job properly right up to the moment of pulling the trigger. Personally, I would not take a shot at a gobbler standing more than 40 yards away. If I were hard-pressed to estimate the range at which I've bagged turkeys over half a century, I would guess it to be less than 30 steps.

A full-choke is best because shots should be directed at the head and neck of the bird. These are vulnerable targets, but the body itself is a veritable fortress of feathers, muscle, sinew, and bone. A dense pattern aimed at the head is almost certain to result in an instant kill if the range is reasonable. Body shots should be avoided since the vitals of a turkey are all neatly tucked away behind great wings and huge breasts. Shots at flying turkeys are always very chancy and should be avoided for the same reason. It is much too easy to break merely a wing and bring one of these wonderful birds to earth—only to have it sprint away on those legs of steel. And remember: A turkey with a broken wing is usually a doomed bird.

A large percentage of the time, body shots prove ineffective. A chum of mine once cartwheeled a big tom at 45 yards with a heavy load of No. 4 shot. It was a body shot. Almost instantly the tom was up and running down the back side of a ridge. My pal got no chance for a second shot. He told me later he didn't believe any bird could take such a hit and still get away.

Later that season, another pal of mine called up a big gobbler and killed it cleanly with a head shot. When he picked it up he discovered some thirty No. 4 shot in the bird's left side and wing. The wounds had turned all yellow and purple. This bird was bagged less than a quarter-mile from where my other partner had earlier wounded the tom that escaped. I leave you to draw your own conclusions.

I like the 30-inch barrel of my shotgun well enough. I will admit there have been times when I would have preferred a shorter full-choke barrel. The overall length of my shotgun from butt to muzzle is 50 inches. That's long and sometimes cumbersome when adjustments in shooting positions must be made quickly and quietly. Still, I know what my gun will do, and I have great confidence when it is in my hands.

Knowing what your gun will do is vital to your success. As I suggested in Chapter 4 on preparing for your gobbler hunt, the only way to test a shotgun's performance is on paper. Go to the range and put up several 4' x 4' squares of paper. The white wrapping paper used in meat markets works very well. Your butcher will be glad to furnish you with paper enough for several targets at little or no cost.

By firing only one shot at the center of the paper, you can determine three things: 1) Whether or not your gun shoots to point of aim. (If so, the densest portion of the pattern will be in the center of the target.) 2) The true choke of the barrel, which is sometimes at variance with what is stamped on the barrel. To ascertain true choke, draw a 30-inch circle around the densest part of the pattern. Ignore fliers. Now count the number of shot holes within the circle. Then compare this number with the total number of shot in the shell. A true full-choke barrel will place 70 to 80 percent of the shot in a 30-inch circle; modified will run 55 to 60 percent; improved cylinder, about 45 percent. 3) Whether or not your gun will evenly pattern the particular shell you fired. Some guns shoot No. 6 shot quite well but refuse to shoot a good pattern with No. 4s. Sometimes just the reverse is true. One brand of ammunition may shoot better than another with the same load of powder and shot.

The only way to solve all these mysteries is to fire a number of test patterns until you arrive at what is best for your shotgun.

Shoot patterns at ranges of 20, 30, and 40 yards. If you use a big magnum, you may want to try some shots at 50 yards to see what Old Betsy will do at extended range.

After all the shooting is done and you have settled on one load, a final test should be made. On a piece of cardboard, sketch out the profile of a gobbler's head and neck. The vital area of the neck covers only one inch and the head just about two inches. Attach this profile to the top of a 3-foot-long stick and push the stick into the ground. Now back off 40 yards and fire a shot. Examine the profile and see if you delivered a killing three or four pellets into the target. Repeat this procedure at various distances. The results of this final test will either boost your confidence in your gun and load or will point up the need for additional testing. Often what looks quite good on a four-foot-square sheet of paper isn't nearly so impressive when fired at a head silhouette.

About shotgun actions, there isn't a great deal to be said. If all goes well on a turkey hunt, only one shot will be required. But there are times, alas, when things do not go perfectly. Then other shots must be taken—and taken quickly. It is then that a shotgun's action is of some importance.

My pump, when plugged, allows me three shots—a legal number in most states where turkeys are hunted with scatterguns. My first shell is invariably a charge of No. 6 shot, followed by a shell containing No. 4s that pattern well at 40 yards. My third round has No. 2s, which I hope I will never need.

I like the single sighting plain afforded by my slide-action gun. Automatics and over-and-unders offer this same advantage. Shooting a turkey is not unlike shooting other forms of big game in that the gun is actually sighted rather than pointed as is done when shooting with a shotgun at upland game or waterfowl.

I do not have a raised rib on my gun, but I am sure a rib would not be objectionable. Very likely it would aid in aiming, especially if two beads were used on it. The rear bead serves as a rear sight and helps with barrel alignment.

Most gun-sight companies now offer shotgun sights. These were developed because of the widespread use of shotguns for deer hunting, particularly in highly populated areas. These sights aid tremendously in improving slug accuracy on deer. I see no reason why they would not also help a turkey hunter deliver his shot into the turkey's head and neck.

Telescopic sights are also offered for shotguns. I do not think any magnification is needed, because of the relatively short ranges at which turkey hunters work. However, some hunters I know like scopes on their shotguns. These have no magnification but do have a large dot reticle that makes the shooter pin the dot on the turkey before pulling the trigger. I've also been told that since no magnification is used, wing shots are not any more difficult to execute.

Most advantages of the slide-action gun apply also to the auto loader. However, I have heard of autos that jammed now and then. My pump has never failed me, though this must sometimes happen to other gunners.

Many turkey hunters swear by the double-barrel shotgun. The chief advantage of these guns as I see it is that two different chokes are instantly available to the shooter. Bruce Brady, my Mississippi turkey-hunting partner, swears by his old 12-gauge CHE Parker double, and a nice collection of beards testify to its effectiveness. Brady's double is bored full in one barrel and modified in the other. It has two triggers. Contrary to what you might think, he uses the full-choke barrel for close shots and holds the modified tube in reserve in the event a wing shot is needed. As far as I know, he has never needed it.

Another advantage of the double is its overall shorter length. Brady's Parker, with its 32-inch barrels (two inches longer than my pump's barrel), is a full two inches shorter in overall length than my Model 12.

Each year hundreds of turkeys are bagged with small-gauge shotguns. It distresses me to report that hundreds more are only crippled and manage to escape only to die a wasted death in some brushtop. I've heard hunters say that they turned to smaller gauges in order to improve the sport of the hunt. Not so. The sport does not lie in the shooting, which if properly done is always at short ranges and under such conditions that a tom doesn't "stand a prayer" of escaping. Once we have outsmarted this wonderful and majestic bird, it's only right that we bring the competition to an end as quickly and as decently as possible. Generally, this objective is best accomplished using big guns and heavy loads. Let us leave demonstrations of shooting ability with small gauges and light loads to the dove fields.

If 16-gauge or 20-gauge guns are used, they should be used with magnum shells. Ballistic tables indicate that both shells are available with 1¼ ounces of shot, which is the same loading as a high-brass 2¾-inch 12-gauge shell. There are approximately 280 pellets in 1¼ ounces of No. 6 shot.

If smaller gauges are used with light loads, the reason should be that the shooter is a woman, a youngster, or some other person who because of his size or a physical impairment cannot handle the heavier shells.

A number of magnum loads are available for 10, 12, 16 and 20-gauge guns. The 10-gauge magnum is 3½ inches and carries 5 drams of powder and 2 ounces of shot. Only No. 2 shot is offered in this load. Remington and Winchester-Western both offer a 10-gauge loading of 4¾ drams of powder and 1⅝ ounces of No. 4 shot in a 2⅞-inch shell.

Almost as potent is the 12-gauge 3-inch magnum, which carries 4½ drams of powder and 1⅞ ounces of No. 4 shot. This is ¼ ounce more shot than that loaded in the 10-gauge shell.

The most effective 2¾-inch magnum 12-gauge load I've used was one manufactured by Smith & Wesson a few years ago. This shell was loaded with 4½ drams of powder and 1½ ounces of shot. The shots were copper-coated and offered in Nos. 2, 4, and 6. I found it to be a very powerful shell, producing unusually uniform patterns with No. 6 shot, probably because they were copper-coated. That coating tends to reduce deformity of the pellets. A shell quite similar to this one is still offered with lubaloy shot by Winchester-Western.

The great majority of turkey hunters use No. 6 and No. 4 shot. I believe No. 6 is the most popular. I use them, but certainly there are no flies on No. 4s. Opinions seem to vary from one section of the country to another. I have hunted in parts of Alabama where hunters would consider it unthinkable to shoot at a tom with anything smaller than No. 4 shot, alleging that the energy generated by No. 4s is essential to cut through heavy feathers and hard bones. In parts of Pennsylvania, turkey hunters look aghast at anyone stuffing shells other than No. 6s into a scattergun. There the claim is that the pattern saturation offered by No. 6s is necessary to skin a gobbler's noggin properly.

When all theory is set aside and we get down to the nitty-gritty, it is a personal decision, and each hunter should use the loading that best delivers sufficient energy and pattern density in his gun.

I know of few deer hunters nowadays who would venture out on opening day without firing at least a few shots through their favorite rifle to be sure the scope is "close enough," as the saying goes. Unfortunately, this is not the habit with turkey hunters, many of whom assume that if they have the most powerful load available they can kill a gobbler as far as they can see it. What a revelation a few practice shots at a paper target might bring.

Actually, checking out your gun should be considered an integral part of the hunt. It's fun, too, and vents some of your enthusiasm as you wait for opening day. If you take along a pal, some interesting competition may develop as you both determine whose gun will shoot superior patterns at various ranges.

I have never killed a wild turkey with a rifle. I have, however, been associated with a good many hunters over the years who preferred the rifle for taking wild turkeys. In some states—Alabama is one—the use of rifles for hunting turkeys is prohibited by state law. In other regions, primarily where the Rio Grande and Merriam's turkeys are found, rifles are widely used. Anyone planning a turkey hunt is obligated to check the regulations of the area he intends to hunt in order to determine exactly which firearms are legal.

In the minds of some gobbler chasers, the man who uses a rifle to take his turkey is a man incapable of calling his bird into shotgun range. This opinion is not necessarily valid. M. L. Lynch, who designed the Lynch Box and manufactured it for almost fifty years, was no slouch at calling turkeys. From time to time Mike used a .22-caliber rifle to take his gobbler. I must add here that I consider the .22 rimfires most inadequate for wild turkeys unless in the hands of a master.

Years ago as a youth in Georgia, I saw Southern mountain men hunting turkeys with small-caliber muzzleloading rifles. But more about muzzleloaders later.

A host of rifle cartridges have been used by turkey hunters over the years. Several of these proved very effective and still persist today. The old .32-20 WCF is such a cartridge. It first appeared in 1882, and the Winchester 73s were chambered for the round. It could have been dubbed the .30-20 since it actually uses a .30-caliber bullet and not a .32. With its mild report and recoil, it was a favorite on varmints and small game and was often called upon (though it lacks the proper power) to double as a big-game cartridge.

The .32-20 was offered for a time with an 85-grain bullet that really stepped along. At present, it is loaded with a stoutly constructed 100-grain bullet to a muzzle velocity of 1290 feet per second, which makes it a fine choice for turkeys if ranges aren't long. Little meat is destroyed with this round. One of the nicest turkey outfits I can remember for this cartridge was the little Savage bolt-action Model 23-D topped with a four-power scope.

In the 1890s, both the .25-20 WCF and the .25-35 Winchester came along. These were widely used by turkey hunters and were offered in several bullet weights. Now the .25-20 WCF is available in only 86-grain bullets, but at a velocity of 1460 still makes an effective cartridge for turkeys. The .25-35 is offered in only 117-grain bullets, which attain a muzzle velocity of 2300 feet per second. This cartridge has a good reputation for accuracy in lever-action rifles. Report and recoil are minimal.

In 1930, Winchester marketed the .22 Hornet and a new ball game began for small-caliber marksmen. Loaded with smokeless powders, this feisty little cartridge hummed its 45-grain bullet along at 2690 fps (feet per second) and gave good accuracy at 200-yard ranges. It had virtually no recoil, and was a quick killer on varmints. Hunters discovered that meat destruction was not excessive when the Hornet hit a wild gobbler.

For a while, the venerable Model 54 Winchester was chambered for the Hornet, as were the Model 70 and a number of other rifles. The .22 Hornet was an excellent choice for turkey hunters, but its popularity diminished rapidly when the racier .222 Remington appeared in 1950.

First offered in the cheap but accurate Model 722 rifle, the .222 exceeded by a hundred yards the range of the Hornet and still had negligible recoil and muzzle blast. It attained a velocity of 3200 fps with its 50-grain bullet. Riflemen found it inherently more accurate than the Hornet. With its increased velocity and energy levels, the .222's hydraulic effect of impact on varmints and turkeys was quite dramatic and destructive as bullet placement was not exact. Shooters seemed quite willing to put up with this loss of accuracy in order to have increased effective range and flatter trajectories.

The .222 is now offered in a wide variety of rifles, both domestic and imported. The little Hornet, alas, is available in only a few over-the-counter guns today. Some of these are the Savage 340-C, the single-shot Harrington & Richardson, the single-shot Ruger No. 3, the clip-fed Anschutz 1432, and a few imported mostly combination guns.

In recent times the Hornet seems to be making a nostalgic comeback of sorts. However, because bullets for the .222 are now available with full jackets (which limit expansion and curb tissue destruction), it is doubtful that the Hornet will ever make a lasting return.

The old .218 Bee would have been a dandy turkey cartridge had it ever been available in other than lever-action rifles.

The .220 Swift is just too hot for use on turkeys unless it is handloaded down to appropriate levels. The same would apply to the Winchester .225, the Remington .22/250, the Weatherby .224, and the various 6mms. In my estimation, the .222 magnum offers little benefit over the .222 as a turkey cartridge. The round was developed in the 1950s when magnums were the craze.

The Remington .223 is simply the commercial version of the NATO 5.56mm round. It offers nothing to the turkey hunter not already available in the .222. Ballistically, it is almost the same as the .222 Magnum. The cartridge has found some favor with turkey hunters around the country because of the availability of military ammunition with full-jacketed bullets.

However, hunters who have tried the G.I. ammo tell me that it is too hot for turkeys and that meat loss is great on body-shot birds. For the hand-loader, though, bullets can be pulled, lighter powder charges used, and the full-jacketed bullets reseated. These custom-tailored loads would be bad medicine for turkeys in the hands of a competent marksman.

I know many hunters who have toted .30/06s and .308s into the turkey woods. These rifles are loaded with military ammo. But as with the little 5.56mm NATO round, these are too large and too hot for Old Brother Tom. Tissue destruction is prodigious, according to the guys who know. Most military ammo is incapable of the minute-of-angle accuracy necessary for head shots.

The idea, fellow marksmen, is to *bag* the turkey—not kill it and leave behind a pitiful pile of remains for buzzards.

Once while hunting Rio Grande gobblers with Glenn Titus in Oklahoma I noted some local riflemen had handloaded mild loads and seated soft-point bullets with the bases forward to minimize tissue destruction. Amazingly, these loads were accurate enough at ranges near 100 yards.

Some Oklahoma hunters who use rifles on turkeys believe that the way to minimize damage to the meat is to pull and then reverse the bullets in the cases, as you see in the two outer ones.

As I said before, when it comes to turkeys I am a shotgun man. Still, if I were to select a rifle for taking turkeys, it would be a light and pretty little .222 with a 2X-7X variable scope. I would work up some super-accurate loads with full-jacketed 50-grain bullets that would produce a muzzle velocity of approximately 250 fps. I realize this load would reduce effective ranges and that trajectory would be affected. To overcome these problems, I would simply pass up shots I considered doubtful, and squeeze off when I felt confident I could put usable meat in the pot.

I like the little .22 Hornet. And if by chance I ran across an old used-but-not-abused Model 70 chambered for this round, I would be equally happy to give it a spot in my gun rack.

In some sections of the wild turkey's range, particularly in the Deep South, rifle-shotgun combination guns are considered the perfect weapon for turkeys. This opinion may be correct if the object is employing just one gun for all combinations of terrain. Combination guns are made principally in two forms: 1) over-unders, and 2) drillings. Over-unders employ one rifle barrel and one shotgun barrel. Drillings usually have three or more barrels. The most common drillings have two shotgun barrels and one rifle barrel.

Two-barrel combination guns are manufactured in the U.S., but I know of no drillings being produced here. Drillings are very well made weapons, and some of them demonstrate such fine points of the gun-maker's art as superb checkering and deluxe engraving. They are also quite expensive if bought new. Used ones are difficult to find and seem to lose little of their original value with resale.

Prices for new three-barrel drillings begin at about $2,500. Imported two-barrel combination guns aren't being given away these days either. Prices for the excellent Ferlach and Krieghof guns range from $950 to over $4,000 as this book goes to press and will probably go higher. Most of these fine guns are offered in any combination of popular gauges and cartridges.

A number of well-made and serviceable two-barrel combination guns are manufactured in this country, and at much lower prices than the imported guns. Savage offers the Model 2400, which has a barrel for 2¾-inch 12-gauge loads and on the bottom either a .222 or a .308 rifle barrel. This gun retails for over $400. Also manufactured by Savage is the cheaper Model 24, which is available with a top barrel for 3-inch 20-gauge loads and below either a .222 or .30-30 rifle barrel. This gun sells for about $140. Both models will accept scope mounts.

A well-made combination gun imported by Ithaca Gun Company is appropriately named Turkeygun. It, too, is a 12-gauge .222 over-and-under design. The gun is supplied with a full-choke detachable choke tube. Modified and improved cylinder tubes are also available. The gun sells for about $340 these days.

Many combination guns I have seen in the field were not ideally suited for turkeys. I'd guess them to be booty from World War II. The shotgun barrels are usually 16- and 12-gauge, which is fine; but the rifle barrel is usually chambered for 7mm or 8mm, or some other caliber more suited for taking big four-legged game. I wonder just how many of these guns that I see in the field are actually loaded with legitimate turkey ammunition. Handloaders can, of course, tailor their loads for turkeys.

The shotgunner aims for the head and neck of his gobbler. Where does the rifleman try to put his shot? Hunters who have considerable experience tell me it is of great importance to hit a turkey properly.

The head shot is out. Anyone who has watched wild turkeys closely knows that their heads are seldom still for a moment but are ever moving, ever turning as the birds remain constantly vigilant, on the lookout for enemies. This bobbing turkey head, need I add, is smaller than a two-inch bull's-eye.

Most of the experienced riflemen I questioned advised waiting for a broadside shot and then aiming for the point where the wings enter the body. This placement anchors the bird and ruins little meat. Others tell me that the bullet should strike at the top of the legs and that a tom hit there can neither fly nor run to safety.

I am also told that shots into the rear should not be taken. In such cases the bullet will most often shatter bone and then exit through the breast, which doesn't add a thing to your Christmas dinner.

It has been suggested that frontal shots be placed at the base of the neck in order to avoid damage to the breast. During a recent spring season, I witnessed a competent marksman attempt just such a shot at about 150 yards with a scope-sighted .223 Remington rifle. His quarry was a fine gobbler in full strut. When the turkey broke his strut, the rifleman knocked him head over tea kettle and feathers flew everywhere. Moments later, the bird rose and flew off into the swamp, where he was never found. He probably died a wasted death.

As I said earlier, I can remember that as a boy I saw men with muzzleloading rifles hunting turkeys in the Georgia hills near home. During the early years of our country's history, this was the principal way wild turkeys were brought to bag.

In recent years, primitive weapons have enjoyed renewed popularity among sportsmen. Most states now have special hunting seasons set aside for hunters who use black-powder weapons. In my rack I have two lovely muzzleloader rifles that were handmade for me by Jack Crockford of Atlanta. One is a .50-caliber, with which I have bagged deer and elk. The other is a .36-caliber suitable for varmints, squirrels, and game up to and including turkeys. I have never killed a turkey with this rifle, but I daresay I could do it. The rifle is very accurate, and I would limit my shot to very close range.

I believe the caplock muzzleloaders have the edge for hunting turkeys because of their faster lock time. But the flintlock may be more sporting.

In caplock muzzleloaders proven safe, there are several loads I consider good for turkeys. They are considered mild loads. In a .36-caliber rifle, I like a patched 65-grain round ball and 40 grains of FFG powder. This load generates about 1900 fps velocity and nearly 600 foot-pounds of energy.

For the .45-caliber, I like a patched 127-grain round ball and 50 grains of FFG powder. This load produces about 1600 fps and nearly 700 foot-pounds of energy.

In the .50-caliber rifle, I think a good turkey load is a patched 175-grain round ball and 50 grains of FFG powder for a muzzle velocity of 1400 fps and about 800 foot-pounds of energy.

Rifles of .54 and .58 caliber, I think, are a trifle too heavy for turkeys.

All of the loads I've mentioned will shoot through a turkey at ranges of 60 to 75 yards, which should be considered maximum with these mild loads. At greater distances, bullet drop necessitates too much holdover to deliver the accuracy needed to make one-shot sure kills. With a muzzleloader, you don't get another shot.

Today, both flintlock and caplock muzzleloaders are available in good assortment. Most of these are imported jobs that retail at prices from about $65 to $300. They are made in a variety of styles, the most popular being the caplock Kentuckys and mountain rifles of the Hawken design. Several domestic firms offer excellent muzzleloaders at prices around $150. Those made by the Thompson-Center Company and Dixie Gun Works I have found to be quite accurate.

Shooters who feel the need I do for authenticity will sometimes insist upon muzzleloaders with barrels of 36 inches or more. Actually, chronograph figures indicate that barrels of 28 inches are just as effective and that only 80 foot-seconds of velocity are gained by adding the 8 inches of barrel.

To be sure, the shorter barrels are handier in the woods. And sighting radius is ample between front and rear sights.

Every year, more and more hunters are successfully taking the wild turkey with bow and arrow. As for myself, I'm not an archer. I tried it once for a short while, but my mentor finally put his hand on my shoulder and suggested I stick with my old Model 12. I followed his advice.

Taking a gobbler with a bow seems to me almost impossible. Experienced archers tell me the new compound bows with their high percentage of let-off at full draw are a boon to the bowhunter who is after turkeys. It is necessary to draw the bow and bring it into position while the turkey's head is obscured by a tree or brush and then to hold the bow at full draw until the turkey reappears. I am told these new bows make this procedure much easier to accomplish.

Still, the turkey must be hit with the arrow—no simple task. Under many circumstances a deer can jump the string, as they say, or dodge an arrow in flight. Imagine, then, how much easier this tactic is for a turkey to perform.

Some archers use blunts on turkeys, but most stick to sharp broadheads. In a number of states, both deer and turkey are legal at the same time; the broadhead lets a hunter be prepared for whichever species presents a shot.

Interest in wildlife photography has grown tremendously in recent years. This development is all to the good, I think. It indicates that folks are beginning to see beauty and great value in animals that they formerly took for granted. But good photos of wild turkeys are very difficult to take. There are several reasons for this, but the main one is that turkeys are just as difficult to get into camera range as they are to get within gun range. In addition, light conditions are very poor when turkeys are most accessible: at dawn and just before dark.

The cameraman who hopes to get fine pictures of the wild turkey in his natural habitat must have himself and his equipment expertly concealed, and he must possess the patience of Job.

For close-ups a relatively long lens (at least 200mm) is required. It must be fast enough to produce good results in poor light. The 35mm cameras are most popular for this work.

For black and white shots, Tri-X film is best since it has an ASA rating of 400, which can be increased if need be. Be certain to advise your processor of the increased ASA rating before the film is developed. For color shots, Ektachrome Professional Film with ASA rating 200 is an excellent choice.

A tripod is often essential, for camera apertures usually must be quite large and speeds very slow in order to gain the required light.

Baited turkeys are the easiest to photograph since you can pick your spot and work at known distances. Elaborate blinds that allow movement are also possible under such conditions. Of course, you must clear your plans with wildlife officials first. Pick a time when the hunting season is closed and the vegetation is exactly as you would like to have it.

14

Sit Still!
Don't Sit Still!

If up to now I've given the impression that it's always necessary to sit like a knot on a log to kill a gobbler, let me hasten to correct it. Innumerable are the occasions when you must move at the right time, but it's important you know when and how to do so.

My neighbor and hunting partner, Dr. Goodwin Tuck, probably heeded this knot-on-a-log advice a bit too well. Tuck and I have long been after doves, ducks, deer, and such, but only within the last few years has Tuck become afflicted with gobbler disease.

Tuck had found a gobbler on the roost, so he sat down nearby, with his back to an old treetop, and called. The turkey answered immediately, then gobbled again. After a few minutes, the bird flew down. From the sound of its wings, the good doctor knew that the tom had landed in an open spot immediately behind his pile of brush. He sat perfectly still, hardly daring to breathe. The gobbler walked around behind him for ten minutes or more, clock-clock-clocking to locate the mythical hen. That's when Tuck should have done one of two things. Either he should have clucked a couple of times to keep that gobbler searching for him—which probably would have brought the bird around the brush pile—or else he should have stood up and turned for a wing shot when the bird became airborne.

As it was, Tuck remained quiet, never moving, and the gobbler finally walked away, apparently convinced that the hen had departed or that his ears had played tricks on him and she'd not been around those parts in the first place.

I've taken many gobblers out of Georgia's Cohutta Mountains and the country to the north across the Tennessee line. Most were hunted and either bagged or missed by orthodox methods. But a few were collected by my getting away from all the prescribed procedures—if there is any such thing in turkey hunting.

If you've just started out in the game, for me to tell you when to change locations and when not to, or when to try something different if what you're doing doesn't work, would take me a whole library of books. And then you'd really be confused! Knowledge in these things can only be gained from long experience with birds and with the terrain in which they live.

Ben Rogers Lee, for instance, is not an old-timer as far as age goes, but he sure is when it comes to wild turkeys. He grew up with the turkey clan. He's hunted them so long he thinks like a turkey. He can talk the language better than anyone else I know. The turkeys think so, too, as do the human judges who decide turkey-calling contests. Ben has won a number of world and other championships.

Ben understands the language as well as he can speak it. When he talks to a bird for a while, he's likely to leave his blind and—in spite of his bulk—race a hundred yards or more through the woods to another spot. And that's where the gobbler comes to him. They seem to have some sort of understanding between them.

Of course, the best rule for the average hunter is to stay put when he hears a turkey. But that's not always the best policy.

I was a faithful follower of this sitting cult myself until the day I took a couple of birds out of the Cohuttas by breaking most of the rules. I'm still a faithful sitter, for that matter. Usually, only the most desperate or curious circumstances (like sitting down on a rattlesnake) will get me to move.

I was hunting along the Tennessee line where the high country stands on end and is broken by sharp ridges and deep valleys. Phil Stone and Lamar Westcoot and I had located a good gobbler a couple of days before, exactly where Hoyt Pippinger, the local game ranger, had said it would be. Lamar came closest to getting the gobbler that morning. The bird was working its way up the ridge toward him, and Lamar reached for the slate call he'd laid beside him on the ground. He felt blindly for his call. When his fingers knocked against it, the slate slid down the steep slope out of reach. Lamar didn't dare bend over enough to retrieve it until the turkey left the ridge and angled off into a hollow. He called when he felt it was safe, but the turkey was either spooked or had something else on its mind, for it kept on going.

Two mornings later, I stood on the crest of a ridge in that same area, straining my ears at the gray dawn. The last of the highland stars winked out, and soft light filtered through the forest crowns. A squirrel barked, and a pair of thrushes churred in the brush. Down in the hollow, a barred owl cackled contemptuously at the day.

That owl's personal reaction to the early symphony of the spring woods soon brought forth an answer. A gobbler on one of the side ridges far below the crest quickly replied. I relaxed against a tree trunk to wait for his second gobble to tell me more exactly where he was. Then suddenly I lost all interest in the bird I'd heard. For from high on the ridge in the opposite direction rolled the shrill *gil-obble-obble-obble* of another bird. It carried along the ground, overflowed the valley, and made my hair stand on end. There wasn't any question about those notes. They were the song of an old tom, and he was in the vicinity of the bird Hoyt had told us about.

I angled across the steep slope, climbing as fast as my aging lungs would allow, yet trying to make as little noise as possible in the dry leaves. Halfway up the hill I paused to get my breath and listen. After a few minutes, I heard the tom again. This time he sounded faint and much farther away, so I guessed he must have gone off the ridgetop on the far side.

Ten minutes later, with my throat aching and my temples pounding from the steep climb, I slumped down on top of the ridge. Almost immediately I forgot my exhaustion—for the tom again gobbled in commanding tones. I remained on the divide long enough to determine the general direction in which the bird might be traveling. Then I paralleled his course around the side of the mountain until I reached a point on the hillside about 100 yards above him. I crawled into an old treetop, sat long enough to get at least a part of my breath back, and reached for a special cedar box I had brought along for the occasion. It had been made for me by John Jared, a guide and shooting buddy over many years. I'd promised him that I would try it on my next turkey and give him an accurate report on its effectiveness. I didn't promise not to throw it away if it cost me a gobbler.

Every turkey call is a little different. And though I'd practiced with this one before coming on the hunt, I had to be careful how I used the slate against the cedar edge.

It was probably more luck than skill that caused my clucks and yelps to come out perfect. I crouched motionless for ten minutes before the gobbler answered from approximately the same spot. I knew he was interested and that he had me pinpointed on a peg. In such a case, the best bet is to wait until he gobbles again and then give him a come-on cluck or two. But he didn't make another sound—which either meant he had been spooked, had lost interest, or else was on his way to investigate. I didn't think he could have been spooked or lost interest, so figured I'd better have my gun in position or reasonably close to it.

I keep the lid of my own gobbling box tight against the box with rubber bands. This arrangement prevents it from making odd noises when it's being carried in my coat pocket or shoulder bag. This time, though, I'd failed to put rubber bands on the box that John Jared had made for me. So I very cautiously (and without taking my eyes off the woods in front of the blind) laid the box down beside me. Apparently I placed it on a stick or some other uneven object, for when I took my fingers off, the box turned over on its side with a weird squeal that made my blood run cold. Knowing that it's imperative to follow any such outlandish noise with a perfect call, I hastily retrieved the box and tried to give forth some notes that dripped with honey—or whatever is a turkey's equivalent.

This time it didn't work. That first sound I'd made earlier would have spooked a barnyard rooster. And I didn't want to take any more chances. So, for a quarter-hour, I crouched as motionless as the snag that was boring into my back would allow. Then I held the box just right and made the most seductive clucks I knew how. When that tactic got no response within five minutes, I tried the ringing-hen call again. To this the gobbler did reply—from 500 yards away on the next ridge.

For another five minutes I sat, undecided whether to go after him or not. I felt that trying to call him back across that cove after I'd scared the very sand out of his gizzard took more genius than I possessed, especially with a new cedar box, or even my diaphragm call.

The morning was still young enough for me to go looking for another gobbler, but this one had become a challenge. Any other tom I managed to kill—considering if I could find one—would be an anticlimax. It had to be this bearded patriarch over on the next ridge or nothing.

So I decided to move. I slid the cedar box into the cloth shoulder bag and made a long detour around the top of the adjoining hollow, pausing occasionally to hear my bird gobble again. He was one of those vociferous types. A dense laurel thicket gave me a break, and I slithered through it like a copperhead. I stopped at the thicket's edge, about 70 yards from where I had last heard the gobbler. After waiting as long as turkey protocol demands, I thought about going to a wingbone or the diaphragm call. But I had promised my friend John to give him a dramatic report on his call, so I decided to go with the box all the way.

Silence answered my call. I could imagine the old tom standing with his head up, listening and trying to decide whether I was a bona-fide hen or that goof he'd left back on the last ridge.

Relief flowed through me when he gobbled again and then after a long pause answered the second call I made. I couldn't tell whether he was moving in my direction or remaining in one spot. He did sound close enough to be within sight, which meant that I hadn't alarmed him too badly during our encounter on the last ridge.

There is no way to guess, even, how this second try might have ended. The fates have a way of playing strange tricks, and most of them seem to favor the gobbler. As I sat motionless, a small whitetail buck walked downwind around the rim of the laurel patch and was within a dozen feet before he saw me. For several minutes he studied me while I sat motionless, not even batting an eyelash. Apparently satisfied, the buck nibbled on by without giving me another glance, until he got on the other side and caught my scent. Then he went through a sudden convulsion as though I'd slapped him across the nose with my dirty underwear. He snorted like the off-note of a steam calliope, swapped ends, and tore down the mountain toward my gobbler.

Why that turkey didn't get airborne and head in the general direction of Canada I'll never know. But he didn't stay around to find out what had scared the "bejasus" out of that deer. When I heard the bird again, half an hour later, he was on the next mountain, so far away that I could only faintly make out his gobble. He was either a loquacious critter or in the mood for a hen.

Exasperated and wishing the little buck was close enough for me to run down and give a thrashing with my belt (which I considered might not be too illegal), I started doggedly on the trail once more. I knew it was stupid and figured about all I'd get out of it was the exercise. But that gobbler was in the direction of camp anyway. Not often do you get three strikes at the same bird, especially a wary old tom such as this one seemed to be.

I sweated out a tough climb over a rugged jumble of big rocks, across a smaller ridge, around a hillside as steep as a church roof, and through a laurel thicket that tried to tear every pocket out of my clothes. There was no way of knowing whether I'd gone far enough, unless I could hear the tom gobble again. So, on a slanting hogback, I sat with my camouflage jacket against a tree trunk to wait.

After I got back some of my wind, I began to realize how uncomfortable a seat I'd chosen. A sharp snag at the tree base jabbed my hindquarters, and the three-cornered rock under me by no means resembled an air pillow. I was about to squirm into a more restful posture when the buck turkey gobbled so close under the contour of the ridge that my neck hairs stood on end. He was right there below me on the slope, but out of sight. I expected to see his knobby head come up over the rise at any second.

I tried to shrink into as inconspicuous a bundle as possible, and I shifted the gun carefully to my shoulder. Sitting down so close to the bird was a real break—nothing else—and I strained every sense to get a glimpse of him before he saw me. I was so sure the kill was only seconds away that I waited with the gun stock pressed against my cheek.

The strain became terrific, both on my muscles and on my nerves. Long minutes passed. I didn't understand how that bird could be so close and yet remain invisible. He was feeding. I could hear his big feet cutting into hunks of humus and leaves. There was no way to know how long I held my gun in that position, but it finally got so heavy my arms began to shake. Moving as slowly as my crying muscles would allow, I lowered the barrel to my knee.

That was when I discovered that I had competition. I heard a cluck and a low yelp. The gobbler heard it too. He stopped scratching in the leaves. I looked hard, hoping to get a glimpse of his head when he raised it to listen. The call came again from across a little hollow. I had only a slight feeling of relief when I recognized the soft notes of a diaphragm call. The guy was good—too good.

My gobbler answered the call and went back to feeding. I couldn't reach any of my calls without making a series of noisy contortions. With my eyes, I desperately searched the forest floor around me for a brier leaf. At that time I'd never tried calling a gobbler with a brier leaf, but I'd practiced on it some and thought I was making progress, though in this department I couldn't touch some of the mountain boys I knew.

On that early spring morning the only brier leaf within easy reach of my hand was a small one no more than twice the size of my thumbnail. Cautiously I reached out and plucked it, and just as cautiously put it up to my lips.

I made three silent tries before the cluck would come. I lay the result to luck as well as practice, but not even a turkey hen could have made a more seductive cluck. The bearded tom must have thought so, too, because he came right back with the most excited gobble I'd heard since he'd answered my call on the first stand.

The guy across the hollow evidently thought he'd been responsible for that emotional outburst. He answered right away with a series of notes so real that I almost revised my estimate again and made him out to be a turkey hen. The gobbler stopped scratching as though he, too, were trying to make up his mind. Then my competitor yelped again. I almost sighed aloud in relief. He'd been too eager and too frequent, and had remained in one precise spot. I knew (and I knew the gobbler knew) that we were being duped.

The tom didn't gobble again for ten or fifteen minutes. He might have been looking for someone to court, but he was feeding. And somehow I got the impression that he just liked to hear the sound of his own voice. During this time he moved around the hill to the left, away from the hunter across the cove, but staying under the contour of the hill, out of sight from me. I worked up nerve to try the brier leaf again. Just two clucks, this time. But they came out right.

The tom answered immediately with a double gobble. For a moment I thought he was poised to come straight to me. If he did, I'd be caught in an awkward position. Immediately in front of where I sat was a small hemlock with so many dead lower branches that it resembled a wooden spider web. The turkey had moved to my left and now my gun was on the wrong side of this tree. A fellow sometimes allows himself to be maneuvered into such a position. Being very careful not to touch so much as a twig, I withdrew the barrel and put it on the other side.

During the couple of minutes I required to execute that maneuver, the gobbler had gone even farther around the hill. I could hear him in the dry leaves, and I continued to keep my gun barrel pointed toward the sounds he made. The hunter across the hollow had gone to work again, but the tom turkey didn't stop scratching to reply. I felt a wave of sympathy for the poor guy, sitting there in such anticipation, but my feeling passed quickly. That old bird wasn't in anybody's bag—not yet.

I could hear his big feet in the leaves. At one point I thought of jumping up and taking him by surprise, but that's one of the surest ways to draw a blank. My arm was numb, and I was about to shift it to get the circulation going again when the gobbler came in sight—almost in the opposite direction from where I'd heard him when I sat down. With his heavy foot, he sent clumps of leaves flying. And when he stretched his long neck to pick up a tidbit, his head went out of sight behind a log. I bumped off my safety and put the sight on the spot where his head should be when he lifted it again.

Then he stood tall and alert in a patch of sunlight. I squeezed the trigger and leapt to my feet—almost in the same motion. The bird had vanished. The apprehension that I might have missed it clean hit me in the pit of my stomach. I made four record-breaking jumps to the top of the ridge. The pile of iridescence was sprawled there, its wings spread out on the ground.

The measuring tape I put on his beard showed that it was one inch short of being a foot long. The bird was heavy too. By the time I'd made the long, rough climb back to the road, I was sure he'd go 25 pounds or more. But on the scales in the checking station, the highest reading we could get was 19 pounds.

There was some discussion whether this might be the "old man" the rangers had seen. They didn't know. But I was sure of one thing: this one would do until the old man came along. And I had added a new dimension to what I thought I knew about turkey hunting.

There are, of course, many reasons why gobbler hunters move. Most important, probably, is to locate the birds. In the early hours, you might change locations until you hear a gobbler. At other times of day, it is often possible to locate turkeys by the sign they leave or by the actions of other creatures in the woods. If you are long on experience, you've already thought of the crow. I've located gobblers a number of times by listening to a bunch of crows. It's not always a gobbler they are after, though. They have a similar affection for hawks, owls, and some other big birds. But, usually, any raucous assemblage of the ebon clan in turkey woods is worth investigating.

I was on a woods road one time with Jim Vessey, who was head man for the Southern Region of the U.S. Forest Service. Jim was a forester who belonged to the old school that believed a forest should have something in it besides pine trees. He was a good woodsman and a hunter, but he had no experience with turkeys.

The old road, which had been the only wilderness highway back in the days of the early settlements, wound through coves and over shallow gaps into a wild back country. Jim and I were hunting it in a rather leisurely fashion. We'd stop in each little gap and then call and listen for half an hour. If we didn't get a reply, we'd move on.

We'd gone a quarter of a mile beyond an apparently unproductive gap and were on our way to the next when a flock of crows set up a clamor that made me stop in my stride. I couldn't explain why, but they just didn't sound like they were after an owl or hawk.

"Let's ease back into that gap we just left," I whispered.

Jim nodded.

The cut in the bank where the road went through was about eight feet deep. By the time we arrived there, the crows were nearer and really raising a ruckus. They were down in the trees, too, and not in the tops, which indicated they might be after a turkey. Apparently the gobbler was on his way to investigate the calls we had made three-quarters of an hour before. Often a hunter will not wait quite long enough to learn the result of his calling. This seemed to have been our problem here.

The target of the crows' hysteria removed all speculation about its identity with a lusty gobble, not more than 75 yards out of the ridge.

"Crawl up that bank," I whispered to Jim. "Don't walk. Crawl. Lie behind that log with your gun pointed down the slope. Don't move. That critter's got eyes like a catamount."

Jim crawled carefully up the bank. He crawled to the log. He arrived where I told him. But instead of flattening himself out behind the log, he rose to a crouching position to remove a large stick that angled across the spot where he wanted to lie down.

The crows immediately left the scene. The turkey finally did gobble again—on the next ridge, half a mile away.

Crows under different circumstances helped me bring in one gobbler. Ray Barnes and I were hunting in the Dutch Settlement in a remote section of the Sylco Range in East Tennessee. I'd seen a lot of turkey sign there.

Back in Chapter 8 I described the Dutch Settlement, which was colonized by a group of Central-Europeans in 1850, about a dozen years after the removal of the Cherokees. The settlers named it Vineland, and records show that a bit of wine was made there, carried by ox cart, and sold outside. After a few years, the colony broke up. Not many years later, the land had returned to wilderness, leaving a few piles of stone from crumbled chimneys and bits of broken china as the only reminders of what had been.

Ray and I walked down the twisting, rutty road by predawn starlight. He built his blind in one of the flats, and I crossed the creek to a sloping hillside. I heard a gobbler far in the distance, but he must have been traveling away from us. I heard him only once. Both Ray and I called periodically until after 9:00 A.M. I was almost paralyzed from sitting so long in one place, so I got up and walked back to the blind of my partner.

"You been listening to those crows?" he asked.

Up in one of the little valleys, at least a dozen of the black marauders were annoying some creature of the forest. We were too far away to tell what.

"There's a standing feud between crows and gobblers," I said.

The year before, I'd almost killed my gobbler when I crawled on my hands and knees through the laurel to where a buck turkey was scratching on a hillside. At least twenty crows were tormenting him—hanging from the trees and bushes, scolding at the tops of their lungs. I had tried to crawl close enough for a shot, but one of the black birds got a glimpse of me. His warning note was enough for the turkey. It ducked into the brush.

"Why don't you go up that hollow and investigate?" I suggested.

Ray shook his head. "You know this country better than I do. I'll slip along the creek on the other side of the ridge. If you happen to spook him my way, I might get a shot."

It was a slim chance, and rather a desperate one for us both. Whatever the crows were after was moving. We had heard them follow their quarry out of one cove, across a low ridge, and into another cove. The chase moved with about the same speed as a walking human. I thought I might intercept the procession on the next flat ridge. But before I reached its crest, the entire group had moved on into the parallel hollow.

I came near giving up the chase and going back to Ray, but there was a chance that I might turn the birds toward him. Anticipating their line of travel, I climbed as fast as I could make it into a long cove that the crows and their victim should reach in minutes. Halfway up the hillside there, I crawled into a laurel clump, waited for them to cross the ridge, and then yelped on my cedar box. Don't ask me why. It just seemed the thing to do.

Two crows came to look for me. But I stayed as still as one of the nearby boulders. After a few inquiring caws, they went back to join their gang. I touched the yelper again—mainly to annoy the crows, I guess—and the group moved across the hillside toward me. The ebon members of the gang were hopping from tree to tree, and occasionally one of them swept close to the low brush, yelling at the top of its lungs.

I was staring at a spot where I thought the turkey should appear. As usual, I was looking in the wrong direction. Suddenly I discovered that the victim of the crows was really a gobbler, after all. He stepped out of the thicket almost at my feet, and I don't know which of us was more surprised. He recovered an instant before I did, and took three long steps before I was able to crash out of the brush and bring my gun up. The bird took to the air, flying as straight up as any quail I've ever flushed.

He was an easy target, and I folded him clean. I vaguely remember panic among the crows, but I forgot them. I've lost too many turkeys by not being on top of one when it hit the ground. This one needed no further attention.

So it no doubt pays a turkey hunter to move when it's necessary to rearrange his strategy, and also to pay attention to everything that goes on in the woods around him. Minor points, you might say. Yet all of this can be very important if you want to develop into a good turkey hunter.

15

The Rio Grande

I still remember the point in my turkey-hunting career when I first decided to make a grand slam in gobblers. I was fairly certain that other hunters had taken all four species—and probably some of the subspecies, too—but I'd never yet heard of anyone taking all four in one spring season. Perhaps no one else considered it a special feat to bag an Osceola, an Eastern, a Rio Grande, and a Merriam's in a lifetime of turkey hunting. I'm sure that to big-game hunters it can't compare with the grand slam in rams, which for many reasons is a much more difficult assignment. Yet I consider a grand slam in gobblers just as honorable an accomplishment.

I had three Osceolas to my credit, but these had been taken while bird hunting in South Florida, when the quail and turkey seasons overlapped and the big birds flushed in front of the dogs. I had never used orthodox methods, and called up and killed an Osceola gobbler in the spring. Spring hunting was not so very old in South Florida.

All my other gobblers—and hens, too, back in the days when they were legal game—had been Eastern wild turkeys, taken in most of the Southern States from Virginia to Texas. I'd always made plans to go after the Yankee birds, with a yen to see if I could speak their language. Over the years I was to learn there's very little difference in the methods and the calls used to hunt any one of the four species.

The chance at my first Rio Grande gobbler came more than two decades ago when I was in Oklahoma on—of all things—a fishing trip. I was there with my outdoor partner of long standing, Byron Dalrymple, to collaborate on a story involving a pickup camper and trout fishing. The trip was delightful, but you can catch trout at almost any time, and I loudly lamented that my work had interfered with my spring turkey hunting. As it stood, I would miss all but a couple of mornings of the gobbler season.

Glenn Titus, outdoor editor of Oklahoma City's *Daily Oklahoman and Times,*

181

was with us on the trip, and he invited me to stay over a few extra days and try for a gobbler with him. But my schedule wouldn't permit it; so Glenn gave me what he called a "turkey rain check," good for any time the Sooners had their season open on the gobbler clan.

I kept that rain check propped up on my desk—as if I needed any reminder!—until early the next spring, when my gobbler-chasing genes began to percolate once more. Then I rolled a sheet of paper into the typewriter to jog Glenn's memory about our date. But even before I could write down his address, he phoned.

"Mental turk-lepathy must be strong medicine," I said.

"Season this year," Glenn said, "runs April twentieth to the twenty-eighth. Just tell me when to meet you."

A few weeks later Glenn met me at the Oklahoma City airport. He had arranged three hunts designed to show off the various types of Oklahoma turkey terrain and the methods used by successful gobbler devotees in his state.

One of our trips was with biologist Tom Logan, who had been assigned to study the wild turkey on some ranches north of Syre, and Byron Randall, a local game ranger. Tom had located several big gobblers in one corner of his study area and thought he could find their roost trees.

We were there before dawn. The morning was not ideal for locating gobblers. The air was unseasonably cold, and after the first few minutes of daylight the wind began to blow. Even an old tom inclined to romance on such a chilly morning would be hard to hear from a distance.

The trees were not yet outlined against the sky as we hunkered down in a sagebrush patch near some roost trees. When the eastern sky eventually lit up, Glenn made out a lone turkey perched in one of the cottonwoods less than 50 yards away. The bird was big, although in that light we couldn't even guess whether it was a hen or a gobbler. We were camouflaged up to our eyebrows, but from that roost the turkey could look right down on us.

With the bird in such a lookout spot, none of us dared move. I sat through a long period of cramped, aching muscles until the first cluck and low call identified the bird above us as a hen. Even then we didn't relax. After all, gobblers might be stationed in the trees nearby.

I conversed with the hen on my diaphragm mouth yelper, and we had a few minutes of interesting small talk until either I said something that displeased her or she saw one of us move. She suddenly pitched out of the tree and flew out of sight over a small rise.

We held our place until a tom gobbled about 200 yards away beyond a low hill covered with shinnery. Glenn and I left the sage patch, walked in the open to the thicket, and cautiously made our way through the scrub oaks to where the patch ended abruptly halfway down the opposite slope. Then the tom gobbled again from the middle of another patch. Apparently he was walking away and keeping his distance.

We were looking around for cover to get ahead of the gobbler when Glenn spotted a small flock of birds through his field glasses. They were feeding in an open patch about half a mile away, but the lay of the land between us was such that we couldn't stalk closer than 100 yards from them.

"What do you think?" I asked.

"Might do well to separate," Glenn suggested. "With the rifle, I'll have a better chance with the birds in the open. If you can get around the bird that's heading west, you might interest him in your yelper. Or you might get in close enough behind him to call him back."

Glenn was shooting a .243, his varmint rifle, and trying an experiment with it. He had pulled the bullets out of the cases, reversed them, and reinserted them that way. His theory was that the hard back end of the bullet, instead of the expanding and blowing a turkey apart, would kill a gobbler without mutilating it.

"I've tried this on the rifle range at up to 100 yards," he said, "and apparently the bullet doesn't wobble or cartwheel. In fact, it shoots almost as good a group backwards as it does the other way, and it leaves a perfectly round hole. I'm anxious to see what it will do on a turkey."

We separated. I went off cross-country, taking advantage of the scattered clumps. I wanted the gobbler to hear my yelping above the wind. The shinnery patches were so far apart and the sage between them so stubby that I never did find a course that would put me in front of the bird without being seen. But I finally managed to get close enough to attract his attention with my yelper.

From the way he gobbled, I knew he'd heard me. Then, for nearly an hour, he remained in one scrub-oak thicket. I was beginning to think I had convinced him of my love and affection, when he finally decided that whatever I was offering wasn't worth retracing his steps for. The last time I heard him, he was somewhere out in the brushy distance.

The gobbling time of morning was over, and the velocity of the wind had increased. So I went back to meet Glenn, Tom, and Byron. Byron knew of several thickets he called "loafing places". He had seen turkeys dusting and relaxing there in the middle of the day. Tom and I gave three of these spots a try but got no results.

On our way out to the main road, we found Glenn and Byron watching three big gobblers feed along the edge of an open field about a mile away. They were studying the birds through binoculars—standard equipment for turkey hunters in this open country.

"You might persuade them to come to a call even this late in the day," Byron said, "if you can get close enough to make them hear you above this wind. Your best bet is to stalk as near to the gobbler as possible and try for a rifle shot."

"I've been wanting to see what that dumdum will do to turkey meat anyway," I agreed.

Glenn put on his camouflage duds and made a detour while I waited on the road with Tom and Byron. Finally Glenn came to a point from which he could get no closer without being seen, and he decided to try a shot. He estimated the range at about 350 yards, but he previously had killed chucks and prairie dogs at long range with his .243. His Bushnell 4X scope was set dead-on at 25 to 275 yards. So, allowing for about a five-inch drop, Glenn took aim and fired at the largest gobbler.

I was watching the turkeys through Tom's binoculars and saw Glenn's bullet blow up a wad of dust at the feet of the big tom. The old bird jumped three feet into the air and took off on a dead run toward Glenn, with the other birds following him. Glenn managed to get in two more shots before the gobblers reached the shin-oak patch. Then he walked out into the field to check the spot where the old gobbler had stood when he fired his first shot.

"I couldn't find any feathers or blood," Glenn reported. "So I guess I missed him clean. I've killed varmints and deer at that distance, but I guess I was too excited. Every time I looked at that old tom through the scope, my heart started going like a bongo drum. It sure as heck ain't anything like target shooting."

That was my introduction to spring turkey hunting in Oklahoma.

I had eagerly looked forward to this hunt ever since the year before when Glenn told me that the turkeys in western Oklahoma were the Rio Grande subspecies. The birds I have hunted for the past forty years in all the Southeastern States have been either the true *silvestris* (Eastern wild turkey) or the very similar Florida turkey. I guess my conversation with Glenn left me with some vague notion that these Latin birds out of Mexico and the Southwest might be more hot-blooded and thus easier to seduce with a call.

The wild turkey is not a new game bird in Oklahoma. In his book *Canadian River Hunt*, General William E. Strong tells of a hunt he made in Cherokee Territory in 1878 with the Generals Sheridan, Crook, and Whipple. On the Canadian River, near one of the spots I hunted, the four military men found one roost that measured a quarter-mile wide and more than a mile long, where thousands of turkeys congregated at night.

Wild turkeys began to disappear soon after the territory was opened for homesteading in 1889. The homesteaders lived on game and cleared away game habitat to plant crops. By the dust-bowl days of the 1930s, the wild turkey in Oklahoma already belonged to history.

Experts disagree over whether the original wild turkey in Oklahoma was the Eastern or the Rio Grande bird. On the Rio Grande turkey, the tips of the tail feathers and upper tail coverts are a golden color beneath the iridescence. On the Eastern bird, these feathers are tipped with a chocolate brown. The metallic sheen on the exposed body feathers of the Rio Grande turkey is more brilliant and tends toward greenish gold or copper, whereas the sheen on the Eastern bird is more a purplish bronze.

Most experts believe that Oklahoma's original turkey was the Eastern variety, but the University of Kansas has some specimens that are said to be examples of the indigenous turkeys of Woodward County, Oklahoma, and these birds have been identified as intergrades between the Eastern and the Rio Grand varieties.

In 1949, the Oklahoma game department began restocking wild turkeys by releasing 21 of the Rio Grande birds. By the next year, the flock had increased to 50. In 1952, some 60 more birds were brought into the state. Since then, 3,800 turkeys have been trapped out of the growing flock and released in other areas of the state. Oklahoma at this writing has a population of 36,000 birds—enough, biologists think, to allow an annual harvest of 8,000.

Clifford King joined us, and we made our next stand at Enid. Cliff is the official photographer for the Wildlife Commission.

At Enid we met Dwain and Dick Bland. (As I mentioned earlier in Chapter 6, at that time Dwain was an electrical inspector for the city of Enid, as well as field representative for a company that sells game calls. Dwain also guides turkey hunters during both the fall and spring seasons. His twin brother, Dick, often helps him out in this respect.)

In spite of the weather, which was icy at dawn and windy the rest of the day, Dwain gave us a couple of the finest turkey-hunting days I have ever enjoyed. He has two favorite spots, and we hunted both. One is the Canton Public Hunting Area north of the town of Canton; the other is on private ranch land in Woodward County, where Dwain had permission to hunt. Much of the private land in western Oklahoma is posted, and you must get permission from the owners before hunting it.

The Canton area covers 16,775 acres, about half of which is made up of the Canton Reservoir. The land north of this fishing lake is slightly rolling, with patches of cottonwood, hackberry, and chittamwood. Dense stands of tall cottonwood trees, willow, elm, and oak cover the river bottoms. Some 2,000 acres of the managed lands are planted to feed patches for the birds.

Except for a sickle of moon above the horizon, there was no light when we separated at our cars. Glenn and Dick headed for a spot where they had found birds on a previous hunt. Dwain, Cliff, and I walked toward the moon until a faint glow began to show beneath it in the eastern sky. In the growing brightness, Dwain stopped to point out the lay of land.

"I'll be in that direction," he said. "There's a high sand ridge over there, and I'll go to any gobbling around or beyond that. You and Cliff hit that big neck of woods that runs out between two fields. A lot of birds travel through it, and I've heard them gobble on the roost in there."

Dwain walked away toward the dawn. Cliff and I stood at the edge of the woods until the light grew brighter. The grass patch at our feet was covered with frost. Though there was no wind, the air was cold enough to jell. I really didn't have much hope.

We waited. About the time that turkeys usually fly down off the roost, we heard a gobbler. The sound came at an angle slightly different from the direction in which Dwain had disappeared.

"He'll probably be working that bird," I said.

The tom gobbled again.

"Let's move about halfway up to it," I suggested. "If Dwain has started working it, we won't be close enough to disturb them. If he hasn't, we may be within range of the gobbler's ears."

We followed the edge of the woods about 200 yards. Then Cliff sat down in a natural blind at the edge of a thicket. From there he could see the open forest on two sides. I backed off behind him, into a thick stand of scrubby trees with no understory of brush. I felt sure that if the gobbler came to us, Cliff would see him and get a shot. So I didn't try to build a blind. I just sat down with my legs under me.

I didn't really expect to see the gobbler. It was gobbling spasmodically, not with any rhythm that might indicate it was answering my yelps. So I figured Dwain was working it. Then the tom shut up. I relaxed and listened for Dwain's shot.

Fifteen minutes passed. I had about decided to call to Cliff and suggest we look for another bird when the tom passed my partner's blind on the one side that was screened by heavy brush. The gobbler walked into a little clearing directly in front of me. I held my fire, hoping Cliff would see the bird. The tom circled through the thicket of trees in which I sat and then stopped on the far edge and gobbled.

I wasn't wearing my camouflage face mask or gloves, and I fervently wished that I had smeared some green greasepaint across my mug as both Dwain and Cliff had done. Greasepaint is a very effective camouflage for face and hands.

The turkey was now out of Cliff's range, so I decided to shoot. I raised my 12-gauge Winchester Model 12, and the gobbler saw the movement. He froze for an instant and then began a slow retreat along the line of trees. The spaces between the trees were so narrow that it was like looking through a picket fence, but I finally thought I had a clear shot and pulled the trigger. The bird disappeared for an instant. Then I saw it running through the trees.

I went to the spot where I had last seen the tom, to look for some sign of a hit. I couldn't find a feather. Then Cliff arrived, and we looked around to see why I had missed at such close range. You can imagine my surprise when I found that the wad of No. 6 shot from the 2¾-inch magnum shell had cut off a wrist-size tree not more than 20 feet from the end of my 30-inch full-choke gun barrel. And I remember laughing at a couple of guys who had pulled that same trick!

That afternoon Cliff and I called in a yearling gobbler that I could have bagged, but I was looking for a more mature bird. Later on we tried to call two old gobblers that were feeding with several hens in a posted grainfield, but the toms didn't show the slightest interest in our entreaties.

On our way back to the motel that night, I suggested to Dwain that the Rio Grande gobblers I had met seemed easier to call and not nearly so spooky as those feathered Einsteins in my home territory. He grinned.

"Turkey hunting in Oklahoma," he said, "is comparatively new for this generation of hunters and birds. The fall season was opened in 1960, but this is only the third year we've had a spring season. More hunting is done with binoculars and rifles at long range than with call and shotgun. Most of our hunters locate the birds feeding in grainfields and then stalk them. Few fellows who hunt this country have learned the pleasure of fooling with an old gobbler when he begins to sound off in the morning. Consequently, these birds aren't yet wise to an artificial call, as they probably will be later on."

"You didn't help my ego one bit," I lamented. "I was beginning to think I had developed into a good turkey hunter."

The next day started cold and windy and stayed windy. We were on one of the ranches where Dwain had permission to bring his hunters. He had seen several big gobblers there, but we drew a blank for the morning. Dwain did spot three toms, but he couldn't get up on them.

After sandwiches, coffee, and a delectable slab of cake put up for us by Dwain's wife, the guide located us in a heavily timbered swamp along a small stream.

"I've seen a good many birds ranging along this creek," he said, "and now that the morning parade is over, our best bet is to wait them out."

His eyes twinkled.

"That is," he added, "unless you'd rather wait and come back in the morning."

I'll have to admit that after the gobbling period ends, turkey hunting loses at least part of its glamour. But sitting out the afternoon in a swamp certainly has more appeal than being caged in a motel room.

I made myself comfortable in a clump of brush, deposited my kit within easy reach, and prepared for a restful afternoon in the swamp woods. I considered that I might even doze a bit, since I really didn't have much hope of seeing a bird. The wind had increased, and heavy gusts tore at the big tree crowns overhead. I was sure that no turkey could hear a call from more than 30 feet away, but I went through the ritual of yelping anyway. Then I put the box down and leaned back against a tree trunk to enjoy the afternoon.

One thing is sure: you can never predict the actions of a wild gobbler, no matter what his pedigree. I hadn't been sitting there more than fifteen minutes when this big bird simply walked out of the brush directly in front of me and came on a beeline for my blind. I did not have my face mask up, but I had pulled on my camouflage gloves.

The gobbler was no more than 20 steps away when I raised the gun off my knee and put the sights on his red head. He paused in obvious surprise and looked me straight in the eye, apparently wondering what sort of critter this could be that made hen notes but in no way resembled a hen. I pulled the trigger and he went down cold.

It was as simple as that—a sort of anticlimax to the hours we had spent hunting the Rio Grande on three widely separated areas of its range.

The Rio Grande gobbler.

The gobbler had a beard and spurs that identified it as a three-year-old. One spur point had been broken off, probably during a fight.

This was my first Rio Grande turkey, and it was beautifully marked. It weighed nearly 18 pounds—large for this subspecies (an Eastern tom of the same age will average one or two pounds heavier). Right then, I was sure this was the prettiest gobbler I had ever seen.

Cliff and I later called in and shot a year-old gobbler. I guess the only regret Dwain had was that we failed to bring in one of the huge old toms that he said were plentiful on his part of the range.

"More big gobblers out here die of old age than are ever killed by hunters," Dwain said. "It's a shame to see them go to waste. Things may change, though, when the local fellows learn how to call wary old birds to within shotgun range."

Although it's true that many of the old gobblers are never shot, the ratio of success for turkey hunters in Oklahoma is by far the highest I know. Records kept since 1960 show that more than 50 percent of all hunters there bring home their birds—a pretty high recommendation for Oklahoma turkey hunting, I'd say.

16

The Apache Gobbler

I looked around me. This was Apache country. Its mountains, canyons, timbered parks, and vast silent distances were much as they had been a century ago. It was so exactly like the land I'd expected to see that I had the strange feeling I had sometime and somehow been here before; that I might have been one of the mountain men who traveled it in those now almost forgotten years.

At 8,000 feet on this spring morning in late April, the air's chill was emphasized by the blanket of frost across the upland meadows. I gave silent thanks that I'd had the foresight to wear my elk-hunting clothes. And even they were none too warm.

My hunting partners were scattered over several square miles of mountain wilderness, in order to cover as much territory as possible. Every man jack of them knew what he was doing and what he was looking for, and at the moment our best bet was to hunt separately.

The object of this expedition, which had brought us a thousand miles and more from home, was Merriam's wild turkey, the Southwest species of America's most highly prized game bird. For almost half a century I had confined my turkey hunting to Florida, Eastern, and Rio Grande gobblers and for years had looked forward to adding the Merriam's to my list of trophies.

In the first frozen light of day, I moved through the forest. No one had told me, but my inclination dictated that these mountain gobblers should be hunted in the same manner that we hunted our Eastern turkeys: find a vociferous tom, and try to call it within shotgun range. I had located many a gobbling bird in Tennessee's Ocoee and the adjoining Cohutta Mountains of Georgia by traveling cross-country, stopping near the crest of each ridge to first give the low clucking sounds turkeys sometimes use to greet one another. If this got no answer, I'd follow it with a series of short yelps, then

189

louder yelps, and often the gobbling call. If the gobbler was close enough, the first cluck got a response, and sometimes the gobbling brought an answer from the next ridge or beyond. Then it was just a question of approaching as close as possible without being seen, and sitting down to make conversation with the bird until it came over to investigate.

Only this wasn't the Eastern wild turkey; it was the Merriam's. I had no certainty that these tactics would be productive. I did know that this was some of the most fascinating country I'd seen in years.

We were hunting the Jicarilla Apache Indian Reservation of northern-central New Mexico. This covers almost three-quarters of a million acres from the town of Cuba to the Colorado line. It's high country, ranging from approximately 6,500 feet in elevation to some 9,000 feet on its highest peaks near the state line. The southern end is covered with sagebrush and low-growing cedars. And as the road climbs toward the northern end of the reservation, the forest cover gradually changes to wooded mountain sides and pockets of pinyon and ponderosa pine with an understory of scattered scrub oak thickets. Spruce and fir cover the highest elevations. The pinyon nut is an important source of game food, and some of the virgin ponderosa forests in these parts were the most magnificent I had seen since my years with the U.S. Forest Service in Montana half a century before.

This was said to be one of the best mule-deer ranges in the West. It produces tremendous trophy heads. More than two dozen trophy racks from the reservation and the country adjacent to it are in the Boone and Crockett Club record book.

I must admit that I considered our party a bit unwieldy for a turkey-hunting group. There were five of us, and we had to depend on a fellow who had been there on two previous occasions and knew the ropes. That hunter, Dwain Bland, had invited Bill Rae and me out to try for Merriam's with him. Dwain brought along two of his friends, Jim Frazee, an Enid furniture dealer; and Max Olsen, a farmer near Waynoka, Oklahoma, with whom Bill and I had hunted the year before.

Dwain and his two partners arrived on a Saturday and spent the night in their camper at Los Indios canyon, some 45 miles southeast of Dulce, the only town on the reservation and the headquarters of the Apache govern-ment. Los Indios is a tremendous canyon just off the fork of reservation roads J-16 and J-17. It begins as a series of flats and climbs several miles almost to the top of the Continental Divide. The road follows the canyon, then swings in a U-turn down the far side of the ridge. A big loop brings it back almost to the mouth of Los Indios. Dwain had found turkeys here in the years past.

The afternoon they arrived at the mouth of the canyon, Dwain and his two buddies scouted and found tracks crisscrossing the dusty road. The next morning the three scattered out to the most likely places. Hunting widely separated locations, Max and Dwain called up young gobblers with small beards. Neither bird made a sound but just suddenly appeared in the forest only yards away. Both men passed up shots, envisioning long trophy beards later in the hunt.

Bill and I met Sunday afternoon in the Albuquerque airport and signed up for a rental car for the 180-mile trip upstate to Dulce. When we went to pick up our baggage, my gun (which had been checked in a hard-plastic case with the other luggage) was missing. I hotfooted to the airline counter and after a bit of frantic (on my part) checking, the ticket agent came in with a teletype message.

"Your gun," he announced cheerfully, "is in the San Juan airport in Puerto Rico."

"You can put that down," I said, "as the story of turkey hunting."

He got on the teletype again, then on the phone, and made a second report.

"It's on the way here," he said. "There's no way we can get it to Dulce, but there's a bus station at Cuba, 80 miles south of Dulce. We'll have it there by eight-thirty in the morning."

"Maybe I can dispatch that old tom with a well-aimed rock," I suggested to Bill.

At dusk we checked in at Dulce's only motel. One of the first persons we encountered was Joe Lucero, one of the four conservation officers who patrol and carry on game operations over the 750,000-acre reservation. Joe was gracious enough to go with us to the Game and Fish Office on the edge of town and issue our New Mexico non-resident licenses and reservation hunt permit. I gave him the story of my misplaced firearm.

"My shotgun," Joe said, "is an old riot gun I picked up and put a Cutts Compensator on. You're welcome to use it. It's bagged a number of birds."

Dwain insisted that I use his over-and-under and let him try the old riot weapon.

Joe gave us maps of the reservation and explained a point or two about them. Then we sat a while and got acquainted. Joe was from Cuba, New Mexico, originally, and had married an attractive Apache girl and moved up on the reservation. He worked at road building for a while, helping to construct the main highway north to Dulce. He transferred to the reservation police department and then to Game and Fish, where he'd worked some seven years. With Game and Fish Director Ed Sandoval, Joe had had a hand in helping build up the deer, elk, and turkey populations. He also told us that his wife had a ranch about 10 miles southeast of town and that turkeys ranged the foothills above it. Members of the tribe who apply are assigned land for ranching in various units of the reservation. Joe insisted that we take a look at his turkey range.

At daylight next morning we left Max to cover a water hole high on the mountain and Dwain and Jim to work down a ridge toward the ranch. Bill and I followed Joe along a winding mountain road into an open valley. The conservation officer pointed to a huge block of boulder perched on the hillside.

"That marks the mouth of a canyon. I've heard the gobbler in there several times."

Bill and I walked around the end of a ridge and stepped into a group of pinyons. The dawn was cold. We stood in the shadows, slowly congealing, and called for a quarter of an hour, low at first and then louder, with no answer except from a raven that came over to investigate.

The canyon floor, open except for scattered tree clumps, was carpeted with grass in the more open spaces. From hillside to hillside, it was nowhere more than a couple of hundred yards wide. We were about to pussyfoot on when, at the limit of my vision, I glimpsed a movement up the draw. By straining my eyes, I made out a turkey hen with her head up. Then she stepped behind a bush and disappeared.

Bill and I called for another quarter-hour without an answer of any kind, so we finally climbed the slope and made a circle to a point where we could look down to the canyon floor, just opposite where we had seen the hen. I clucked my call, and she answered with a cluck. That was all. We never saw or heard her again. Nor did we hear a gobbler or see sign, though I worked my way to the head of the canyon, stopping in likely places to call and wait long intervals for an answer.

That was the only hen we saw on the trip. From her actions, I'd say she appeared to be nesting. I mentioned this to Joe Lucero later in the hunt.

"All are on the nest now," he said. "Prior to open season we had several weeks of warm weather, and so the birds mated early. You never heard such gobbling and goings on. It wasn't uncommon to see bunches of toms and hens together in the meadows. Then this cold spell started last week and it seems that all the birds shut up."

From Joe's place we went back to the motel for breakfast and then drove to Los Indios canyon, where both Max and Dwain had drawn beads on gobblers the morning before. We spread out up and down the canyon. Bill took his stand on a partially open hillside for several hours and the only movement he saw was when Dwain came out of the forest below him, crossed the road and angled toward the tall ridge beyond.

I was farther up the canyon, hunting out the ridges. About the middle of the afternoon, I heard a bird gobble in the distance. I gravitated toward the faint sound. But Dwain was nearer. He called the bird to him and drew first blood.

It was the first Merriam's I had heard and the first I had seen close enough to study, though years ago while hunting for lions in the Gila Wilderness in the southern part of the state, and later for elk on the Coconino National Forest in Arizona, I had encountered several tremendous flocks of the big birds. My hunting partner on the lion hunt had told me that although the Merriam's is found from Colorado through eastern Arizona, New Mexico is the region of greatest abundance and that its natural range is synonymous with the pinyon and ponderosa pines in rough, rugged country.

All wild turkeys are, of course, beautifully marked with combinations of feathers that vary from almost black to almost white, with browns, coppery bronze, greens, and purples showing in the iridescent coat. The Merriam's carries the lightest coat. The rump feathers and upper tail coverts range from pale buff to almost white. Its distinctive coloration makes it easy to identify. It is very close kin to the Mexican turkey that was carried back to the Old World and domesticated four centuries ago.

"That riot gun of Joe's sure shoots good," Dwain commented wryly.

After taking photos, we covered the lower end of the canyon until dark without seeing or hearing a bird. And after much too little sleep, we were back in the same spot the next morning with the same results. We met at the camper about 10:00 A.M.

"That one gobbler Dwain took must have left all those tracks," Bill observed.

The decision was made to have breakfast out of the grub box in the camper and to take a nap before hunting the far upper end of the canyon in the afternoon.

"While you're all sleeping," I said, "I'll drive over to Cuba and pick up my gun."

"I'll go with you," Bill offered.

We looked at the map and decided that J-17, a direct route south to Cuba, would give us a further look at the reservaton and also save us a long ride back to the paved highway. We didn't know at the time what a narrow, crooked, and often almost impassable road it was, especially beyond the Jicarilla boundary and through a corner of the national forest.

At one spot we were bumping along at about 5 mph, trying to dodge a series of holes, when a magnificent gobbler stepped out of the woods, so close I had to put on brakes to keep from hitting him. He walked slowly across the road a few feet in front of us and stopped not more than 25 feet away to give us the eye.

"Where's your gun?" I asked Bill.

"I left it at the camper. Where's your camera?"

"Same place," I said.

We watched the turkey saunter unhurried and unalarmed into the woods.

"He knew we wouldn't bushwhack him anyway," Bill commented.

While we were in Cuba, the wind began to blow. When we came back up the highway, the blow had developed into a fair-sized dust storm. By midafternoon we arrived back in Los Indios. Our hunting companions had pulled out. Even though we had only my retrieved gun, we decided to hunt the upper end of the canyon, where we had seen tracks in the road.

This was some of the most impressive forest in the entire reservation, with magnificent ponderosa and open, grassy parks with scattered oak clumps. Bill and I settled down at the edge of a park for a while. But I doubt that any gobbler could have heard us more than 50 yards away above the roar of that wind. We thought the wind might diminish by late afternoon, but instead it grew stronger. The sky was so overcast with an off color that it could have presaged a change of weather. Remembering how Joe had warned us against being caught on the dirt roads in that back country in a rainstorm, we decided to make for the pavement.

Dwain and his buddies had ridden out the afternoon, looking for a new location. Before sundown they saw seven gobblers in the high country south of the Lake La Jara-Stone Lake road. There appeared to be an abundance of tracks on one of the narrow side roads through the big timber. First light on the following morning found us parked in a narrow gap above the high valley.

"We'll spread out," Dwain suggested. "You and Bill take the north side of the road; we'll work the high timber on the other slope."

Bill and I had just stepped off the road in the dim light when we heard a turkey gobble. It sounded as though it might be on our side, so we started climbing and made our stand where we knew the gobbler could hear us. I called, and the gobbler answered. After a few minutes we heard yelp notes that I recognized as Dwain's diaphragm call. When the gobbler answered, I realized it was on the wrong side that Dwain had set up as a boundary. So I shut up, and Bill and I sat and heard the whole show until a blast from Max's gun climaxed the mountain drama.

"Maybe we can find a gobbling bird of our own," I said.

We struck off through the woods, angling toward a low ridge in our assigned territory. On top of the divide, we paused where we could see a flat beyond the ridge and I went through the cluck-yelp-gobble routine over a period of fifteen minutes, listening and watching the flat between calls, shivering in the frozen breeze that had blown in with full daylight.

"Let's move a bit farther down the ridge," I whispered.

When I swung and looked behind us, a gobbler stood in the open, not more than 30 yards away. Apparently it had stalked our calls. When I turned, it saw my movement, streaked for a clump of oak brush, and disappeared before I could swing my gun into position—just as any Eastern or Midwestern bird would have done. That bird never uttered a sound. We had made the mistake of looking for a gobbling tom, instead of setting our stage for a silent one.

We hunted the remainder of the day in this valley. Around the middle of the afternoon, Jim Frazee had a young gobbler walk silently within a few steps of him, then turn and stride away. Jim's gun was on the ground, but he had time to pick it up and bag the bird some 45 yards away.

The Oklahoma hunters had filled out and were anxious to start for home, but Dwain agreed to get up before daylight the next morning and show us a mountain where he had taken his gobbler the year before. We covered two sides of the road, heard not a putt or peep, and were back in town before sunup to give the Sooners an early start.

Bill and I had breakfast, filled our car tank, and headed back to Los Indios canyon. The sun was high when we arrived there after 8:00 A.M., the gentle breeze warmer than at dawn.

"Looks as if we'll have the place all to ourselves," Bill observed.

We decided to hunt as a team. A few days before I'd found a little gap near the end of the ridge. By locating there, we had the possibility of attracting a bird from the flat on either side.

"Let's give this a couple of hours," I suggested, "before we move on."

We settled down. Bill was located where he could cover the gap and a large portion of each side. I sat against a rock slab farther up the hill, but at an angle where I could see only a fraction more of one hillside than my partner.

Bill let me open the party by clucking—in case a gobbler was close. After that I yelped softly. Then we both joined in with loud yelping of our boxes and followed that with gobbling. I strained my ears for five minutes. Then, over the rustle of breeze, I thought I heard a tom gobble somewhere in the distance.

We waited another five minutes and then went through the call routine again. After another period of waiting, we heard a tom gobble far out in the big wooded flat in front of our stands. After ten minutes I caught Bill's eye and nodded slightly. He read my thought. He yelped his box, and the tom turkey answered almost immediately. Very deliberately my partner put his box down as if to say, "O.K. He's yours. See if you can bring him in."

My most effective seducer at that time was the Turpin yelper. I went to that entirely, but used it sparingly. The gobbler worked cautiously nearer and arrived at the foot of the small ridge below us in a position that should have brought it into the flat right below where Bill sat. For at least twenty minutes it stayed there, making all the sounds of a romancing tom. At last I gave the low cluck of an ardent hen. Maybe it was a mistake. The turkey, instead of coming on in the direction it had been traveling, cut at an angle that brought it under the brow of the ridge on my side and away from my partner. After a minute I dared one more low yelp; and when I heard the gobbler walking in the dry duff, I put the gun to my shoulder. He appeared on the brow of the slope no more than 15 feet away, his head bright red in a patch of sunlight.

I waited, holding my breath, the bead on his head. Just as I was about to squeeze the trigger, a second gobbler about the same size stepped into sight a few feet behind the first. I held my fire, waiting for the tom in front to walk on over the hill, where he would be visible to Bill. But it didn't work quite that way. Both gobblers stopped and stood tall, as though they either sensed something was wrong or could hear the beating of my heart. By ducking and running, both would be out of sight almost before I could shift my sights and pull the trigger. This had happened to me before.

I sensed that if I didn't take him now, I might not have another chance. I swung my gun barrel and blasted the bird farthest away from my partner, hoping the tom ahead would either run over the hill or fly; in either case Bill would have a shot. The lead gobbler did neither. He turned and ran back to the bird flopping on the ground. Then the bird I had shot disappeared over the little rise. I could visualize it wounded just enough to get away, so I jumped to my feet and sprinted downhill. The second gobbler gave a startled *squawk* and flew—not toward Bill but back in the direction from which both birds had approached. My gobbler was stretched out against a log.

Like the guy he is, Bill was sincerely enthusiastic in his congratulations and not nearly as disappointed as I was that he did not have a shot.

"It's team effort anyway," he pointed out. "They could have come up either side of that ridge."

We field-dressed our bird and hung it in the shade of a thick balsam tree. Then we climbed the mountain, taking our time, pausing at all the hollows to yelp and listen. Deer and elk tracks, as we had found them wherever we went in this highland forest, crisscrossed everywhere. We had seen animals of both species many times, and usually they stood and studied us curiously while we in turn watched them. There were tracks of wild horses, too. We had encountered such horses throughout the reservation. Joe Lucero had told us that a percentage of these were rounded up each spring and sold. The older Apaches resented this practice fiercely, saying that with all the wild horses gone, the Great Spirit would have no reason to send the rains.

This entire upland timberland was alive with the Abert squirrel, that grayish treetop creature with distinctive tassels on its ear tips who makes his home high in the pinyon and ponderosa forests of the Southwest. There was also an abundance of the Steller's jay and ravens that Bill and I had often encountered farther north in the Wyoming timber ranges. One bird I could never see to identify was a woodpecker with a queer cadence that hammered out a *br-r-r-r—tap—tap—tap* on old tree shells. It sounded like turkey—but then so many of the woodland noises sound like turkey when you're after the big birds.

We had this country to ourselves. In a week of traveling by car and afoot over hundreds of square miles, we saw only four persons—one a vaquero (cowboy) on road J-17 near the southeast boundary, and three Apaches with bundles, traveling together from somewhere to somewhere.

As we approached the top of the mountain, I was sure I detected movement in the far edge of a spacious park. I wasn't sure I had seen a turkey duck out of sight, so we sat and called for an hour without any response. When we moved to make a picture in the high park, the bird gobbled beyond the park. We maneuvered and called for another hour, but we were never able to get an answer. My conclusion was that the bird had seen us when we entered the park—and again when we moved for pictures. Such is gobbler hunting.

We spent our last predawn hours with Joe Lucero in the high valley where Max and Jim had taken gobblers two days before. Joe parked in the gap, and Bill and I covered the big valley for four hours without raising a bird. As luck would have it, we hadn't been gone down the side of the ridge more than thirty minutes before Joe heard a gobbler in the adjoining valley, but on the wrong side of the mountain from us. He said it gobbled for a couple of hours before it finally went over the far ridge.

The Merriam's gobbler.

"Ain't that the fate of a Scotsman such as I!" Bill said with a groan.

All the same, we both agreed that the country, the people, and the new hunting experience with the Merriam's had combined to give us one of our most delightful gobbler safaris ever.

17

The Osceola

In looking back over the years, I discovered that I had killed three Osceola wild turkeys, but none in the orthodox manner of calling them up within range of my scattergun. Two were taken on quail hunts when they flushed in front of the bird dogs, and one curious old long-beard had walked up to look me over when I sat camouflaged and immobile while watching for squirrels at the edge of a swamp.

These three were identified as the true Osceola by people who should know. Two others that I did call up and bag occurred in the twilight zone where the Osceola range spills over into that of the Eastern wild turkey and may indeed have been of pure Osceola strain, although I doubt it. I wasn't taxonomist enough to decide for myself, and no biologists happened to be around to classify them. So I chalked them up as hybrids. Let me add: the lack of positive pedigree in no way impaired their table qualities.

Though at that stage of my life I'd already taken all four species of the North American wild turkey, nevertheless I wished to become better acquainted with the Osceola gobbler. Among the several things I wanted to know about him were: 1) Was he hunted any differently from the others? 2) Would he respond to the same calls? 3) Was he less cagey or more of a prima donna? and 4) Did his habits and habitat set him apart from the three other species?

There was only one way to find out: go and beard him in his known abode.

I'd made one hunt specifically for the Osceola with Jim Floyd, who headed the public-relations department of the Florida Game and Fresh Water Fish Commission; and Jim Poncier, wildlife officer of DeSoto County, in the south-central part of the state. Our territory was the 38,000-acre cattle ranch of Judge Vincent Hall, and the time was the end of the first week in March.

I had but one thing in mind then: to make a real grand slam by killing all four species of wild turkey in a single year.

At that time, neither of the two Jims was experienced in turkey hunting, and I myself felt like a stranger in a strange land. This was a vast flatland of wild pasture, marsh with head-high reeds and other vegetation, a few creeks winding through it, and scattered clumps of forest confined mostly to sandy hillocks rising only a few feet above the surrounding flats. There were some patches of tall pines, but mostly the tree cover was scrub oaks with scattered palmetto under them.

During the first afternoon we scouted, bouncing our butts over rutty sand trails that seemed endless and, as far as I could tell, led nowhere. In a dozen places I searched the ground unsuccessfully for a sign, though I had been assured that the ranch contained several flocks of turkeys. It certainly had an excellent deer population. Tracks were everywhere. I selected what appeared the best possible site, a strip of tall pines bordering the marsh. Adjacent to the pines lay a 30- to 40-acre sandy knoll of scrub oaks and palmettos.

We were there before daylight. Jim Poncier let us out of his four-wheel-drive, said he would pick us up at noon, and roared away into the darkness.

The dawn was cool and so still that I'm sure in this flat country we could have heard a gobbler a couple of miles away. I listened. I owled. I rattled my gobbling box. For all the good it did, I could just as well have been trying to sing them a bluegrass song. We sat out our blinds in that scrub-oak patch watching armadillos, skunks, and jaybirds, but never heard a turkey sound.

That afternoon a cold wind of gale proportions blew in from the west; by the next morning it was laced with rain. We stuck out another spot for about four hours, but all we got was soaking wet in spite of our rain suits. That weather lasted through the remainder of the day and night. At noon the third day, with the forecast for more of the same, we gave it up.

Judge Hall told us that the weather had been extremely warm in late January and early February, and he had heard a good many gobblers then. He figured the nesting season was about over and that by now the turkeys had more prosaic things on their minds, like eating.

It was with much reluctance that I gave up my idea of a grand slam that year. I also had to admit that I didn't know any more now about the Osceola than I'd known before going south.

At least I had slightly better luck with Charley Dickey. Charley is an old friend and outdoor partner over many decades. As a Florida resident, columnist, freelance writer, and photographer, he makes it his business to know everybody with outdoor connections in the Sunshine State.

"Most of my experience," Charley admitted, "has been with the Eastern bird. I've never hunted the Osceola but would admire to give it a try. Let me find out where we can try for one, and I'll call you."

I was excited about the prospects of another and—I hoped—more favorable bout with the Osceola. I did my homework like a kid boning up for a college exam. I already knew that the Osceola (Florida) turkey was considered one of the distinct subspecies and that the true form of this bird ranged southward below a line drawn across the state stretching roughly from De Land to Crystal River. North of this line the Osceola was more likely to be integrated with the Eastern wild turkey.

The true Osceola turkey averages a bit smaller than the Eastern bird. Though some specimens of 22 pounds or more have been taken, the Osceola runs closer to 16 pounds, some two or three pounds lighter than the average Eastern. And the Osceola's color is slightly different. Dr. John W. Aldrich says that the hues are similar to the Eastern turkey's but show "greenish and reddish metallic reflections on exposed portions of body feathers [while its] purplish reflections on [the] secondaries [are] more brilliant, resulting in a less purplish bronzy, more greenish golden or coppery appearance."

I always thought the Osceolas I saw in the wild were a bit darker, though this impression may have been caused by the narrower and broken white bars on the wings, which make the bird seem darker when its wings are closed.

Charley Dickey, closer to the scene, made the arrangements for our hunt. To give us a better chance, he decided on two locations: one near the top of the Osceola range, the other close to the bottom. Our first stop was to be near De Leon Springs in Volusia County, about 30 miles west of Daytona Beach. One of Charley's friends, Fred Voight, owns an 11,000-acre tract there. It lies across the St. Johns River from the Ocala National Forest and snugs up against the Lake Woodruff National Wildlife Refuge, which also boasts a heavy population of wild turkeys. Fred Voight told us there had been no hunting on this place and that we should have no problem getting a gobbler there.

The plan was to try for tom turkeys for two or three days along the shores of the St. Johns. If we failed to score, our ace in the hole lay another 300 miles to the south, on property leased for hunting by George Matthews of Palm Beach. His lands lay smack up against Lykes Brothers Fisheating Creek, a 178,000-acre game unit administered by the Florida Game and Fresh Water Fish Commission.

Fisheating Creek Wildlife Management Area contained one of the finest turkey populations in the state, with 100,000 acres open to public hunting. For my sake, Dickey had gone the whole route. He pursuaded Lou Gainey, who had worked at Fisheating Creek for eight years in charge of its turkey program, to take a vacation from his job and hunt with us. This was welcome news. Lou and I were old friends. We had worked together on other projects in past years.

For starters, Charley and I hunted the Voight tract for two days. We were there at the proper turkey-hunting times—from long before first light until well past flying-up time. We covered a sizable portion of the property but found no evidence of the big birds—no tracks, droppings, scratches, or feathers. Although the area was posted, guarded by gates, and supposedly protected, human footprints and empty shotgun hulls told us that it had been heavily hunted, probably over a period of several seasons.

"This one sure looks like a water haul," Charley admitted.

On the third morning, Charley was tied up in a business meeting, so Billie LaConte, a local realtor, made arrangements for me to hunt with Paul Dreggore who had the reputation of being "the best doggone turkey hunter in the whole county."

Before first light, Paul and I drove across a tremendous open pasture and walked in to the edge of a swamp that lay along a small creek.

"These birds," Paul said, "either roost in the big pines at the upper end of the pasture or in the swamp at the lower end. Where do you think we should go?"

"You're in your own ball park," I countered, "and I'm sure you know a heck of a lot more about their habits than I do."

"Maybe we should get right in the middle," he decided. "From there we can hear any turkey that gobbles in the pines. If the birds are at the lower end, they usually come into the pasture to graze, then pick their way up the edge in this direction."

After I'd kicked around inside a palmetto clump at the edge of the meadows to look for rattlesnakes, we sat down in the clumps.

"You do the calling," Paul suggested.

"Why me?"

"I figure you're better at it than I am," Paul said, "so I didn't even bring a call along."

I couldn't decide whether to feel complimented or frustrated. I'd never talked to an Osceola gobbler. The question was whether they'd understand my Middle-Georgia Crackerese.

One of the things that struck me when the light was bright enough to see more than a dozen yards was how deep and thick the clump of palmettos was in which we had submerged ourselves. No eyes could spot us there, but we didn't have even a peephole to look through. It was as though someone had wrapped a green curtain around the clump.

Long ago I'd made up my mind never to be caught again in a situation like that. With my small hand pruners, I went to work on the heavy fronds and cleared out enough to give us a view in every direction. Palmettos, which occur throughout the range of the Osceola, make excellent blinds, though usually the fronds must be rearranged.

When we didn't hear any turkey sounds after flying-down time, I clucked, yelped, and gobbled the box over a period of about two hours. No response. Had I been after the Eastern or other species I knew fairly well, I'd have been gone from that blind long ago.

"Let's make a little circle along the creek," Paul finally suggested, "and swing around to those roost trees. We seem to be parked in a dead spot here."

This is Osceola country, and the palmettos give a hunter some good opportunities for merging into his surroundings.

We found that the top of the sandy bluff above the creek was marked with turkey tracks. We saw fresh human footprints, too, where two hunters had apparently passed through that morning.

"That may be our answer," Paul commented.

We were sure of it when we found a pickup truck parked at the edge of the woods. It hadn't been there when we came in before dawn.

From the rim of the woods we studied the meadow in detail. Far at the lower end, about three-quarters of a mile away, three turkeys grazed about 10 feet out in the pasture.

"Guess we came to the wrong end," Paul observed.

"I usually do," I said.

We cut back into the woods along the creek and made a long stalk to a thicket about 75 yards from the grazing birds. Two were gobblers.

The lay of the land and a mass of brier thicket were arranged in such a way that we could get no closer to the gobblers along the edge of the pasture.

"Why don't I cut through the swamp," I said, "and try to reach the point where they came into the field? You stay here in case they feed on up the edge of the pasture, as you say they often do. Then we'll have them blocked from at least two sides."

Paul agreed and settled down in the brier patch. I waded the rim of thicket into the swamp. I followed the little creek in hope of reaching the point where the birds had entered the pasture. I wasn't more than halfway to my destination when a shotgun blasted 100 or more yards away, across the swamp. I didn't find the turkeys we were stalking. I didn't expect to. Paul Dreggore said the shot had come from a poacher.

"One thing I've learned for sure about hunting the Osceola," I told him grimly. "The people after his bird are no different than you'll find anywhere. Most real good spots are plagued by poachers."

After that failure Charley Dickey and I moved on to deep South Florida, to the tract of land that adjoined the Fisheating Creek Game Management Area. We met George Matthews and his son, George Jr., at the Matthews camp, a big house trailer that George had improved with an expansive built-on room that contained refrigerators, cooking and dining arrangements, spare beds, and an extra shower.

There are parts of America you'd have to see to believe. This was one of them. It is the kind of range in which the Osceola thrives. The country is as flat as you'll find on the western plains, and it seems almost as large. The vast palmetto flats are studded here and there with a lone pine or clump of tree-tall cabbage palmettos that only accentuate the depth and breadth of this land. Here and there a gum or cypress swamp winds through it. Occasionally you'll find a patch of scrub oaks, and now and then a stretch of pine forest. Mostly it's palmetto flat.

Fisheating Creek might be considered the headquarters of the Osceola management program in Florida. It takes its name from the stream that meanders through it, though the origin of the name seems to be lost in antiquity. For many years the Florida turkey has been grown and studied there. And it had been trapped there to stock other regions, both in and out of the state. Lou Gainey had told us that some of the Osceolas raised wild at Fisheating Creek were trapped and stocked in states as far away as Louisiana, Texas, and Ohio.

Much of the wild and ranch land in South Florida now has fair to good turkey shooting as a result of the work done at Fisheating Creek. Such was the situation on the lease adjoining it, where we had been invited to hunt.

A dense fog hung close to the ground next morning when we gulped our last cup of coffee and climbed aboard George Matthews's Bronco for a long ride across the palmetto flats. The ruts and cowpaths George followed didn't make for the smoothest trip. At times it was necessary to hold on tightly to keep from being bumped out of my seat. It amazed me that in this heavy fog George had any idea where he was going. This was cow range, and occasionally we had to stop and open a gate or a wire gap, so I knew he couldn't be too badly lost.

Although it couldn't have been that long, we seemed to ride for hours. Finally George screeched his torture chamber to a halt and pointed out a gnarled old tree that stood in a bunch of scrub oaks.

"Right beyond that tree," he said in a low voice, "is a shallow marsh.

Between the tree and marsh you'll find a blind in a palmetto clump. We've seen gobblers pass by here a good many mornings and have taken a few. It's a good spot. We'll be right over yonder, about a mile away."

I crawled out of his rig with my gun and shoulder bag, and George roared away through the mists, following a trail I couldn't see. It took five minutes before he went out of earshot.

As my eyes adjusted to the dim light, I felt my way past the tree, to where I found an obscure blind built in a cluster of palmettos. Someone had left an old tin bucket there as a seat.

The fog grew a little brighter, and I knew that daylight was on the way. I made myself as comfortable as possible on the bucket and strained my ears against the morning. The birds around me began to stir, and a crow called in the distance. The light grew brighter. The fog around me thinned out and began to lift.

Above the music that a few birds were making in the brush, I heard a gobbler. He sounded a long way off. I stepped out of the blind to go to him, walked a few yards, and stood at the edge of a cypress pond that was crowded with trees. I waded into it until the water came over the top of my boots, then turned back. The pond stretched in three directions as far as I could see.

I pondered the situation. I had a compass bearing on the bird, but I had no idea how far away it was or what lay between. If I took off into that wild hinterland, George Matthews and the others might spend a week looking for me. Once again I was forcefully reminded of the need to know the territory in which you hunt.

That tom gobbled only once. I was just as satisfied that he didn't sound off again. For regardless of the consequences, I'd probably have gone after him.

I spent the next four hours in my blind, calling occasionally and looking hard every time a songbird fluttered in the brush. George came back after midmorning to pick me up. It was only then I learned that I was no more than a couple of hundred yards from the wildlife refuge, where no hunting was allowed. Had I gone after that gobbler, I'd have crossed the forbidden line and been caught for trespassing. I couldn't work up much enthusiasm for a South-Florida jail. It sure pays to know your country.

Neither George, George Jr., nor Charley Dickey had seen or heard a turkey, but back in camp we found a delightful surprise. Roy Burnsed and Tom Bevan, two young men with the Game and Fresh Water Fish Commission who were there to make a wild-hog study on the cattle ranch, had gone out before working hours to hunt turkeys. Each had brought in a young gobbler. It was the first turkey Tom had ever called in, though he had bagged a couple while hunting quail. Roy's gobbler was the first he'd ever killed.

Charley got a chuckle out of all this. Where we had been camouflaged to the hilt, both the neophytes had worn white sneakers and cowboy hats.

"This only proves," Charley said, "that we don't know know to dress right when we go after gobblers."

"All turkey hunting," I agreed, "must be alike everywhere. I've had my eye wiped a few times by fellows who'd never seen a gobbler, and once by a guy who, as far as I knew, had never been in turkey woods."

The two young game officers had taken their gobblers out of a flock of eight birds. After a round of picture-taking, Lou drove Charley and me back to the same area so that we could scout around until dark and—we hoped—roost some of the remaining birds. Legal shooting ended at 1:00 P.M., so we left our guns in camp.

The spot seemed about perfect for turkeys. A thick wooded stretch half a mile wide separated the palmetto flat from a wide cypress swamp that was bordered on one side by a low hardwood ridge.

Charley and I found a place on a little knoll overlooking the swamp and sat down to call. For a couple of hours our only entertainment was furnished by a couple of barred owls that met in a tree next to the one under which we sat, and carried on a low, intimate conversation.

"We should separate," I suggested late in the afternoon. "We'll have a better chance of hearing some turkeys fly up to roost."

Charley moved a couple of hundred yards to a spot where his ears could cover more territory. I walked down the swamp for half a mile and stopped near a clump of tall pines that seemed to be good roost trees.

Periodically I clucked and yelped until after flying-up time. I got no results except that in the distance I thought I heard the *flop-flop-flop* of heavy wings. But the sound was so faint and far away that I could not be sure of the direction.

Charley had a different story. From where he sat, he could see the vicinity of the blind we had vacated. In the late hours, two turkeys—one of them a big gobbler—had walked up clucking, apparently trying to find whoever had called earlier from that spot. Charley yelped a couple of times on his diaphragm call and put it back in his pocket.

"Since I didn't have a gun to shoot, I decided not to disturb him. It being so late, I figured those birds would roost somewhere close around."

"Story of my life," I said amicably. "They came to where we'd been calling. If I had killed all the gobblers I've walked away from, wild turkeys would probably be on the list of endangered species. But one thing for sure. I'm more convinced than ever that hunting the Osceola is no different from hunting any other kind."

By starlight the next morning, we were back in the same location. Lou left us in the darkness so he could walk up the swamp about a mile to a roosting site he knew. Charley and I discussed our strategy.

"If these act like all other turkeys I've met," I said, "then whatever we do is likely to be wrong. Leaving our blind yesterday afternoon to separate is an example."

Since Charley hadn't heard the birds fly up and only knew the general vicinity in which they were supposed to roost, we decided to concentrate our efforts in that area. In the half-light, I built my blind on the edge of the swamp, about 150 yards below where Charley had seen the gobblers. He moved to the side of a knoll that angled into the swamp some 200 yards beyond our afternoon blind. Then he set up his stand 40 yards or more from the edge of the swamp, though at the time I had no idea exactly where he was.

The world around me awakened with its usual sounds. I gave any gobbler within hearing plenty of time to announce his presence before I clucked softly, listened, and then yelped my diaphragm. No answer. I tried louder notes on the Lynch box, just as I would have done in Eastern territory. The reply came back immediately in a lusty gobble, from the direction in which Charley had gone. Seconds later, another tom gobbled—from almost the same place.

This situation put me in a quandary. Had I been alone, I'd have moved up the rim of the swamp, closer to the gobblers. But that spot had to be near where my partner was. Any move in that direction might have thrown the proverbial monkey wrench into his hunt. I even thought of slipping out quietly and making my way down the swamp in the other direction, to where I thought I'd heard turkey wings the afternoon before.

My final decision was to remain in the blind. There was a possibility that if Charley, for any reason, spooked the gobblers, they would run or fly in my direction. If he called one close enough to kill, the other might fly over me. Then, too, any other gobbler coming up the swamp to investigate the goings on was likely to follow the edge and walk right past my stand. So I hung tight.

I yelped a couple of times more so that anything within hearing might get a fix on me. Then I put the call in my pocket and turned the show over to Charley, who was stationed nearer the gobblers.

The dramatics went on for almost two hours. The voices of the gobblers would seem to fade and then come back strong. And each time my anticipation grew keener to hear the blast of Charley's gun. From the sounds, I could only guess what was happening.

Charley told me about it later. Too late, he realized he had set up his blind too far from the edge of the swamp. The 45 to 50 yards in between was probably too open for a cagey old gobbler to cross, especially when he couldn't see a hen on the other side.

"He would come to high ground right on the edge of the swamp," Charley said, "and strut and gobble there. But there was no way I could convince him to start up that little rise. The gobbler traveling with him was even more shy. He came into the open a couple of times, but the rest of the time remained in the background, gobbling only now and then.

"Still, I might have killed one bird," Charley continued. "After the two gobblers flew to the ground, a young tom left its roost tree in the same area and came directly over my blind. I believe I could have killed him, but I'd have had to shoot through the thick tree branches overhead, so I didn't

The Osceola gobbler.

chance it. The way the big gobbler was coming through the swamp toward me, I knew I'd have him in the bag in a matter of minutes, anyway. Only it didn't work out like that."

"These Osceolas don't have a lock on being cranky," I said.

Since our time was up, we didn't have another go at the big gobbler. I felt that with one more morning we could have brought him in, but that same brand of optimism once kept me after another gobbler for three solid years before I got him close enough for a lethal load of No. 6s.

Although Charley Dickey and I failed to score, I considered our hunt a success. Our small party had taken two handsome toms. More important, I had learned a lot about the Osceola and the country in which it lives. Only the terrain proved different. As for the techniques and calls, they were about the same as those I'd been using in other parts of this nation on other birds for more than fifty years.

18

Each Bird Is
a Character

In many ways, gobblers come mighty close to being human. I know that statement may be open to discussion, but discussion seems to be a lot of what gobbler hunting is all about anyway. Biologists say that gobblers act by instinct and can't think. All the same, if one of the old patriarchs wore pants and a tie, I'd sure hate to come up against him in any kind of business deal.

Each bird develops its own character and personality and becomes a separate and distinct individual. Over a period of years, a turkey is likely to acquire a pattern of behavior. I have known gobblers with such set routines that you get to know where—or at least close to where—you might find them at almost any time during a day or week. Jimmie Shirley, over in western Alabama, once drew a map to show how I could intercept a tom after daylight when he came off the roost. I was there; and sure enough, the turkey was there. I didn't kill him—but that was no fault of his or Jimmie's.

If you hunt a bird long enough, you get to know its range and habits, and even to recognize its voice. I stayed after one a number of years and would have known him if I'd met him coming down Peachtree Street in Atlanta. He probably told some of his wives the same thing about me.

Some biologists say that one of the most common faults of writers and other lay people is attributing to animals the power to reason, when in reality the dumb creature acts only by instinct.

The people who live day by day with animals in the wild are likely to reply that this attitude indicates that about all the biologist knows is what he's read in books. This assertion is not true, of course. Many of these scientists have had vast experience in the woods, or wherever else their scene of operation. But if they persist in sticking strictly to the instinct theory on gobblers, then they don't know as much as they should about them.

Don't fool yourself into believing that turkeys are so dumb they can't figure things out on their own. For many years, I hunted the birds on a large Southern plantation. Fall turkey hunting on some of those plantations is a ritual completely different from either fall or spring hunting almost anywhere else. During the evening preceding the hunt, plantation hands scatter out through the turkey woods to locate the group of trees where birds fly up to roost.

The party of gunners may number from a few to a dozen or more. They leave the plantation house in the darkness before dawn. A part of the ritual is to ride to the stands in a mule-drawn wagon that has wooden seats for the gunners. The wagon is stopped short of the blinds where the hunters will stand, and each gunner is led afoot to the spot that has been selected for him.

About flying-down time, the beaters start in the woods, with the turkeys between them and the stands where the shooters have been placed. The beaters whistle, sing, and hit on the trees with sticks. The turkeys fly down, run ahead of the beaters, and then take to the air when they spot the firing line, manned by gunners.

This is the general ritualistic procedure of plantation hunts.

One drive on a plantation where I hunted was set up so that when the birds flushed, those that escaped the shot strings flew across a wide creek. This was a safety barrier, as water often is for any kind of game.

After two or three drives on this course, a different strategy was planned. Instead of all the gunners being placed between the roosting site and the creek, a number were stationed across the creek to be in line for the birds that got past the first line of shooters.

There is some doubt that what happened after this last drive could have been due entirely to instinct. The entire flock of turkeys, finding that the water course was no longer a safety feature, left their range and moved 3 miles away to the swamps along the river. To me, anyway, that proves turkeys can think.

As it is with people, some turkeys are smart and some are stupid, although the stupid ones don't usually last long. Every veteran turkey hunter has seen wise old toms pull stunts that could in no way be classified solely within the realm of instinct. And by so doing, these gobblers continued to live. Such turkeys gain a local reputation and are often known by all the hunters in an area. Some become associated with the men who hunt them. I've stood on a ridge or in the swamp with a local shotgunner, and when we'd hear a bird gobble around daylight, I'd look at the guy with shining eyes. But he'd only shake his head.

"That's Joe's turkey." Or: "That one belongs to Pete Dobson. We'll leave it alone." And the other shooters would do the same for him if they knew he was after a certain bird.

I've known cases, too, where a hunter finally decided it wasn't in the cards for him to corner some cagey old tom—so he "gave" it to a friend. In another instance, a couple of fellows became disgusted with their own efforts and "swapped" birds. One of these was an old mountain friend who afterward said ruefully, "I wisht I'd kep' the bird I had. I'll see if I can git him to swap back."

I've thought many times—and said so a good many times—that the most expected thing in gobbler hunting is the unexpected. You never have any idea what a bird will do, and probably he doesn't even know himself. He reacts to the contingencies of the moment, and seldom will any two birds react the same way. This trait is most evident when you unexpectedly come face to face with a gobbler.

I once met a tall gentleman dressed in iridescence on a wilderness trail that ran through North Carolina's Joyce Kilmer Forest. That was back in the days before the magnificent stand of virgin timber had been set aside in perpetuity. Word was out that the U.S. Forest Service had sold this part of its forest to the lumber industry. A friend at a New Year's party in Knoxville suggested that if I wanted to see it before it was converted into a slash, I'd better go straightaway and have a look.

So I drove by that very day on my way home. This January first was bitterly cold, dark as twilight, with a mixture of sleet and snow. The only two cabins in the vicinity were on Santeetlah Creek and belonged to a mountaineer named Brownlow Blevins and his son.

On my hip I carried a .22 Colt Woodsman. Why, I don't know. But maybe I had some vague notion about protection from the bears or "painters"— mountain vernacular for panther—a few of which lived in this country.

My companion and I were pussyfooting along a trail through the giant poplars, oaks, and such when we came face to face with a gobbler. All the rules said he should have stayed on his roost in such weather, but I suppose he hadn't read the rules.

We stopped eyeball to eyeball at twelve steps, and the gobbler stood there long enough for me to draw my pistol and get a bead on his head. I couldn't see his tail feathers to identify him as wild and was trying to decide whether he belonged to one of the Blevins families when he made that decision for me. He stepped into a patch of laurel that completely engulfed him.

I've taken gobblers under all sorts of weather conditions. Once in western Alabama, Turkey Johnston, Jimmy Shirley, and I met a severe thunderstorm in the predawn woods. It was a dilly, as only an Alabama storm can sometimes be. Lightning flashed. Thunder rolled. The rain fell literally in sheets.

The afternoon before, I had heard a gobbler fly up to roost. So I knew now approximately where he was. Day was not yet a peep of gray when I slid into my rain suit and felt my way along a dim trail that followed the crest of a ridge. I was well aware that I should have been elsewhere, such as in the office of some head-shrinker, waiting to have the part of my anatomy located between my ears examined. The lightning was getting too close for comfort. The wall of sound erupted only seconds after each high-voltage display. Wind and rain slashed at the trees. I turned my gun barrel down to keep it from being filled with water.

Two or three times I thought of returning to where we'd left the car, but I knew where that bird was perched out on the end of the ridge, and I wanted to be there come daylight. I kept trying to convince myself that the storm would blow on over about daybreak and that after such a wild night my gobbler would be hungry for company.

First light was slow in arriving. The lightning and thunder had moved on out of the immediate vicinity and with it the wind. The rain had abated to a mere downpour. The light increased, and I was beginning to wonder whether I should make the first move or wait on the gobbler. He beat me to the draw. Thunder rolled through the forest, and he answered it with a lusty gobble. After a few minutes, I called. I hoped the sound was loud enough for him to hear and locate me. He answered immediately, and seconds later he again answered the thunder.

The tom gobbled a dozen times on the roost. I called only once more to make sure he wouldn't forget me. I never did hear him fly down, and he did not gobble on the ground. But suddenly he stood out there in front of me in the downpour, looking a bit bedraggled I thought. My gun was almost in position, and the woods were open around him. I knew I'd have a shot, no matter what kind of evasive action he took. So I put up the gun and shot him while he stood there and made no attempt to fly or run. Because of the way I was hunkered down, I don't believe he recognized me as a man.

On my first hunt in Mississippi many years ago, I killed a big gobbler only minutes ahead of a tornado. Bruce Brady and Dr. Jim Stribling of Brookhaven were with me.

This was really Jim's bird. Jim had roosted it the afternoon before and graciously dictated that I should be the one to go after it in the morning. I think he felt a bit of sympathy for me. I'd been in that part of the state for several days and had failed to lay eyes on a Magnolia gobbler. I was beginning to wonder if any such creature existed. We'd been with a good team of hunters, too, including Ed Norwood and George Pullen.

Those Mississippi hunters have a pattern all their own that gives a Deep South flavor to gobbler hunting. The first morning we met by starlight on the blacktop parking lot of my motel. Under the motel floodlights, everyone brought out a Thermos of coffee, and Ed Norwood set two large paper sacks on the hood of his truck.

"Smells good," I observed. "What is it?"

"Your breakfast," Ed explained. "You can either eat it here or after the morning hunt."

"This guy," Bruce put in, "spends half the night frying country sausage, making biscuits, and putting them together as sandwiches. It's sort of a ritual, and you'll never have a better breakfast."

The national forest boundary lay only a few miles from town. Where the road forked, we separated, Ed and George going in one direction, Jim, Bruce, and I in another.

"We'll meet you back here with a couple of gobblers around midmorning," they called.

After a pair of miles, we parked our car on a wide shoulder of the road.

The first gray tints of dawn were beginning to streak the eastern sky when we separated. Jim climbed a slope that led into a valley beyond, and Bruce and I followed an overgrown woods road that skirted the brow of a hill and then dropped off on a long gentle slope to a creek swamp that lay somewhere ahead of us.

In the growing light, I could see that—even this late in the season—the trees were not fully leafed out. A glaze of frost lay on the ground. Air stirring out of the northwest carried a touch of icicles on its breath.

"These birds have already been gobbling," Bruce whispered, "and I hope the weather won't discourage them too much."

With dawn growing brighter, we paused in a fork of the logging road and stood for thirty minutes, slowly congealing, our ears strained to pick up gobbler sounds.

"A yelp or two might raise something," I suggested.

Bruce clucked a couple of times, paused, and then gave the quick notes of an ardent hen. He uses no artificial call. With only his vocal cords he imitates the sounds of a turkey better than anyone I've heard. Bruce says he learned this from Jack Dudley, another Mississippian, who not long before had yelped and gobbled his way into a world turkey-calling championship.

When Bruce received no response to his calls, I gobbled my Lynch box and we waited long minutes, hoping to hear the rattle of an answering gobbler.

"None seem to be within hearing distance," Bruce finally said. "If it's all right with you, let's split up and go looking for them."

His suggestion appealed to me for several reasons. I was cold and needed to get my heat pump going. Then, too, no matter how much you like a guy or enjoy being with him, gobbler hunting is truly a lone man's game. You can thus plan your moves without always having to consider how it might interfere with the other fellow. And when you make a mistake, you know that you've got nobody to blame but yourself. Also, nothing is so sweet as walking up to your hunting pals at a rendezvous point with a long-bearded gobbler swung over your shoulder.

Since we'd heard no turkey sounds, I walked fast for a couple of hundred yards to warm my blood. The trail I was on wound through hardwood forest, skirting a sidehill to the rim of a long open cove. I propped myself against a tree where I could see up and down the cove. And after I'd let the sound of my motion settle down, I made a couple of hen clucks on my Turpin yelper. Five minutes passed before I yelped again, a little louder. The woods around me were still. I went through my regular calling pattern. After ten minutes, I clucked again for the benefit of any feathered gent who might be snooping close around. Then two or three minutes later I rattled my box with the shrill cacophony of an old gobbler.

After another ten minutes of silent woods, I was about to move on. But then the corner of my eye caught a movement. Shifting only my eyeballs, I made out the shape of a turkey but could not further identify it until cautious steps brought it within clearer range of my vision. I saw that it was a tall, trim hen.

She clucked tentatively, studying me, walked on a few feet, scratched at the leaves, and pecked at something she'd uncovered. Then she strode on, passing within 30 feet of me. For another quarter-hour I remained motionless, listening for sounds that might indicate she had gone to a gobbler. I heard nothing more.

Until past midmorning, when the toms usually stop gobbling, I covered a big scope of country, calling and rattling my box. Then I went back to meet my partners and have breakfast of coffee, sausage, and biscuit while propped against the back side of Ed's truck. Bruce had seen two hens. Every one of us had found plenty of sign. No one had heard a gobbler, though.

"It just may be too cold," Jim Stribling stated. "These woods are full of birds."

By now the day was much warmer and wispy clouds moved across the upper atmosphere. Bruce looked up.

"Bad weather travels high," he observed. "Hope it holds off for a day or two. I don't know which would be worse—a frosty morning or a stormy one."

After lunch, we scattered out to cover as large a segment as possible of the Homochitto, stationing ourselves in the vicinity of known roosting sites. Sometimes a tom will gobble before going to roost. When the afternoon is still, you can hear the flap of wings for several hundred yards when the big birds fly into a roost tree.

I selected a long ridge below one of the hilltop game-food patches. The pines there were tall, heavily limbed with thick foliage—an ideal roosting site. When the birds are not gobbling, a hunter can accomplish little by moving around, so I made a blind overlooking a section of hillside and settled myself for the afternoon.

Every twenty or thirty minutes I clucked, listened for a while, and then yelped—softly at first, in case a bird was close. Then I gave a series of loud yelps that might attract turkeys feeding several hundreds of yards away.

The afternoon proved uneventful. Smaller birds and squirrels were moving and helped me pass the hours. And of course there was always the expectation that a tom might slip in to investigate my calls. But none did. It was almost black dark, and the flying-up hour past, when I walked back along the trail to where we had agreed to meet on a main road.

By the headlights of the cars, we swapped reports. Ed had heard a turkey fly up somewhere below the slope on which he sat, and Jim Stribling had roosted two birds about a quarter of a mile apart on the rim of a creek swamp. One he knew was a tom, for it had gobbled twice in answer to an owl's call, after flying into its roost tree.

"That'll at least give us a head start in the morning," George Pullen commented fervently.

We made our decision to concentrate on those three birds the next morning.

When we pulled off the road before daylight, not a star showed and lightning played across the sky to the west. The air was heavy and smelled of rain. With his flashlight Jim led the way down an old road and around the edge of a field. The morning was just gray enough for me to make out Jim's outline when he stopped and pointed.

"The turkeys I heard are somewhere beyond that corner of the field," he said. "You and Bruce go to them. I'm gonna cut across here to the river swamp."

"What's the matter with you two going to the gobbler you heard?" I asked. "Let me look for a new one."

"I'm familiar with this country," Jim replied. "I know better than you where to look."

Bruce and I felt our way the last quarter-mile through the meadow to a line of low pines, where we paused to listen. A strip of open meadow lay in front of us, and beyond that stood the black silhouette of tall trees.

"Ten to one that gobbler is roosting in one of those," I offered.

"I hope that in a little while you'll find out," he whispered.

We stood in the growing light while lightning winked over the horizon and thunder rumbled along the earth. Minutes passed, and more minutes as the forest around us came to life. Then, loud and resonant, a tom's gobble rang across the open meadow.

"That's one of them," Bruce whispered. "You go to him, and I'll step down this stretch of woods and listen for the other bird."

"You take this one," I insisted.

Being the sportsman he is, Bruce wouldn't hear of that. And since it was probable that he would run into the other bird farther down the swamp, I didn't stop to argue. Instead I cut through the forest bordering the upper end of the meadow. While I was making that circle, the tom gobbled twice more on the roost.

There is always a question of how close you should try to get to a buck turkey before you sit down to call.

I have spooked birds by trying to approach too near. And I have failed to interest them when I stopped too far away. This time I tried to find a happy medium of 150 to 200 yards.

Before you sit down it's always smart to pick out the best blind you can find. You want to be well hidden, but not so concealed that you can't see beyond the immediate cover. This little swamp was so open that finding a suitable blind was difficult. In the half-light, I went from one spot to another, including a fallen dead treetop, but none seemed right. The fifth place I looked at seemed the best so far. It was a large pine, growing on the edge of a shallow gully. Within 30 or 40 feet were just enough low bushes to hide me, and yet things were open enough around them for me to see the approaching bird—if I could get its attention. Behind me was a screen of bushes and beyond that an open space of grass and scattered pines.

While I was moving around, looking for my stand, the gobbler flew down.

I didn't hear him fly. The next time I heard him he was on the ground and farther away than he had been in the roost tree. I clucked, but I'm sure he was too far away to hear it. I gave the higher notes of a hen, and he came back immediately with a gobble. At least he knew I was there.

I waited. The bird gobbled again from a different angle, and I knew he was circling. To give him an even better fix, I clucked a couple of times, then made a short series of low hen yelps. He came back, making the swamp woods ring. By now he was almost behind me, and I knew he would come in from that direction.

The approaching storm sent its scouts ahead with a few splattering drops of rain and a gust of wind that stirred the topmost branches of the entire swamp. Thunder rumbled, and the air felt heavy enough to produce a downpour at any minute. Because I had no idea what effect rain would have on this turkey, I did something that under ordinary circumstances I never would have dared. I slid from my sitting position into the shallow gully, wormed my way around, and came back facing the pine. I had to guess which side of the tree to put my gun on and hoped I was making the right choice. I put the stock to my shoulder and the barrel against the tree trunk at about the height of a turkey's head.

The tom had gobbled about a minute before I made my move. Then he shut up completely. Ten long minutes passed. The horrible thought grew that the bird had seen me change positions. A few more drops of rain fell. I couldn't make a cluck or yelp to find out where the gobbler might be. I had done my calling on a Lynch box and Turpin yelper and had failed to put the diaphragm call in the roof of my mouth. More minutes passed. By now I was sure I had made a mistake in moving. I considered reaching for my diaphragm call and even my Turpin yelper, but I'd had enough experience with gobblers to abandon that idea as soon as I thought of it. When an old gobbler shuts up, he's either going the other way or coming to you. In either event, you might as well stay put. So I continued to wait.

I was wearing yellow-tinted glasses that are supposed to pick up twice the amount of light regular cheaters do. I'm sure that within range of my vision not even a wood tick could have moved without my seeing it. It was one of those moments when eternity seems to hang by a thread or single note of sound. The woods were almost breathless.

A thick screen of brush lay beyond my gun sights. I had my eyes on this but occasionally shifted them without moving my head to glance at the right of the tree trunk, in case the bird should slip in from that direction. Then, in the clump of brush directly ahead, I saw what appeared to be a leaf that changed position. It could have been a vagrant wisp of wind or a raindrop, but I kept an eye on it. It moved again, only an inch, and I knew that I was looking at a very small fraction of yellow-white color on top of the gobbler's head.

I remained motionless, trying to decide how far away the gobbler stood. With only that spot of color to judge by, I had no idea. So I waited what seemed to be an interminable time. It must have taken the gobbler ten minutes to move four feet. And still all I could see was the top of its head.

Another few feet would put him in the open, and then I would have to shift my gun barrel a few inches. If he saw that, he'd disappear as though the ground had swallowed him. I still had no idea about distance, but with the raindrops becoming thicker and thicker, I decided to take a chance. Lining up the front bead on the small patch of head I could see, I squeezed off a shot with the same care I would have used in shooting a rifle.

The head disappeared and I was immediately on my feet, runnng toward the spot. I've lost some gobblers by not getting there fast enough. But my bird was flopping on the ground, no more than 30 yards from where I had crouched.

In the meantime, Bruce was busy on his own. Farther down the swamp—too far for me to hear—his gobbler had sounded off. My partner, approaching as close as he dared, took his position at the base of a big oak, with a screen of bushes in front of him.

Later that day, Bruce gave me details of his affair with this particular bird.

"I removed the cedar box from my pocket and chalked it," he said. "I was undecided about trying to call with my natural voice. Suddenly the big tom opened up again. I put the box down, cleared my throat, and gave a seven-note yelp, the notes clear and rising in volume.

"The turkey fired right back. I forced myself to wait two or three minutes before making another call. This time I tried three yelps, lower in volume, and followed them quickly with two clucks.

"I'd hardly got out the second cluck," Bruce went on, "before the gobbler shook the woods again. This time he sounded 50 yards closer. I sat back and waited, certain he was on the way. After five minutes and still no sight or sound of the tom, I began to think I'd made a mistake by not using my box call. Finally I clucked twice, paused a moment, and then clucked again.

"Almost at once, off to my left, I heard the sound of footsteps in the leaves. Cutting my eyes in that direction, I saw the big turkey sprinting directly toward me. When he closed to within 25 yards I whirled and fired my Browning Sweet Sixteen at his head and neck. His momentum carried him tumbling toward me."

I heard the shot on my way to meet Bruce, and he arrived at the rendezvous spot minutes after I did, with that gobbler slung over his shoulder. It was a beautiful bird sporting a ten-inch beard.

By now the rain came harder and the wind was blowing big. To keep from getting soaked, we walked along the edge of the woods for three-quarters of a mile to where we had parked our car in the yard of a small church. We reached the church porch a few seconds in front of a heavy downpour that completely blotted out the woods only a hundred yards away.

Jim Stribling arrived empty-handed in the storm, which was beginning to increase in velocity. He was as wet as if someone had held his heels and dunked him in a pond. He brought a jug of coffee out of his car, and we

Two trophies that you save from an outstanding gobbler: his beard and his spurs.

Another trophy you're likely to save from a big gobbler is the tail. The process is to sever the tail at the "bishop's nose" and then spread the tail and dry it into a fan. This trophy from any of the species is colorful.

three huddled on the front porch of that little church. The wind had increased to such force that the rain was now blowing parallel to the ground. The church trembled under the impact, as though it were afraid of being blown away. I shared its feelings. Jim had pulled his rain suit over his wet clothes to save himself from being completely congealed. The hot coffee helped.

We remained there for half an hour until the storm seemed to have blown itself out. Only after we had pulled out and were on our way to town did we discover how close a call we'd really had. Less than 400 yards up the road, out of sight from where we'd crouched on the church porch, a tornado had cut a swath across the countryside, tearing big trees out by the roots and devastating others. The twister had also blown down an unoccupied tenant house less than a quarter-mile away. Had the tornado shifted slightly, the church would have been directly in its path.

On all fronts, the Great Spirit had been good to us that day.

19

Gobblers Make Men Do Strange Things

If there's any critter that swims, walks, or flies that can put the double whammy on a man quicker than a wild turkey gobbler, I don't know what it is. Guys who are normal and otherwise fairly sensible will often seem to lose the handle completely when faced with some unusual situation in turkey woods. Even the old-timers are likely to fall under this spell. I've seen turkey hunters do some of the most incredible things. I've done a few myself, some so ridiculous I later had to laugh. I suppose that helped me relieve the guilt of acting so stupid.

I was on a quail hunt one time in southern Georgia with Ellis Arnall. Arnall was Governor of Georgia then, and I was Director of the State Game and Fish Commission. Both of us should have known better.

We were hunting on horses. One of the bird dogs ranging in front of us jumped a turkey gobbler out of the brush. Instead of flying, the big tom streaked afoot at an angle toward us. I'm sure one of us could have killed it if we'd simply stepped out of the saddle, pulled a gun from the scabbard, and seated a couple of shells—all of which could have been done in a matter of seconds.

You'd never guess what we did: two full-grown men. As if someone had given the signal, we jumped off our horses and took out after that gobbler *afoot*. With the speed at which it was moving, I don't believe we could have caught it on a horse! And heaven only knows what we'd have done with the bird if we had overtaken it. The least desirable thing I can think of is getting into a fist-wing-beak-and-spur fight with an outsized turkey gobbler.

I don't know whether that old tom thought we could outrun it. Anyway, it took to the air and flew across the creek. The Governor and I walked sheepishly back to our horses, where our hunt manager was all but falling off his saddle from laughing.

"What would you have done with that bird if you'd caught it?" he asked.

Neither of us had an answer, not even a smart one.

221

Many years ago I was hunting with a friend in Buckingham County, Virginia. In those days the turkey population was at low ebb and not many states had seasons. Most of these fell in the fall. Virginia was one state that maintained a fair turkey population and was one of the first to begin its restoration program. In 1937–38, Mosby and Handley, whose state jobs centered on the wild turkey, estimated a population of more than 22,000 birds in 73 of Virginia's 99 counties. Buckingham headed the list with the largest number of hens and gobblers.

My partner and I had taken a couple of the big birds there by finding areas of heavy use and concentrating on those. Once we scattered a flock and managed to call one to us. Another we got while it was flying over us at treetop level.

Another time we were following a fence that ran along a strip of woods, and we almost collided with two young gobblers. I'm sure they were as surprised as we. Instead of flying, both birds tried to duck under the fence. One made it, the other didn't. With one bird trotting away through the woods, my partner cut down the other hung there in the fence.

"This one wasn't going anywhere," I said. "You had plenty of time to take him. So why didn't you shoot the one running off?"

"Why didn't you?" he countered.

That's another time I didn't have an answer. I was so busy being amazed at my partner's stupidity that I didn't even think about my own.

In a way, I feel toward turkeys about the way one of my old Okefenokee Swamp fishing guides said he felt about bears.

"I ain't afraid of what they'll do to me," he said. "I'm afraid of what they'll make me do to myself."

Probably the results would never be so drastic with a gobbler. But under the right circumstances, a turkey can sure make a fellow come up with the most amazing reactions.

Brooks Holleman, for instance, is one of the best turkey hunters I know. He left a successful investment business to devote his life to the big birds. And it is Brooks who's largely responsible for re-establishing wild turkeys in one section of Alabama.

Brooks didn't tell me this story. His wife Martha did. With at least a modicum of chagrin, Brooks later acknowledged the correctness of the details.

Brooks had been after a certain gobbler on his place at Turkey Hollow for a good couple of years. It rather irritated him that the bird seemed to know all the tricks and have all the intuitions to keep him beyond the lethal range of a shot string. In addition, the gobbler apparently was one of those rare individuals who seem to lead a charmed life. Brooks was sure of it after his last encounter with the old tom.

Martha was at the farm, and she went into the woods with him. Otherwise, we probably never would have heard a true account of this hunt.

When Brooks heard the gobbler, he quickly built a blind of cedar boughs, making it roomy enough for himself and Martha. Both wore camouflage clothing with head nets. Apparently they were invisible in the cedar clump, for that morning the gobbler was not even suspicious. Brooks yelped a couple of times, and the old tom came within 75 yards. There it paused to study the lay of the land. Brooks gave him two soft clucks, and the gobbler started walking toward him.

"Don't even wiggle your big toe," he muttered under his breath to Martha. "I'm gonna let him get close enough this time to where I can't miss."

Brooks had his gun propped on his knees, with its sights following the head of the gobbler. There was no strain, and no further motion was necessary. The turkey came on, one slow step after another, his eyes seeming to study every leaf, every insect that moved. The gobbler was in the open most of the way. Brooks, with his 3-inch magnum shells, was assured of a kill at 40 yards. But he didn't pull the trigger. He let the bird continue to walk toward him.

When it stopped at less than 20 feet away with the gunsights dead on its head, Brooks squeezed down on the trigger. Somewhere in that fraction of a second, the turkey moved to take another step forward. As one of my old mountain friends used to say, "His head steps before his feet do." The tom moved his head just enough to let that column of shot go by. The range was too short for the lead pellets to have begun patterning, and the situation was more like shooting a rifle.

Brooks was so sure of his gobbler that he suddenly stood up in the blind. The startled turkey came straight off the ground as though propelled by booster jets. My old shooting partner could easily have killed that gobbler in midair, but he didn't even shoot. He was so shook up and exasperated that, instead, he threw his shotgun at the turkey.

I know exactly how he felt. I've had the same inclination a dozen times myself. You wouldn't give way to such an impulse with any creature other than an old gobbler.

Bob Card and I have tramped a lot of miles and sat through countless hours together in turkey woods. Bob is a calm, down-to-earth, logical sort of fellow who thinks around the next corner instead of just one step ahead. As far as I know, the only creature that ever blew Bob's mind was a turkey gobbler.

Bob was working a tom turkey one morning in East Tennessee when two other birds got into the act. Each time he yelped, three birds answered. They were converging on him from three directions. It seemed only to be a question of which one would get there first. But then all of them hung up about 75 yards out. In the next two hours, they talked back and forth with one another and with Bob. They gobbled, yowked, and putted, and two of the toms finally cut through the woods at an angle and got together behind Bob's blind.

Bob yelped in dulcet tones. He clucked. He begged. He cajoled. The birds answered but stayed put. Bob could not get them to come any closer.

A bird might eventually have walked within range, but Bob's patience finally steamed over. He jumped out of his blind into the open, rattled his box as loud as he could make it gobble, and yelled, "Shut up, you sons-abitches, and let *me* talk awhile!"

They did.

Bob Card wasn't even peeved with himself.

"I'd do it again," he declared, "just like I did the first time."

I could only shake my head in wonderment at what strange things a tom turkey will often do to a man.

In this same Tennessee region, I called up two gobblers. That morning I was making what sounded to me like sweet notes. The buck turkeys thought so, too. They walked in without hesitation. I had my gun up and ready. I had plenty of time to look them over. One was an old long-beard, half a head and neck taller than his young companion. Both were well within range.

For some unaccountable reason, as though an irresistible force had moved my hand, I swung the gun barrel from the head of the old gobbler over to cover the two-year-old. Then I pulled the trigger. The big tom disappeared in a flash through the treetops.

No psychologist I ever met could explain that strange twist, though one or two who were turkey hunters studied me as though they were about ready to call the men in the white coats. I'm convinced that I'll go looking for them myself if I ever pull that same stunt again.

An odd experience that any turkey hunter can—and often does—have is to call up another hunter. This situation can be dangerous, too. In my opinion, any guy who goes sneaking around through the woods with his scattergun and thinks he can slip up on a gobbler just can't have much savvy about turkey hunting and might be fool enough to blast away at the first movement he sees that resembles what he thinks he's stalking.

Very seldom will an old-timer who knows his stuff get that close to a talking bird. If he hears a gobbler, or sometimes even a hen, he may move partway to the sound. But he stops far enough away to get the bird's attention and call it to him.

Nor does it usually take a seasoned hunter long to recognize if the notes are being made by another hunter, no matter how accurate they sound. After a while, he realizes that all the notes are coming from the same spot. No turkey, unless he's on his strutting ground, is going to remain in one place for any great length of time and give the same yelps in probably the same series again and again. The hen that's supposed to be making that music either moves toward a gobbler (if one is near), goes farther away, or else changes locations (if she is feeding).

I am usually able to recognize the type of call a hunter is using. A box has a tone all its own. So do a slate call, a diaphragm, and a snuffbox. A brier leaf in the fingers of someone who knows how to use it is the most difficult to distinguish. But even that soon gives itself away by holding in one spot over any length of time.

It's the guy who doesn't know these things who frightens me. If he's a reasonably good woodsman and moves slowly and quietly enough, he can slip up on your back side almost before you know it. And that may be too late.

I've been pinned down by other hunters so much that I should be getting adjusted to the idea. So far I haven't. When some fellow moves in quietly and begins to yelp, you can usually tell what kind of hunter he is from the sounds. But not always. Also, you can usually tell whether you are within range of his load.

Bill Rae and I were hunting once under the shadow of Big Frog Mountain in Tennessee. We'd heard no gobbling at daylight on one of the high points. So we took off down a long ridge from which our ears could cover a vast scope of country on both sides of the high "lead," as the main ridges are called in that country. I followed my usual procedure of pausing every couple of hundred yards to cluck, listen, yelp, listen, and then gobble my box in resonant tones.

After we'd gone through this process on one high point, I suggested something to Bill.

"We might have been traveling too fast," I said. "Let's wait here for twenty or thirty minutes just in case an interested bird is somewhere around. He might come to investigate."

I placed my partner near the top on one side of the knoll, and I sat down against an old log just on the other side. I gave the box one more healthy rattle before I settled down to wait.

The answer came much sooner than I expected, from right down the slope under me. It was the soft, accurate yelp of a hen. After about five minutes, it came again from the same place. This time I was sure of what I had first suspected. The guy who had moved in below me had a slate call, and he knew how to use it. My ear couldn't pinpoint the sound to tell me how far away he was, so I sat perfectly still, straining my eyes. While I was looking, he called again. This time the notes sounded as though they had come from beyond a contour along the side of the ridge.

Moving as slowly as I could, I lay down beyond the log, in case he decided to come on up the hill. I stayed there motionless for a quarter-hour. When the hunter remained where I had first heard him and continued to call, I crawled away from the log, keeping it carefully between us. I went over the ridge crest, which wasn't more than a dozen feet away. Far enough down the other side, I stood up and walked over to Bill.

"Let's get out of here," I said, "before one of us gets lead poisoning."

We made a long swing back to the game trail that cut just under the crest and was open enough for us to be easily identified as humans. I kept up a conversation with my partner so that there would be no mistaking us for turkeys. About 50 yards below where I had sat on the knoll, we came upon three hunters crouched near the game trail. They had the appearance of veterans.

We exchanged a low greeting, and one of them angrily asked, "Didn't you hear that gobbler?"

He said it as though accusing us of walking and talking down the trail, scaring off some tom turkey he'd almost had under the sights of his gun.

"Why no," I replied. "We haven't heard a turkey all morning."

"Well, there was one here," he insisted, sure now that we had run off his bird.

"Good luck," I said. "I hope all three of you get a good one. We're going to hunt on down the ridge."

I suppose it was a dirty trick. But I couldn't resist pausing out on the tip of the ridge about 200 yards away and gobbling twice on my box, with a well-spaced interval between. Then Bill and I cleared out for another part of the range, figuring that if we bumped into those guys again, one of them might take a shot at us just on general principles.

You never know quite what to do when some other hunter moves in on you. My own rule has been to get out as quietly as possible and leave the territory to him, if I can do so without being seen. There have been times when I had to hunker down and make myself as invisible as the leaves and background of my blind would allow, until he gave up and went his way.

Only once or twice have I spoken out to alert a caller in such circumstances. Then the guy was close enough for me to talk or whistle in low tones, and when I could see him and watch his reaction, just in case I startled him into thinking he'd heard a turkey. Such a response would, of course, have come from only a rank novice. Usually it's easier to shut up and let the other guy drift on. I spoke to a fellow recently in such a situation after I recognized his calling as that of a veteran hunter. Then I waited till he stood up in his blind to move on before I showed myself. Of course, it's always possible that a nearby hunter is working a gobbler that I haven't heard. So, everything considered, I generally decide to keep quiet in such a situation.

Dwain Bland, whose turkey-hunting home territory is more open than where you generally find the Eastern or Florida birds, says there is always the danger of being bushwhacked by some rifle-toter using iron sights. The guy is likely to see movement farther away than he can clearly identify—and take a chance.

"All of us who hunt that country by calling up the birds," Dwain added, "would like to see every turkey rifle equipped with a scope. Even then we'd say a little prayer that the fellow with the rifle has good eyes.'"

Dwain knows as well as the rest of us that gobblers sometimes make men do strange things.

20

How Not to Clobber
a Gobbler

I'd just missed getting a long-bearded tom that had been gobbling up on the ridge behind George Shuler's cabin.

"I had that bird dead to rights," I confided, using an old mountain expression. "He was coming in. Then, at just the wrong time, a buck deer walked by, caught my scent, and snorted. The gobbler stepped behind a tree, and I never saw him again. Turkey hunting's gotta be at least 80 percent luck."

"Getting a gobbler ain't luck," George said with a sly smile. "It's something that's preordained."

I didn't know George was acquainted with such a fancy word. But in one sense he had to be right. Sometimes no matter how much a man knows about turkeys and turkey hunting, it's just not in the cards for him to come down the trail or out of the swamp with one of the big birds over his shoulder. At least a hundred unanticipated things can go wrong between the first contact of hunter and gobbler and the last, and that's the way it often goes.

At other times, a gobbler seems so bent on self-destruction that he'd come on in if you stood up and waved a flag at him. Although the wild turkey has a reputation as the smartest feathered creature in existence, sometimes he pulls such stupid stunts you'd think he was almost human.

After George brought up that "preordained" stuff, I felt compelled to tell him about the only gobbler I'd been able to bring out of the woods that season. I had bungled my job in the worst sort of way, but the tom turkey had bungled his as well.

For many years Dempsey Cape and I have hunted together for a couple of days each season in one of the East-Georgia counties. This has been going on so long that it's become a sort of ritual with us. Seldom have we ever failed to bring out a couple of birds, but they come hard. This section is heavily hunted. The last hunt had been one of our most unusual experiences with gobblers over half a century of hunting them. It certainly tended to prove George Shuler's belief that bagging a tom turkey is something that goes beyond mere luck or talent. There is simply no other way that such an unusual chain of circumstances could have fallen into place and fit together like pieces in a jigsaw puzzle.

To begin with, had we known what kind of weather we were getting into, we'd have postponed our trip until a later date. The night before, the earth had been deluged with rain. The rain was still coming down when Dempsey picked me up at 4:00 A.M. for our 80-mile ride to the turkey woods. We discussed the weather briefly over a cup of coffee.

"No self-respecting turkey will gobble in weather such as this," I observed.

"Man on the radio says it's supposed to clear up," Dempsey said, "but we'll give it up if you want to."

"I've got a kitchen pass at home for a couple of mornings," I said, "and we sure shouldn't waste it."

The weather prognosticator had been right. The rain slacked to a drizzle. And by the time we arrived at our destination shortly before first light, it had stopped altogether. But the fellow had failed to tell us that the storm would be followed by a strong, cold wind that roared through the trees, dominating all other sound.

As any hunter of any forest game species knows, the worst time to hunt is when the wind blows. It plays tricks on the eyes and ears and understandably makes every creature in the woods nervous.

Dempsey and I were in a stretch of back country where he had heard half a dozen gobblers on one of his scouting trips the week before.

"The woods are full of the critters," he'd reported.

But that had been the week earlier when the dawn hours were bright and warm and quiet. On this morning, we might have been in the forests of northern Siberia as far as turkeys were concerned.

At daylight, we stood on the rim of a narrow creek swamp where Dempsey had sat and listened to a couple of toms gobble half the morning the day before season opened.

"They're here," he whispered. "I know they are."

And they very well might have been. But I wasn't sure we could have heard one if he'd been perched on a limb directly over our heads. The wind made sounds I might have considered wild music under any other circumstances. Now it was only irritating noise.

"I've known them to gobble in weather such as this," I said. "But it's unusual, and we'll have to be close to hear it."

"Let's start looking," Dempsey suggested.

From daylight until an hour before noon, we ranged the swamp and the bordering upland hardwood forest, following our usual routine of pausing frequently to cluck, listen, yelp softly, listen, yelp louder, listen, then gobble our boxes, trying to get an answer. Not a turkey sound could we hear above that banshee wind. Dempsey is one of the best turkey hunters I know. So very hesitantly I made a suggestion.

"I don't think we wait long enough after we yelp and gobble," I said, "especially this late in the day when the gobbling period is past. It's unlikely one will answer at all, with conditions as they are. We've been waiting only about five or ten minutes after we call. I believe we should allow more time when we stop and call. If a gobbler happens to be in the vicinity, he just might come close enough to investigate."

"Good idea," Dempsey agreed readily. "Up ahead there's a creek that flows into Little River. Several times we've heard gobblers there. We'll wait out that spot a little longer."

If anything, the wind had only grown stronger. By now it was really roaring. It made a fellow feel that he'd have to hold on to the tree to keep from being blown out of the woods. We built quick blinds about 30 feet apart. I waited a few minutes for Dempsey to start calling, then got out my Lynch box and diaphragm call. I omitted the cluck with which I usually start a series. A gobbler would have to be quite nearby in such weather to hear that, or even to hear a low yelp. So I simply yelped the box as loud as I could, calling at the same time with a diaphragm, giving the call a double tone that is often successful at calling in an old gobbler.

I was hoping the loud yelp might somehow penetrate the sound of wind. The first gobbler I'd ever taken in Oklahoma had been under similar conditions, when I'd sat in a narrow creek swamp and given the box and diaphragm all I had. I told this story in Chapter 15—how I had put the box down, made myself comfortable, then looked up and saw a tom turkey standing 20 yards away, eyeing me curiously.

I didn't expect to repeat that drama here. After six or eight minutes I tried the loud call again, then put the box down. I am one of those who believe that under almost any circumstances you can call too much.

A number of minutes passed. Then both Dempsey and I heard a sound, buried in the roar of the wind, like a small dog jumping a rabbit or deer out of its bed. The wind was so strong that what we heard was hardly an identifiable sound. But it did occur to us that either the race had been mighty short or had gone quickly out of hearing over the brow of the hill. Neither of us gave it another thought.

A few minutes later, Dempsey left his blind and stepped over to where I sat.

"It's a hell of a long way back to the car," he said. "No need for both of us to make that hike. Why don't you hunt up the creek to where an old road crosses at a ford? I'll pick you up there."

Where he left me, the hill pitched off sharply for a hundred feet to the creek. It was easier to make a long angle from the rim on which I stood to the swamp along the stream. My Model 12 turkey gun is equipped with a sling, so I slid this over my left shoulder to free both hands for helping me keep my balance by holding on to tree trunks as I went down the slope.

I kept the diaphragm in my mouth, and for lack of something better to do, I guess, I paused every dozen yards or so and yelped. I wasn't expecting to see or hear anything in that wind.

The lower edge of the hill was humped up into a long narrow knoll about ten feet higher than the slope on both sides of it. When I walked casually around the end of the knoll, I was looking at a turkey gobbler, not more than a dozen feet away. I'll take an oath that he was every bit as startled as I was.

The gobbler seemed to recover first. I suppose he must have been so astonished or confused that he didn't even fly. He simply turned slowly and walked away along the open floor of the swamp.

That's when I began going through the gyrations of some Mack Sennett silent-movie character. For the life of me, I couldn't get that gun off my shoulder. The strap stuck like flypaper to the buttons and folds of my hunting jacket. I practically disrobed myself tearing it loose. The turkey continued to walk with both eyes on me, no doubt amazed at my wild contortions.

Then I went through another frantic period. I had shot that Model 12 for fifty-five years, but to save my soul I now couldn't find the safety. It just didn't seem to be anywhere around that trigger guard. All this must have occurred in a fraction of a second, but it seemed like minutes. Meantime, the gobbler was simply walking away, no doubt in a state of shock.

Just as I put the bead on his head, the gobbler changed directions, walking to the left toward the ridge and moving a little faster. I put the bead a fraction below his eye and followed it for a few feet to make certain. Just as I pulled the trigger, the head went behind a tree I hadn't even seen. My whole load went into the tree. You'd think I'd never seen a gobbler before, much less shot at one.

There could have been only one reason why that tom turkey didn't take wing or duck behind one of the trees he passed and run straight away, keeping the trunk between us. Like George said, "it was preordained."

My next shot was through a screen of brush at the whole turkey. The shot pattern knocked the bird down, but apparently didn't hurt it much, for it got up running. My third and last shell in the gun knocked him down again but left him very much alive.

I wish I had a movie of the next few seconds. I ran toward the gobbler, trying to scramble another shell out of my shoulder bag. A big gobbler is enough to excite anybody, but this was ridiculous. The only item I could feel in the bag was my waterproof matchbox, which is about the size of a 12-gauge shell. But that won't fit in a gun barrel. I tried it. Neither will a Chapstick or a pocket knife. I tried those, too, all the time running toward the gobbler—who looked well enough to fly or run out of there any minute now. Somehow or other I found one shell, managed to keep from dropping it in the leaves, and got it in the gun. By this time I was so badly shaken that I almost missed the old tom's head at close range.

I had done everything wrong, but so had the turkey, only more so. Had he flown straight up off the ground when we first met—as 999 out of every 1,000 turkeys do—I'm sure I'd have stood there with the gun on my shoulder and watched him go. If he'd run and ducked behind one of those big trees at the edge of the swamp, he'd have simply vanished. Yet even after I shot that first load into the tree, he did not fly, but continued to walk hurriedly along. When I turned him over on the ground, I could see he hadn't been winged or wounded. He was sound all the way through.

I had arranged the turkey on my shoulder for the long walk up the creek when Dempsey yelped from the crest of the hill where he'd left me when he went for the car. I returned his yelp and he came on down to the swamp.

"Why, damn you," he said. "I can't leave you alone for a minute without you doing something like this behind my back."

As near as we could figure, the dog bark we thought we'd heard had been the *yowlk-yowlk-yowlk-yowlk* of the gobbler. I'm sure we could have recognized it on a calmer day. The sound had come from directly behind us on the hill. Either the bird was circling naturally to the call and had come off the hill into the edge of the swamp or else he had seen Dempsey go up the ridge and ducked down the hill, where I met him. That the bird was waiting in such a spot; that I had remained out of sight on my way down the slope, pausing now and then to cluck or yelp; that a man's footsteps in the leaves sound like those of a turkey walking; that the bird had walked off instead of flying— those are the main pieces of the jigsaw by which I bagged this gobbler. He was a good one, with an 11-inch beard and sharp 1½-inch spurs.

But wait—that's not the whole "preordained" sequence of events.

Dempsey said, "I'll hunt up the swamp with you, and we'll call into some of the hollows."

He picked up my turkey, attached his carrying strap, and lifted it over his shoulder.

"You're not going to carry my bird," I said.

"You're damn right I am," he said. "It'll bring me luck."

He wouldn't give it up, and I had no intention of fighting him for the privilege. He was younger and stronger than I was.

We didn't hear or see any more birds in the swamp or on the way to Dempsey's truck. It was after noon when we drove to the hunting camp of a friend in the next county, where we planned to spend the night and hunt out from there the next morning.

"We'll hunt around here late this afternoon," Dempsey said. "What are you going to do between now and then?"

"I'm going to get a little shut-eye," I said.

"I think I'll do some scouting," he replied. "Be back for you around four o'clock."

He walked out to his truck and opened the door to get in.

"Aren't you going to carry a gun?" I asked.

Dempsey shook his head. "Oh, no. I'm just gonna look for a few tracks and other signs."

"Carry the gun," I said.

So he came back to the cabin for his shotgun. When he drove off, I hit the sack and died for half an hour. When Dempsey drove into the yard, I'd have bet my last turkey shell on the outcome of his scouting trip. Somehow I just knew it. I was right. He brought in a two-year-old gobbler and dropped it on the kitchen table.

His story wasn't quite so bizarre as mine, but it helped prove that all the turkeys in that part of the country must have been a little crazy that day.

The wind was every bit as strong as it had been that morning. Dempsey said he left his truck on an old woods road and walked downhill to a creek swamp. He stood in an open spot in the edge of the swamp and went through the ritual of clucking, yelping, and then gobbling his box. He stood there for ten minutes, listening, then turned to walk up the swamp to look for tracks in a muddy flat he knew. Not more than 20 yards away, a turkey had its head down, pecking at something on the swamp floor.

Dempsey squatted, putting himself out of sight behind some low brush. He inched forward and pulled himself erect behind a tree trunk, with his gun on the turkey. He recognized it as a hen. She went on picking, paying him no mind. Then he let his eyes range. About 15 feet from the hen stood the young gobbler, its head up. The bird had already seen Dempsey, but it made no attempt to run or fly. Dempsey put his sights on the gobbler's head and killed it.

"You and I should write a book," I said. "How To Bag Gobblers On Windy Days When They Ain't Gobbling."

"I've got a better title," he replied. "Shot In The Ass With Luck."

Sometimes the crazy things that people and gobblers do come out in favor of the hunters. Sometimes it's the other way, as with my old friend Charlie Steinwinder in western Alabama.

Charlie started hunting back in the days when the use of tame turkeys as decoys was legal. One morning he borrowed a barnyard turkey from one of his neighbors, carried it into the woods with him, and staked it out in front of his blind. Shortly after daylight the hen began to sing, but she wasn't getting much response. Charlie thought he heard a gobbler in the distance, so he left his blind and went to find it. His meanderings got him completely lost. Then he did hear a real turkey, not too far away. It was yowking like an old gobbler, so he crawled on his hands and knees for a hundred yards through the brush until he could see the bird. It had apparently heard him, for it stood with its neck stretched up. Steinwinder was close enough to down it. Immediately after the shot, he went running up. The first thing he saw was the string tied to the turkey's leg. He had killed his own decoy! Charlie never did say how he got out of that fracas with his neighbor.

Charlie was head engineer on perhaps the world's shortest railroad, a four-mile line belonging to the Bellamy Lumber Company. From a motor car, he did a lot of checking on the rails and roadbed, a stretch of which ran through a planted field. One day he saw a gobbler there, just beyond range of the shotgun he always carried with him. He knew that if he stopped the car, the gobbler would run or fly. It seemed to be feeding toward the tracks, so Charlie went on out of sight around the bend and reversed his route to see if the tom had fed within range. It hadn't, so he went out of sight in the other direction and turned around again.

"I made thirty trips up and down that road," Charlie admitted, "before that gobbler was close enough to kill. I shot him—but I had burned up so much gas that my motor car stopped halfway home. I had to push it the rest of the way, turkey and all."

It was the only gobbler he ever killed.

One odd incident put an end to Charlie's turkey hunting.

"After that," he said, "I figured it just wasn't in the cards and gave up."

Like most of Charlie Steinwinder's turkey-hunting mornings, this one had been full of frustrations. Just after daylight he heard a turkey gobble on the roost. Charlie worked his way to within 200 yards of the spot and hurriedly built a blind. When he made the plaintive note of a hen, the tom answered immediately, and moments later it flew out of its roost tree. When it thudded to the ground less than 100 yards away, Charlie mentally put his game in the bag.

There was reason enough for excitement. Charlie had hunted the Alabama woods for three long seasons and had brought home just one of the big birds. This was about as close to success in the woods as he'd ever been. Out of sight, beyond the thicket, he could hear the bird strutting and clucking. Charlie eased his 12-gauge into position for a quick shot.

Off to his left somewhere, a real turkey hen yelped. The gobbler in front of him responded with enthusiasm. Charlie clucked his own caller, and the buck bird's shrill reply sounded so excited that Charlie waited with his heart pounding in his ears, expecting at any moment that tom to step around the bush in front of him. He held the gun until his arms ached and the sun touched the treetops over his head. Then the turkey gobbled again, 400 yards away. He had gone to the bona-fide hen.

Later that morning Charlie stalked a second bird, only to find that the notes he followed were made by another hunter with a very effective cedar box. Now it was past midmorning. Most of the birds had stopped calling. Charlie was on the way to his car, which was parked on an old logging road.

Tired and discouraged, he stopped at a small spring creek for a drink of water. He propped his gun against a bush, got down on his hands and knees, and put his lips to the cool water. The movement of his clothing shook the lid of the cedar gobbling box in his pocket. It squawked.

Instantly the note was answered by a gobbler a few yards away in the swamp brush.

Charlie kept his nose in the creek. The turkey was so close he didn't dare raise his head or shift his body. So he did the next best thing. He wiggled his hind end, and the flapping coat pocket sang out once more: *yowlk-yowlk-yowlk!*

He could hear the turkey walking in the leaves, right above him. Charlie reached back for his gun, splashed out of the creek, and came up shooting. But the gobbler was already high in the air, climbing for the treetops. Charlie shot under it, twice.

"That," he mourned, "might be considered one of the prime ways how not to kill a gobbler."

I assured Charlie that every turkey hunter could think of at least one other "how-not-to" in the process of trying to bag a tom turkey. There are dozens of things a gunner may do wrong and a hundred hazards beyond his control, such as the sudden appearance of a wildcat or other predator that's after the same gobbler.

Every gobbler is a brand-new experience, different from all the others. A squirrel may habitually use the same limbs in the same trees. Rabbits circle in a predictable way. A quail is likely to fly like all its brothers before it, and you can anticipate the pattern of ducks over decoys. But no two gobblers act the same.

A few springs ago, Jimmie Shirley and I stood on a high hill in western Alabama at daylight, listening to the owls. We could hear them in three directions. When an owl hoots at daylight, a tom will usually answer from its roost. In gobbling season, that's one way to locate a bird.

The woods grew brighter, light enough for the turkeys to fly down, but we hadn't heard a bird of either sex. So we decided to separate, Jimmie going in one direction and I in another.

I crossed a swamp creek and climbed into an adjoining series of ridges for a couple of miles. From the top of a high point, I heard three gobblers. The nearest was no more than a quarter of a mile away, and he seemed to have the shrillest voice, the sign of an old bird. I stalked to the brow of a narrow swamp and found a natural blind where bushes grew in front of a tree stump. I made myself as comfortable as possible, waited for a few minutes, and then yelped like a hen. He answered at once, so I settled back to play the game.

For two hours or more, the tom continued to gobble. But gradually he shifted from a position immediately below me in the swamp to the right and at an angle going away. When I was reasonably sure he wasn't interested in my small talk, I moved 20 yards, parallel to the course he'd taken. Sometimes it's necessary to get completely around and in front of a wise old bird. Twenty-five yards from my original stand, I set up shop again and gobbled my box to imitate another tom infringing on this range.

Although his reply was a challenge, I waited for another quarter of an hour without hearing another peep out of him. Then he gobbled again, on his way down the swamp, toward the spot where I'd originally called. Since most birds will go to the place where they heard the first call, I was sure this one had the same goal. The gobbler was still deep enough in the swamp to allow me to crawl back to my first stand.

Minutes passed, and more minutes. Then I heard him stalking through the brittle leaves like a man walking. I put my gun up to be ready for a neck-and-head shot when he showed through the brush. But be broke the rule of coming to the spot where he'd first heard me. Instead, he walked in a beeline to the second stand. I could hear him in the brush, 20 yards away, popping his vocal cords angrily, as if he intended to whip the male intruder that had dared to enter his domain. But the vegetation between us was so thick I couldn't see him.

At a time like this, you wonder what to do. And when you wonder, the best advice is to sit completely still. I did so, for an interminable time, until the sounds indicated that the gobbler had crossed an old logging road and was going away.

That's what I thought, anyway. So I made my fatal mistake. For some reason, my mouth yelper was in my pocket. I moved my hands to hit the cedar box a sharp cluck to tell him exactly where I was. Apparently, he was closer than I realized, and must have seen me. Anyway, the gobbler I'd worked so carefully for more than two hours left the country.

Just two weeks later, in the mountains of Tennessee, I called a turkey down a ridge toward a shallow gap. I had moved into the spot from a hilltop 30 yards away, where I'd made my original call. The only logical course the bird could take to the hilltop was through the gap where I'd made my second call. So I knew I had him.

Logical? Yes. But logic doesn't always win the day in turkey hunting. The gobbler detoured around the gap and walked uphill to my first blind, from the opposite direction. I could hear him on top, strutting and gobbling. I tried seductive hen calls and abusive gobbler language on the box, but he never came any nearer.

In gobbler hunting, your mistakes are often as fascinating as your successes. And a turkey, hunter as I said earlier, is the only species of hunter I know who laughs and brags about all those times he goofs.

Not too long ago a friend told me how easy it is to be a successful turkey hunter. He had just killed his first gobbler.

He had spent a lot of time around tame turkeys on a farm near his home, practicing on a yelper made by one of his mountaineer acquaintances. When the spring gobbling season opened, he made a date with his mountain friend and drove up before daylight to his cabin. The mountaineer's wife told him that her husband had gone on, but left instructions for the guest to climb the nearest ridge behind the house, sit down there, and work his yelper.

On top of the ridge, he heard a tom, reasonably close. So he hunkered down and touched his box. The gobbler answered. Behind him, he heard a hen yelp. So he yelped again and sat perfectly still. In minutes the gobbler stuck its head up over a log. My friend already had his gun up, so he shot the gobbler through its head.

As he walked over to pick up his prize, some guy behind him yelled, "Why, you blankety-blankety so-and-so-and-so!"

My friend had innocently moved in between the bird and another hunter who'd been working the gobbler before he got there.

"I picked up my kill and got out of there in a hurry," my pal said.

After I'd chased gobblers long enough to think I knew all about it, I invited a Yankee friend to go with me into southern Georgia, where I was going to demonstrate to him the precise art of turkey hunting. One of the tricks I'd learned was that if you can hear a flock of birds fly up to roost at dusk, you won't have to go looking for them in the morning.

We maneuvered around the swamps for a day, and late in the afternoon I located what I considered an ideal roosting site. The sky was overcast and producing intermittent drizzles, but the woods were quiet enough to let us hear a turkey fly up to roost within 300 yards. At just the right time, I heard the heavy beat of wings as a big bird flew into a tree. Then we heard a dozen more fly up.

From where we sat, we couldn't see the birds or be sure whether they might see us, so we didn't move until black dark. That's the correct procedure, as every turkey hunter knows.

Next morning we were in the same spot before daylight. I placed my partner where he'd be in position for a shot when the birds flew down out of the trees. Then I concealed myself in a thicket 30 yards behind him and yelped just before I figured the birds would leave the roost.

We didn't have long to wait. I heard the familiar *flop-flop-flop*. But my heart really went down into my boot tops when a buzzard, instead of a turkey, flew out of that tree. What we had roosted was a flock of buzzards!

Too embarrassed to face my friend, I left him where he was and crawled on my hands and knees out of the thicket. I walked into the swamp. Twenty minutes after I left, I heard him shoot. I hurried back, found him on the same stand, and asked for details.

"I missed," he said.

But he hadn't missed at all. Later that day, I found a deceased buzzard near his stand, along with an expended shell. I never mentioned it, of course, and he wisely said nothing about my roosting a flock of buzzards instead of turkeys.

The best gobbler hunters I know make no attempt to call a tom from one ridge to another, or out of a swamp. They try to either get as close as possible without being seen or else determine the direction the gobbler's traveling and try to get in front of him. Once placed, they conceal themselves in a thicket or hastily built blind and stay there.

I was in an old downed treetop on a ridge. A tom had talked to me from a small hollow 100 yards away. Although he'd answered my call, he continued to move away, down the hollow. I made love to him with dulcet notes, then threatened him with a gobble. Over a period of time, I clucked, purred, and yowlked, but he continued on his way. Finally his voice had grown so faint that I knew he was headed for the next ridge. So I deserted my treetop and walked down the ridge toward where I'd last heard him. On a sharp contour, where the ridge broke off into a valley, I met the gobbler coming back to me. The reason for his faint voice had been the hill bulwarked between us. He flushed too far away for a shot.

A good turkey hunter knows most of the tricks of an old gobbler. He's aware that a cagey tom will walk quietly and completely around him to come up on the blind side, or that a gobbler will make noises to indicate that he's on his way into the next county, then tiptoe back without making a sound, to see what's going on.

One of my partners in the Southern swamps had followed a big gobbler for a couple of seasons. The man was one of the best callers I know, and a dozen times he'd had the bird walk completely around him, but never close enough for a kill.

Opening week of the second season, he spent every day trying to see that tom over the sights of his gun, but the old Einstein was much too cagey. On the eighth morning of the season, my partner stopped his car on a dirt road that ran along the rim of a swamp where he'd played hide-and-seek with the gobbler the afternoon before. As he started to get out of his car, his elbow hit the horn button, emitting a short burst of sound. The gobbler answered immediately from its roost tree down in the swamp. My friend sat for five minutes, thinking it over. Then, out of sheer curiosity, he touched his horn again. The gobbler answered.

The hunter figured that since he had the bird spotted, he might get close enough to call it off the roost. He opened the car door quietly, slid the barrel of his shotgun out for safety, then loaded the magazine and chamber to keep the metallic sounds of loading within the confines of his automobile.

As he was about to slide off the front seat to the ground, the gobbler suddenly flew off its roost, sailed straight for the car and landed 30 yards away in a little clearing. My friend recognized it as the same bird that had so consistently outwitted him for two seasons.

"That was such an insult to my calling and to my turkey-hunting ability," he said angrily, "that I had no qualms about shooting him on the spot!"

No matter how many turkeys a dedicated gobbler hunter has killed, he can give you the minute details on every one. A few kills may be orthodox, when the bird works in at least some of the expected ways. Others are unusual. Consider, for instance, the morning I had covered a scope of country from daylight until eleven o'clock without ever hearing a gobbler or finding a fresh scratch. I was disgusted and completely worn out. I knew the high mountain coves were full of birds, but not one had sounded off.

It was almost noon when I sat down with my back to a tree and yelped my box a couple of times. I had little hope of an answer, since it was so late in the day. With the warm sun on me, I fell asleep.

If you're an old gobbler hunter, you already know the rest of the story. I dreamed that a long-bearded bird had found me and was *phutt-phutting* just out of sight behind a bush, where I couldn't get a glimpse of him. The dream was so real it woke me; and, luckily, I must have opened my eyes without moving.

There stood a tom turkey, 40 feet away, resplendent in the sunlight. Apparently he'd come to investigate my hen call. If he'd seen me, he gave no indication. He scratched a couple of healthy chunks out of the forest humus with his big feet. When he put his head down to peck at what he'd found, I raised my gun. When he put up his head again, I shot him.

If I hadn't gone to sleep, I doubt that I'd have had the patience to sit still long enough in that spot, not when I didn't expect to see a bird.

And impatience, certainly, is not a trait that helps you clobber a gobbler.

21

Not All Turkey Hunters Are Liars

Generally you can count on it. Where a group of normal men such as hunters and fishermen are together, the subjects under discussion may be varied, but sooner or later one topic certain to come up is—women.

An exception to this general principle is the dedicated, dyed-in-the-wattle turkey hunter. Normally, in season and out, he's got one thing and one thing only on his mind—turkeys. He'll tell you how he bagged a wise old gobbler, or just as enthusiastically relate how he failed to bring it in. He has a hundred stories, and you've got to catch him between breaths to get in one of your own.

The group on one trout-fishing trip I took had three turkey hunters. Did they talk about trout? You bet your sweet tail feathers they didn't. We spent the whole weekend trying to outdo one another in the gobbler tall-tale department. One guy had even brought along his turkey call, which was decidedly unfair to the rest of us. I made up my mind to never again let such a thing happen, unless I was the one who had the call.

Similar things happen on any kind of outdoor trip. On a turkey hunt, you'd have to hear it to believe it. I sat in what Jack Dudley calls his turkey club house near Scooba, Mississippi. This is his family old homeplace that he has remodeled into a camp for the hunting seasons. It's a gathering spot for local and visiting chasers after gobblers.

Jack is another of those fellows who grew up with turkeys. From the time he could toddle, he ranged with the family barnyard flock and learned to speak their language as well as they could. From the time he could pick both ends of a gun off the floor, he has associated with the wild-turkey flocks. His knowledge of the language and the fact that he doesn't need any artificial devices to speak it has won him many championships, including the "World." Jack has made records and tapes and developed some calls and other handy equipment for a hunter in the woods.

That evening in Jack's camp was typical of many I have known. Men

239

dressed in jungle camouflage kept coming and going. Some of us were Jack's guests, others were neighbors dropping by. Everyone had a few stories to tell about his turkey experiences, and everyone had his favorite call he was anxious to show off. The calls included every type of device that could make a creditable sound. There were many kinds of boxes, slate calls, wing bones, diaphragms, and even one artificial brier leaf, made of an unusual type of plastic. Many of the calls were "store-bought," but just as many were hand-made.

From sundown until midnight the scene was one of organized bedlam—if such a condition can exist. Each man spoke his piece, told his tale, or worked his call, never less than three or four at a time. Any flock of turkeys within hearing would have left the roost and come over to investigate, and even then wouldn't have believed their ear pans. I listened carefully, but not a subject was discussed that evening in which wild turkeys were not in some way involved.

I've watched and listened to this same scene or its equivalent so many times that you'd think it might get boring. But like turkey hunting, it never does.

We were carrying on this way one night in a motel room in Brookhaven, Mississippi. The time was near midnight, and crowded into my small room were half a dozen of us who should have been in bed hours before. We'd left a message at the switchboard for us to be called at 3:00 A.M. to get us to the turkey woods on time. Anyone listening outside the motel would certainly have concluded that a hen-and-gobbler convention was going on.

I thought I heard a rap on the door, but I wasn't sure until it came again, louder and this time more insistent. When I opened the door, a guy stood there in his pajamas. I didn't dare stare at it, but the object in his hand looked like a pistol.

"I can't stand this any longer," he said.

"Gosh," I apologized. "I'm sorry. When a bunch of turkey hunters get together, I guess they haven't got much sense, or much consideration for the folks around them. I'll run this crew out, so you and I can both get some sleep."

"It's not that," he said. "I was just wondering if you'd let me join the party."

The thing in his hand wasn't a pistol. It was a turkey call he'd made. All he wanted to do was show it off. I opened the door wider, and he came in and introduced himself all around. Someone fixed him a drink, and he flowed into that party like a spring branch joining a stream through turkey woods. We were still going strong at 3:00 A.M. The only thing left to do was to grab a cup of coffee on our way to beat the first light of dawn. At this season of the year, who needs sleep?

When the addicted get to talking gobblers and such, they have no sense of time or place. Seldom does one go to bed, unless he collapses and some of his buddies put him there. On top of this, he can't understand why *everybody* doesn't feel the same way!

A couple of my old turkey-hunting partners came through town one night and called me at about ten o'clock from their hotel room. Risking divorce and sure of getting a lot of domestic flack later, I put on my clothes and drove downtown. After greetings and a short practice session on our instruments, I couldn't resist the temptation to call Zeke Holleran, another of my local partners, who worked the graveyard shift on the local paper. I knew Zeke wouldn't want to miss this one.

Zeke didn't ask for an hour or so away from the paper. He couldn't think of a valid reason. He just walked off, knowing he could manufacture some reason later—if he still had his job, that is.

If you've ever sat in on a turkey session, you can well imagine how quickly the droppings began to fill that hotel room, with each tall tale being topped by one at least a wee bit taller. Zeke himself finally came up with the climax buster.

"I worked on that gobbler for a year," he said, "before I even saw it. From its tracks and droppings, I knew it was a tremendous bird. And possibly as smart as it was big. Finally I called him up, but he stayed just out of range, and there wasn't anything I could do to get him any closer. Finally he walked away, for no reason at all, as far as I could tell. I haven't seen him since, but I'd sure like to have that gobbler mounted in my den. He's at least 4 or 4½ feet tall."

"Aw, come on," one of the fellows said. "There ain't no way for gobblers to get that big. You must've been looking at somebody's runaway ostrich."

"By damn," Zeke said, "this one was! And I got a witness."

"Who?" I asked.

"My wife. She was right there in the blind with me."

"Legally," I said, "no wife can testify for or against her husband. But I'll take her word over yours any time."

I looked at my watch. It said two o'clock, and I knew all decent people—outside turkey hunters—were supposed to be in bed at that time of night. I reached for the phone. I shouldn't have done it, I know, but the corn squeezings that my two turkey-hunting associates had brought out of the mountains with them was powerful stuff.

I dialed Zeke's home. He didn't protest. He just sat there with a sort of silly grin on his face, as though he could already visualize what kind of castigation he might expect at home. In a sleepy voice, his wife answered the phone. I wondered if I had made a mistake when I told her who I was.

"Mrs. Holleran," I said, "I'm terribly sorry to disturb you at this time of night, but there's a very important question here that you can settle."

She was wide awake now. I imagine she could see Zeke stretched out on a sidewalk somewhere.

"Nothing's wrong," I said quickly. "We just needed something verified. Zeke was telling me and a couple of other fellows that you were with him when you two saw a gobbler that stood 6 feet high. Was it really that tall?"

"Every inch of it," she replied, without hesitation.

"Boy," I said, when I hung up the phone, "you've got the kind of wife every turkey hunter should have."

Of course, some of the stories are so bizarre that they're ridiculous. But they still go the rounds. Like the old classic about the Alabama hunter being so good that he called a gobbler up to the other side of the log behind which he was stretched out on his belly. The turkey's legs were within arm length, so he reached under the log and caught one of them. The gobbler flopped around a bit while the hunter held on, wondering what his next move should be. He could think of nothing practical, except to turn the gobbler loose and then call it around to the other side. Which he did.

It's a wonder that in my early hunting years I ever killed a turkey of any kind. I made so many blunders, fumbles, and wrong decisions that I'm sure any bird I brought out of the woods was solely because I had the sympathy of a benevolent Providence. I still make mistakes, but now I know enough to make them in a refined sort of way. In other words, I'm experienced enough to put a little "English" on them.

To show how ignorant I was, I once spotted a bunch of turkeys through the swamp trees before they saw me. My eyes and ears were a damnsight better then than they are today. The birds were feeding along a little slough that ran through an edge of the swamp. An inch at a time I lowered myself behind the clump of brush through which I had seen the turkeys. A sensible move would have been to crawfish away from that spot and make a long detour to get around and wait in ambush to scatter the flock, then sit down and call one when the birds began to regroup. Did I follow such a course? You bet your life I didn't. I thought I was Injun or blacksnake enough to crawl within shotgun range. I did it, too. When I arrived, the turkeys were somewhere else.

I had another experience in the same stretch of swamp. That morning I was a member of a deer-hunting party. Hounds were used to drive deer out of the swamp to standers placed on an old woods road that paralleled the strip of swamp along the river. That was the popular method of deer hunting thereabouts a generation ago, when whitetails were not nearly so abundant as they are today and so were more likely to live in the thickest places, where no man could get to them except with dogs. Today, dogging deer is still one of the methods of hunting in some regions of the South. This is party hunting with its own special rituals, many being throwbacks to the old ante-bellum plantation days.

Often a stander came out with a turkey that had been flushed from the swamp ahead of the dogs, and this was considered as much of an achievement as bagging a buck.

On the stand next to me that morning was a young fellow who had brought along his turkey call. He kept it in action over the two-hour period of the hunt. Some of his notes were authentic enough, but they were what I would classify as rather inconsistent. He'd begin with the notes of a hen and end with the sounds of a gobbler trying to get over a case of the hiccups. In those days I didn't know much about calling turkeys but I thought I knew how one was supposed to sound.

After the hunt one of the dog handlers told me that his hounds had scattered a flock of turkeys. He gave me the location. In the middle of the afternoon, loaded with brunswick stew and barbecue, which usually follow such whitetail affairs, I made my way back to the edge of the swamp where the turkeys had been flushed. I settled down in an old downed treetop, where I could see the surrounding swamp floor and along the rim of a bluff bordering the swamp.

The afternoon was sunny and cool. The normal life of the swamp moved around me. I gave a series of yelps and settled back to enjoy the movements and soft music of the lowland forest. I was in no hurry.

I have no idea how long I relaxed in the treetop. I was brought sharply out of whatever reverie had invaded me by several short yaps of a dog beyond the section of bluff that I could see. I thought it might be one of the deer hounds, yet it didn't ring quite true enough for a hound. Thinking that it might be a turkey, I yelped several notes. After a few minutes I received a reply that wasn't like a turkey, dog, or anything else I'd heard. Then the thought hit me like a load of No. 6s: It must be that kid who'd been on the deer stand next to mine. Well, at least I could give him a few moments he'd remember.

I clucked a couple of times and yelped again softly. He came right back with that odd call. It was nearer than when I'd first heard it. Then I suddenly realized that I might be promoting an unhealthy situation. If the kid crawled up to the rim of the bluff, he just might take a pot shot at me or at the spot where I'd made my call. I thought about standing up behind the tree and watching the bluff until I could see him, but then I decided it was better to stand in the open where I couldn't possibly be mistaken for a turkey.

I leaned my gun against the downed treetop, and crawled up through its heavy branches to where I could stand up in full sight.

"Hello," I called. "Seen anything?"

There was a sudden commotion just beyond the contour of the bluff and the opening was suddenly filled with a large gobbler, less than 30 yards away. I almost fell out of that downed treetop.

After more decades than I care to count, I'm still puzzled how the call of that lad on the stand next to me and the gobbler that came down the bluff could both be so off-key and sound so much alike. There was a possibility that the turkeys in that section of the swamp had a dialect of their own and that the boy had learned it from them, but I wouldn't wager on it.

Some hunters brag about the long shots they have made. They always fail to mention the cripples they have left behind. When it comes to shooting, a turkey is not in the same bracket with such creatures as elk or sheep or antelope. With such four-legged game, you may often expect long-range shots, and usually you have the gun for that job. A turkey is a quarry to be called in and taken at close range. Fifty yards should be the maximum range for the most powerful shotguns, and then you would do well to know what kind of shot pattern you get at that distance. Thirty yards is much safer.

One gobbler I know of was killed at an incredible distance. The shot was more of a fluke and was even intended as a trick one of my hunting partners hoped to play on another. The two men involved were Dr. Robert Hines and Bob Card, old settlers around Cleveland, Tennessee.

Doc and Bob are two of my favorite people, indoors or out. For many springs we have hunted the Ocoee in East Tennessee together. We don't break any world records with the number of gobblers we bring in, but I look forward to that trip each year with more enthusiasm than I would have for a Kodiak-bear hunt in Alaska.

Doc and Bob often amuse themselves by playing harmless little tricks on each other. For laughs. Or to "get even" for some similar trick that's been played on one or the other. This seems to be the order of the day when they are on a turkey hunt or trout trip back in the mountains.

One season not long ago they were coming in from a fruitless morning hunt in Card's Bronco. He's a Ford dealer, and you wouldn't expect him to be riding in any other four-wheel-drive vehicle. They were discussing the dawn hours and comparing notes on how each had been outmaneuvered by a cagey gobbler, when a young tom ran across the road in front of them. By the time Card skidded to a halt and both men had jumped out and loaded their guns, the young gobbler was disappearing into the brush on the far slope. Doc says you couldn't have reached it with a rifle. But he did have a sudden inspiration. He threw up his shotgun and fired at the spot where he had last seen the gobbler.

"I got it! he yelled. "I got it, Card! It's right up there. Go get it for me."

Bob put his gun in the car, sprinted down the slope, crossed a small branch, and started up the steep side of the mountain.

"Where is it?" he called.

"On up the mountain," Doc said. "Keep going."

Card scrambled farther. The slope grew steeper.

"Keep going," Doc yelled.

"You couldn't kill him this far with a .30-06," Card shouted.

"Just a little farther," Doc called. By now Card was almost out of sight in the brush.

"Here it is!" he yelled. He brought back the young gobbler by the neck.

"You could've knocked me over with one of the tail feathers," Doc admitted later. "I had no real idea I'd hit that bird. All I wanted to do was give Card a little exercise."

They examined the bird. By some freakish circumstance, the young gobbler had been killed by a lone lead pellet in the head.

That's just another reason why I'll believe anything anyone tells me about turkey hunting—and why I expect them to believe me.

22

Hunting Partners

Gobbler hunting is generally a lone game in which one man must match his woodsmanship against one gobbler. And yet hunting partners add immeasurably to the enjoyment of any turkey trip.

After all, there's got to be somebody around who understands the language, who will listen to your perfect call (if you will listen to his), to whom you can brag, and who will lend a willing shoulder on which to cry.

Most of your association with these partners will be during the ride to and from hunting territory, in camps and motel rooms, over coffee at four o'clock in the morning. And you know your partner will be waiting when you arrive back at your transportation point for lunch at noon or after dark when the afternoon hunt is over. You know he's there, too, if you get into trouble in the woods, like being lost, breaking a leg, or accidentally shooting yourself. Partners are nice to have around.

Often, two partners find much pleasure in hunting together. They may be an old pro and a tyro. Both profit from the experience. The beginner can learn a lot, and I know no single veteran at this game who does not find an immense satisfaction when some rookie who has carefully followed instructions finally bags one of the big birds.

Two old campaigners may team up together. Many times they can help one another—through knowledge of the terrain and areas the turkeys are using. Almost any experienced hunter can find the birds in strange country if he has days enough to look for sign and other indications. But when time is limited, one of a hunter's greatest assets is a partner with knowledge of the land.

Almost anyone who's been after gobblers long enough could write a book about his turkey partners and the hunts he's had with them. I'm certain that no one could sport a finer list than I do. Many of these I've already mentioned in this rather lengthy report on my turkey activities over the years. Still, certain ones stand out as special.

245

Bill Rae seems to have trouble believing that he has actually taken his first Alabama gobbler.

By now a few of the best have been lured by the Master's turkey call from out of the Great Beyond. Others are still around and continue to practice their siren sounds on the turkeys themselves.

Typical of the many magnificent partners I have had over the years is one Turkey Johnston, who hails from Tuscaloosa, down, up, or over in Alabama, depending on which direction you live from there. Needless to say, the name given him by his parents was not "Turkey." He acquired that on his own.

For many years, Turkey, Jimmie Shirley, and I hunted together each spring in western Alabama on the old Allison Company lands, which eventually became the property of a giant pulp-and-paper company that systematically destroyed it by removing the hardwood forests and replacing them with pine trees. That spring hunt was a ritual, and I felt it was necessary in order to help me survive the remainder of the year.

I won't try to guess how many seasons ago it was that the Allisons graciously invited Clarence Streetman and me to hunt turkeys on their property. To be certain that we would get—or at least see—a gobbler, they assigned two of the top turkey hunters in that part of the country to guide us. One was Bob Hutchinson, one of their foresters. The other was Turkey Johnston, who was an insurance agent in Tuscaloosa and in no way connected with the Allison company, except as a perennial guest who needed no pass and had a key to all the gates. Turkey was said to be on clucking terms with every bearded patriarch on company lands. So Clarence and I drove over to hunt a territory that, as far as gobbler hunting went, was entirely strange to me.

We arrived shortly after lunch. By the time the supper bell rang, I was thoroughly convinced that Turkey Johnston was every bit as elusive as any bearded gobbler ranging the river swamps. All afternoon, Clarence Streetman and I had been hot on his trail, and we'd almost caught up with him a couple of times. A truckdriver told us he had seen the lanky hunter on a backwoods road, and in another distant part of the swamp we learned that he had stopped to talk with a log-loading crew. The trail ended there.

Clarence and I followed the supper-bell music to the big dining room in the company hotel. We took seats across from Clint McClure, Allison's chief forester, at the end of a long table loaded with steaming platters. Clint looked up and smiled.

"Turkey'll be in sometime tonight, for sure, unless he's roosted a flock somewhere and decides to sleep with them."

Conversation around the table, which had been interrupted briefly when we came in, fell naturally and easily back into the groove. I gathered that every man around us was a devout turkey hunter, and each had his own pet story of a gobbler he had killed, or the largest one that got away. Clarence and I were fresh meat, and they recognized us as willing ears.

After supper, we moved our conversation, lock, stock, and iridescent feathers, out to the front porch. I got the impression that a fellow's social standing around those woods and swamps was measured by how he could handle a box and other tools for taking the toms. Someone had left a note on Turkey's door, and I was disappointed that he had not appeared by bedtime. Bob Hutchinson agreed, in the event Turkey had been sidetracked somewhere, to go along and show us some of the more productive turkey woods.

Clarence and I borrowed an alarm clock, set it for 3:30 A.M., and put it on the table between our beds in the guest house—as if I could ever oversleep when gobbler hunting is the day's first order of business. It seemed, though, that I had just closed my eyes when I heard footsteps on the front porch. I was struggling through semiconsciousness when a door slammed and bright light flooded the room. I opened my eyes to find a gangling fellow, dressed in a camouflage suit, standing over us.

"I'm Turkey Johnston," he announced. "Thought I'd better come on over. Alarm clocks just ain't reliable."

Using all my muscles, I sat up in bed and glanced at the clock on the table. Its hands were poised at 3:00 A.M. Then I shook hands with Turkey Johnston.

"We followed you all over the place yesterday afternoon," I said, "trying to roost you."

He grunted.

"Don't reckon I was aimin' to be found. But I brought good news."

He told us that at sunset he had been in a distant swamp. He was crouched against a lean-shanked oak when a flock of birds fed past him, just out of range. When they were safely out of sight, he dug for his cedar box. But before he had a chance to use it, they began flying up to roost. He couldn't tell whether they were close enough to see him if he moved, so he kept his seat under the oak until black dark. Then he moved out of the woods as quietly as possible to keep from flushing the birds off the roost.

"We'll be hunkered under that same tree, come daylight," Turkey said.

To be doubly certain he would find his way back before dawn, he had left a scrap of paper hanging on a bush at every uncertain fork or turn of the trail. His paper supply was exhausted before he got back to the Jeep, so he shredded his handkerchief and left it in bits to mark his way before first light cracked through the swamp forest.

While Clarence and I were getting into our hunting clothes and lacing our boots, Turkey went back to the kitchen to stir up orange juice and coffee. Bob Hutchinson came in with the information that one of the loggers had seen a group of gobblers just at dusk in another swamp miles from where Johnston had roosted his flock. The local hunters decided that since two guns were enough at each spot, Clarence and Bob should make a try for the birds the logger had seen.

In Turkey Johnston's Jeep, we turned off the main road and into a dim, overgrown lane that could hardly be called a road. With brush dragging at us, we snaked along the almost impassable path. Then we shot suddenly over the brow of a slope and downhill toward a yawning ravine. In the yellow car lights, it looked like the end of the trail. Turkey gunned his machine and lurched toward the earth cavity. I closed my eyes and waited for the crash, sure our hunt was over before it even had a chance to begin, but we shot across the ravine at such speed that I thought we'd jumped it. I didn't find the answer until later in the morning when Turkey showed me two parallel logs over the chasm. They were laid the width of Jeep wheels apart, forming a bridge.

Turkey parked his Jeep at the edge of a swamp. Then, helped by his two-cell flashlight, we literally felt our way along the faint trail Turkey had marked the night before. As we walked, Turkey continually picked up bits of handkerchief cloth and paper off the bushes and stuffed them into his pocket. We waded long pools of ankle-deep water, and then through a hole that slopped over my boot tops. I sloshed behind Turkey another mile along the ancient swamp byway before he picked up his last scrap of paper. Here he put his flashlight into his hunting-coat pocket and substituted a miniature keyhole light, with hardly enough beam to show us the ground.

"We're getting close," he whispered.

We turned off the overgrown swamp road into a game trail and followed it for a couple of hundred yards to where he'd marked it earlier with a broken branch. Turkey put out his light, and we stood for three full minutes in the game trail, trying to adjust our eyes to the total blackness. Not a star showed in the overcast sky. The treetops around us were only vague and misshapen blobs of black, scarcely distinguishable from the heavens behind them. Turkey pointed out the general direction from which he had heard the flock fly up to roost at sundown.

"About a hundred yards in there," he said, in a voice that I could hardly hear, "you'll find a tree with a big bushy top."

I nodded.

"Go to it only two or three steps at a time, so if the turkeys hear you, they'll think you are a browsing deer and won't be alarmed. Somewhere around the tree, locate a spot where you can hunker down and stay out of sight."

"O.K.," I said, trying to keep my voice as barely audible as his, "but let's get one thing straight. If you have a chance at that gobbler before I do, don"t pass it up."

Turkey hesitated, and though I could not see him, I felt that he was grinning at me in the darkness.

"I wasn't aimin' to," he said.

I moved away, trying to walk like a browsing deer. Even though the swamp earth was wet, it was carpeted with a layer of leaves and brittle sticks. It seemed to me that in the predawn stillness I made an uncommon lot of noise, though Turkey told me later that I seemed to vanish completely, causing him to wonder if I had gone more than a few yards off the game trail.

In the blackness, I had no idea whether I was in line with the mythical bushy tree—every tree looked bushy—but I made my way slowly in what I thought was a straight line for a hundred yards to a thick-butted water oak. I felt around it with my hands and decided there was at least enough vegetation to screen me from the sharp eyes of the forest. With my back to the broad tree trunk, I settled down as comfortably as possible to wait.

Dawn came slowly. It slipped into the swamp woods so furtively that I was hardly conscious of when the trees began to lose their silhouettes and take on shape and color. A cardinal on my right opened the morning choir, and that served as an overture for the feathered serenade that grew in melody and volume with the growing light, finally climaxing in an explosive *ga-lobble-obble-obble* a hundred yards deeper in the swamp forest.

By the expanding daylight, I discovered that my position was not as good as I had thought. Except for a few scrubby patches of swamp growth, I could see and be seen for a hundred yards around me. The large tree bole I had chosen in the darkness was isolated. It was too late to change positions or try to build a blind. The only thing I knew to do was—as Turkey Johnston put it—"hunker down" and make myself as inconspicuous as possible.

Above the ringing dawn melody, I heard one of the big birds fly down off its roost, and then another. That seemed to be the signal for a general exodus from the trees. The sound of wings was a couple of hundred yards away. One of the birds hit the ground gobbling, and I waited about ten minutes before I cautiously reached for the cedar box in my pocket. As I was stripping off the rubber band that held the lid tight, Johnston yelped. It was the first time I knew he was stationed about 50 yards to my left. The quality of his call was good enough for me. I deposited my own rectangle of cedar against the tree trunk behind me.

The gobbler replied to Johnston's box before he got through yelping it. I couldn't see the bird from where I sat, but his voice indicated that he was a big one. I forgot about my cramped position and my cold feet some ten minutes later when the tom turkey stepped into view about 150 yards away at the other end of a narrow corridor through the trees and brush. He spread his big fan and strutted, but he did not answer the call.

Off to the right, I made out the smaller, darker body of a hen. Johnston yelped again and was answered almost immediately by a bona-fide hen, this time behind my tree. When she yelped, the gobbler yowked and strutted, dropping his wings and performing a little dance that carried him out of sight into the brush. Two more hens were suddenly visible. And from what I could see and hear, I figured there were seven females altogether, challenging Turkey Johnston's flirtation with the big gobbler.

Now I'm an old and a reasonably experienced turkey hunter, and I have taken a few birds in my time. But such a sight never fails to skyrocket my blood pressure. By moving very slowly, I shifted my position to get down even lower against the tree trunk. That slight movement startled the hen behind my tree—who'd been obviously closer than I thought. With a roar of heavy wingbeats, she took off through the treetops.

I thought the jig was up for sure, but the sudden departure of the hen did not seem to disturb the rest of the scattered flock. When Johnston called again, the outsized buck turkey came into view in another swamp corridor, yards to the right of where I had last seen him. He spread his tail and dropped his wings. The woods rang with his most resonant challenge.

The gobbler seemed to be circling to the call. It seemed to me that if he completed the parabolic arc he had started, that would bring him close enough for my shot string. To say he was taking his time would be a gross understatement. For an hour, I sat as motionless as a mortal man can sit. My legs had long since lost their feeling from lack of circulation, and the cheeks on both sides of my caudal appendage ached from the pressure of their contact with the earth, which grew more unyielding by the minute. To add to my misery, half a dozen mosquitoes found me and went to work on my face. I watched them come in one by one for a landing and felt them drive their rapiers in to the hilt. In plain sight of the birds, as I was, I could do nothing but sit there motionless and suffer—consoling myself that at least this experience might prove character-building.

I was wondering how much the human flesh can endure when a buck turkey I had not seen appeared in the picture. He was less than 100 yards away and coming straight for me. My systolic pressure soared again, and I forgot my aches. He wasn't as large or as stately as the old buck, but even at that distance I could see his beard. It was short and heavy, with the appearance of being dragged off against the ground, though I was sure this wasn't true.

The gobbler came on, stopping to pick at tidbits on the swamp floor, raising his head to survey the domain around him. In the background, still twice the distance of a lethal load away, the big turkey continued to strut.

Tom No. 2 got within 32 steps of me—we paced it off later—before he saw me reclining against the tree. I knew he'd spotted me by the manner in which he suddenly stopped, lifted his head and slowly raised it higher and higher until he seemed to be standing on tiptoe.

I didn't bat an eyelash while for a long minute he simply stared in my direction. I could almost tell when he finally decided I was a human and realized that his situation was definitely unhealthy. One long stride carried him out of sight behind a tree. The instant he vanished, I raised my gun, ready to take his measure when he appeared in the open again.

I couldn't see the gobbler, but Turkey Johnston could. He said the bird stretched its neck until my lanky partner thought he would pull it loose from its moorings. There was no doubt that the bird was alarmed and that he intended to keep that tree trunk safely between us. He hadn't seen my hunting mate, who was 50 paces from him in the other direction. Turkey knew that if the bird flew or ran it would spook the rest of the flock, with the possibility that neither of us would get a shot. The distance was long, even for the 12-gauge magnum in Turkey's hands. But he fired. The woods rang with the blast; the gobbler fell kicking against the earth. The rest of the flock stood still with heads up until Turkey jumped up to run toward his bird. Then they took off in all directions.

I was glad of the opportunity to stagger stiffly to my feet and follow my partner to his kill. He looked back at the tree against which I had sat, and shook his head.

"Gad," he said. "I wouldn't have pulled the trigger if I had known you were *that* close."

"Who pulled the trigger," I said, "makes not the slightest difference. That was just about one of the grandest shows I ever watched in gobbler woods."

To make our morning hunt a complete success, Clarence Streetman came in bug-eyed with a young gobbler he and Bob had lured within range of their guns. The two guys were muddy and wringing wet from the waist down. They gave a graphic presentation that needed no words to tell us what kind of swamp they had to navigate to get to their flock of birds.

We solemnly shook hands all around, and Turkey Johnston squinted at me.

"Sure hope you can get back over here and help me look for that old gobbler that got away this morning."

"Come another spring," I said, "I might do just that. In the meantime, if you get another crack at him, don't wait for me."

Turkey's eyes crinkled around the corners.

"Don't worry," he said. "I wasn't aimin' to."

Turkey Johnston and I had many such colorful hunts together. Jimmie Shirley, after he retired as manager of the company store, joined us. I don't remember a spring when we failed to bring gobblers out of those woods. One of our most fascinating mornings was when circumstances dictated that Turkey, Jimmie, and I should team up on one gobbler.

Turkey and I were hunting together. Jimmie had gone off in another direction. It was just growing light when my partner and I heard two gobblers answer the owls. The light wasn't bright enough for the toms to fly down, and we knew they had gobbled from a distant roost. We took a compass reading on each and found that one was north of us and the other about northwest. We stayed on the hilltop hoping to hear a tom closer to us. Every veteran turkey hunter at one time or another has been lured away by a distant gobbler only to hear another gobbler sound off from the very spot he left.

So we sat while the light brightened. The woods filled with music, and tom turkeys in the distance gobbled until I couldn't stand it any longer. I stepped over to where my partner was perched on a mound left by the roots of an upended tree, but he beat me to the suggestion I was about to make.

"The northwest one is closer to Jimmie," he said. "Let's you and me go after the other. I don't believe there's a gobbler or hen in our neck of the woods."

I didn't need any urging. We retraced our steps down the logging road to the creek and climbed the opposite hill. We paused at the crest, and soon heard a tom turkey gobble loud and clear from the swamp that lay beyond a stretch of slashings. We crossed the slashings on a muddy skid road and were starting downhill toward the creek bottom when Turkey stopped and bent over a track in the soft earth. I stopped behind him, and he straightened up.

"Jimmie is ahead of us," he whispered. "I believe we're after the same bird."

"Maybe we'll have enough firepower to surround him," I said quietly. "Or perhaps we shouldn't disturb Jimmie and see instead what we can do with the other bird."

"Let's give Jimmie a hand," he suggested.

Though ordinarily I consider a gobbler hunt a one-man deal, I have often hunted successfully with a partner. Now I was curious to see how a team of three hunters would fare.

My partner clucked, and Jimmie gave him an answering cluck from somewhere deep in the swamp. Turkey nodded, and I followed him across a little creek and through an oozy flat to where Jimmie was waiting beside a wide canebrake.

"There's a small ridge ahead that breaks off into the swamp," Jimmie whispered, pointing. "The gobbler is just beyond it. We can get him if we work this thing right."

He nodded to me. "You go to the point of the ridge just where it begins to level out to the swamp floor," he said. "Turkey will go to where the ridge flattens out on top. I'll be somewhere in between you two. Call just as you would call if you were hunting alone. We'll probably make that tom think a whole flock of hens are after him. If he comes straight in or circles, one of us should be in a position to take him."

I took my stand against the massive base of an oak, put on my camouflage gloves, pulled the camouflage netting over my face, and hunkered down against the damp earth. Turkey Johnston found a brushpile at the first break of the ridge, and Jimmie settled down in a clump of sprouts just around the hillside from my oak.

Jimmie clucked his box, and I heard the gobbler strutting and strumming under the brow of the hill. Then the second gobbler, which had worked slowly toward us from the time Turkey and I started down the skid road, made the woods ring about 200 yards off to my left. This development was disconcerting. Should I concentrate on the bird beyond Jimmie or turn and face toward the second tom? Since this was a team effort, I decided not to turn, at least not until the bird on my blind side came so close I couldn't ignore him.

The short hairs on my neck snapped on end when I heard a sudden flapping of wings that was not loud enough to be made by a gobbler flying away. It might have been hens on the ground, I thought. The flapping was repeated several minutes later, keeping me as tight as a coiled spring and also mystified. (Jimmie later explained that from where he sat he could see several wood ducks moving about in the trees.)

I clucked my mouth yelper a few times to let the two gobblers know I was in the ball game, then turned the calling over to my partners, who apparently were carrying on the right conversation with the tom below us.

Moments such as these are filled with suspense. When a tom pauses for long periods between his gobbling, you never know whether he has detected you and slipped off or is making a cautious approach. You are glued to the spot. Your bottom aches, your legs get numb, and your eyes hurt from trying to see everything within an arc of 180 degrees without moving your head.

I heard a stealthy step behind me. The gobbler? It was so close that if it flew or ran I could pivot in time to have it well within the range of my 12-gauge Winchester Model 12 with its 30-inch full-choke barrel. I swung around. Jimmie was there, not more than half a dozen steps away, motioning to me.

My legs were so numb that when I stood up I stumbled. But somehow I made them work. Jimmie put his mouth close to my ear.

"He's gone around the base of the hill," he said. "There's a little gap beyond the treetop where Turkey is sitting, and the chances are better than even that he'll circle through it so he can look this country over from a high point before he tries to find the hen he thinks has been clucking to him. If he comes down the ridge, he'll walk right into Turkey's blind. If he circles through the gap to the swamp, we'll be waiting for him. Follow me."

In a half-crouch, I stepped in Jimmie's tracks for 100 yards to where we were within range of the open hillside just below the gap. Jimmie pointed to the base of a tree, and I lay down behind it in such a way that I would be in a position to bring my gun up smoothly and quickly to cover at least 120 degrees of the hillside above us. Jimmie sat behind me in a patch of brush and clucked. The woods were silent for five minutes before he followed his cluck with the low, plaintive sounds a hen makes.

Another five minutes passed, and I had about decided that the tom turkey had seen us move when he answered from the vicinity of the gap, just about where Jimmie had said he would be.

Then there was another long period of suspense. On the hillside, Turkey Johnston gave a low yelp on his diaphragm mouth call. A few minutes later, Jimmie called again. Immediately behind us, the swamp exploded with sound.

Both Jimmie and I were facing the wrong way to spot the bird, and for a moment I wondered whether our tom in the gap had somehow gone around us without being seen. I thought of slowly rolling over on my side to face the swamp, though I knew better. But I might have tried it if the tom we had been after all morning hadn't gobbled from the very place where we had last heard him in the gap.

Two turkeys were somewhat just out of range on opposite sides of where we lay. We didn't know whether the bird in the swamp was near enough to see us, and again it took all my will power to keep from turning my head. I knew that if the swampside gobbler saw the slightest movement, it would give a sharp *phutt-t-t* of alarm and both birds would vanish.

Turkey Johnston yelped again, and then we went through a long period of

Like horse racing, turkey hunting gives rise to various opinions. Here, Turkey Johnston (left) shows his favorite call, a diaphragm yelper, to Jimmie Shirley, whose choice is the Lynch call, a box type.

quiet expectancy. My right leg was cramped from the awkward position I had taken behind the tree, but I could do nothing about it.

Jimmie and I had no way of knowing that the gobbler on the hill had come into the open where Turkey could see it, but just out of range. He watched while it strutted, walked in a circle, and stood up tall, apparently searching for danger or for the hen that had been making those dulcet tones.

About twenty minutes passed. Then Jimmie yelped again. Both gobblers answered immediately, and the one behind us sounded close. We waited. The bird on the hill strutted again, then straightened up and took a dozen steps toward us. This maneuver brought it just to the limit of the range of Turkey's gun, which was laid over the limbs of the brushpile and aimed within a couple of degrees of where the gobbler had appeared.

The bird stood there for five minutes and then took a couple of steps as though it intended to retreat along the ridge. Our partner in the brushtop decided that it was now or never. Moving slowly, he lined his sights up on the bird's wattles and pulled the trigger.

The peaceful scene erupted into pandemonium. The gobbler flapped into the air and took off with a roar of wings. In its startled flight it struck a limb sticking up through the brush, and this turned its flight into a downhill course directly toward where Jimmie and I were crouched.

"Take him!" Jimmie shouted to me.

I stumbled up on my numb legs, but when I tried to bring my gun up, its barrel got tangled in some limbs I hadn't noticed when I sat down.

"Kill him!" Jimmie shouted.

I had to take one step backward and one sideways to clear the shotgun, on which I use a sling for turkey hunting. The gobbler had started low off the hill, but now it was climbing through the tree tops at jet speed. I swung my sights in front of the bird and led it by a good 3 feet. I pressed the trigger. The bird folded in midair like a quail and crashed into a patch of swamp canes about 40 feet from where we stood.

"Boy, I was just about through giving you a chance at him," Jimmie said. "You beat me under the wire by just about one second."

Turkey Johnston came down the hill with a big grin on his face.

Turkey Johnston (left) and Jimmie Shirley look over a gobbler taken in Alabama by the author.

"The same instant you pulled the trigger, I took my second shot at him in the air," he said, "and for a second or two I thought I'd knocked that bird down from a hundred yards away. I gave myself a pat or two on the back."

"One thing for sure," I said. "If ever a gobbler was taken by team effort, this one was."

"This is just about the most interesting gobbler hunt I ever had," Jimmie declared.

"Each one is," Turkey said.

23

The Thanksgiving Bird

It was the most conspicuous, delectable, and unforgettable of all the foods served at that first Thanksgiving celebration at Plymouth in 1621—well over three-hundred-and-fifty years ago. Since then it has been known as The Thanksgiving Bird.

Naturally, these three-and-a-half centuries have seen some changes. The first Thanksgiving bird was the wild turkey. Today the chances are about 99.99 percent that you'll sink your molars into one of the millions of domestic birds raised annually on wire or in confined areas.

I know a number of turkey hunters who put a wild gobbler on their table when the end of the harvest season rolls around. When I luck an old tom in the spring season, it goes into my freezer, just in case I can't meet up with one in the fall.

There's a lot of difference in the taste of a domestic bird raised on mash and such and a wild bird that forages on wild fruits, seeds, and a variety of other edibles out of nature's larder. Some have called the meat "gamey," and you want to ask, "Compared to what?" The meat is richer, more flavorful, more tender, and juicier when cooked right than its domestic cousin's.

On the other hand, one of the worst pieces of wild meat I ever tried to eat came off a wild turkey. It had been cooked by a lady who detested wild meat of any kind. I am sure she had never been hungry. She especially despised wild turkeys because during turkey season she lost complete control over a husband who was definitely a milquetoast throughout the remainder of the year.

I'd liked to have known what she did to that bird, but I never had the temerity to ask. I'd have had more luck gnawing the sole off my hunting boot. I tossed the piece I was unable to chew to an old mountain hound hanging around our cabin. He snatched it up and ran off with it. In five minutes he brought it back and left it where he'd found it.

Another time after a morning hunt I met an old mountaineer friend on the trail and went home with him to breakfast. We sat down to buttermilk biscuits, scrambled eggs, and as delicious a slab of fried meat as I ever put between my teeth. He read the question in my eyes.

"Turkey breast," he said. "We slice it off, then hammer, batter, and fry it. Wild turkey ain't fitten cooked no other way."

"What about the rest of the turkey?" I asked.

"We boil it," he said. "Eat most of the dark meat and make the leavings into hash and soup."

"You said 'hammer' it. What does that mean?" I asked.

"It ain't very tender," he said, "especially from an old gobbler, if you jest whack it off and drop it into the frying pan. So we lay it on a clean oak board and beat it flat and thin, like you would a piece of tough steak. That no way hurts the flavor. And instead of being chewy, the meat melts in your mouth. We flour and cook it in a skillet, like you'd fry a piece of chicken."

There must be as many ways to cook a wild turkey as there are to get him within lethal range of a shot pattern. Almost everyone familiar with the bird has his own idea of how it should be made more palatable for the table. Then, naturally, at least a few of the recipes are by various culinary geniuses who probably never laid eyes on a wild turkey. Luckily, these concoctions seem to be in the minority.

Each cook is likely to have his or her own idea how to roast a turkey out of the mountains or the swamps. One will say it should be seared at high temperatures and then the oven turned down to moderate heat. Another may use a very low temperature from start to finish. Some use aluminum foil or brown paper; others cook the bird in an open pan, basting it generously throughout the process.

The wild turkey is "stuffed" at the whim of the stuffer. What he pokes inside that hollow carcass is a matter of personal preference. Stuffings may include giblets, mushrooms sautéed in butter, onions, oysters, chopped parsley, thyme, bread crumbs, celery or celery salt, a few tablespoons of wine, salt and pepper to taste, or a cornbread dressing that includes a few of those items. Take your choice. You're the one who's gotta eat it. Just don't doctor it up so much you spoil the rich flavor of the meat.

Unless you have the same attitude as the lady who cooked wild game only under protest, there is hardly any way, outside of serving it half-done or burned to a crisp, that you can destroy the fine eating qualities of a wild turkey.

My wife Kayte's recipe is the one with which I'm most familiar. We argue about most things now and again, but never a cross word do we have over her wild-turkey cooking. The sweet, juicy meat she gets out of a woods gobbler is the best I've ever tasted.

Kayte's like some of the other natural cooks I've met, who go by feel, or instinct, and never by exact measurements. It's difficult to get a precise recipe from someone who cooks with "a dab of this, a pinch of that, a smidgen here and there."

Here's the way, as near as I can understand, she does it:

Have dressed turkey thoroughly dry.
Make a mixture of sifted flour and either peanut, corn, or saf-
flower oil, thick enough (about like heavy honey) so that when you
smear it on the carcass, it will stick and remain in place while
turkey is being cooked. Coat bird with this.
   Put salt to taste, plus a light sprinkling of meat tenderizer *inside*
the body cavity.
   Place turkey in roasting pan, set oven on "Broil," and brown bird
lightly on all sides until flour-and-oil paste forms a crust.
   Reduce oven heat to 200-250 degrees Fahrenheit.
   Pour 1 to 2 cups of water on bottom of pan and cover with lid.
Baste every 30 minutes—more or less—with juices that have
cooked out of turkey into bottom of pan.
   Kayte usually counts on 3 to 4 hours, but she judges the turkey
done when the meat begins to pull away from the bone. To make
certain, she slices to the bone of a drumstick or thigh, and checks
the meat there.

   Kayte doesn't stuff her turkey with dressing, but makes this in a
separate dish. Here's how:

The standard cornbread mixture is baked (Southern hoe-cake
style) on top of the stove. Kayte makes this up while the turkey
roasts.
   Cook 1 to 2 cups of giblets separately, and chop into small pieces.
   Hard-boil 3 or 4 eggs. Peel and chop up.
   In a mixing bowl, crumble cornbread and add giblets and eggs.
Also add one small onion (minced), one-half pint of raw oysters, a
cup of water chestnuts chopped coarse, and enough turkey juices
from roasting pan to give dressing the desired consistency.
   Place in baking dish and cook dressing separately in oven.

   That's the way Kayte says she cooks a wild turkey. I can't verify it. I stay
out of the kitchen around Thanksgiving time.
   Kayte's recipe is a relatively simple one. Others I've found are more
elaborate and call for diverse ingredients. Some approach gourmet cooking,
and I'm sure they are delicious.

In the May 1976 issue of *Outdoor Life* magazine, Jane Gould, noted food editor, presented three recipes for wild turkey, which should add a touch of spice to the wild meat. These were as follows:

Roast Wild Turkey with Cornbread Stuffing

For the stuffing:

6 cups cornbread (use any standard recipe) coarsely crumbled
¼ lb. butter
½ tsp. salt
1 tsp. thyme
1 tsp. marjoram
1⅓ cups minced onion
1 carrot
1 celery stalk
1 lb. sausage meat
¼ cup parsley, finely chopped
¼ cup Madeira or dry sherry
Cream
Thin slices of fat pork

In heavy skillet, cook onions in melted butter until tender and slightly colored. Turn into a large mixing bowl. Cook sausage meat in skillet until lightly browned (breaking up lumps). Drain fat, and combine sausage meat with the onions in the bowl. Add cornbread, salt, spices, and parsley to the bowl. Mix well, stir in Madeira and enough cream for desired consistency.

Stuff and truss turkey, place it on a rack in a large roasting pan, and cover the breast with thin slices of fat pork. Slice an onion, a carrot, and a stalk of celery, and scatter around the bird. Roast 25 minutes per pound, uncovered, basting every 15 minutes with drippings and butter.

For the gravy:

½ cup dry white wine
3 cups turkey or chicken stock
1 cup light cream
Salt and pepper

Use only 1 to 2 tbsp. of fat. Stir wine into drippings, scraping up the brown particles. Then add the stock, boil a few minutes, add the cream, salt, and pepper.

Turkey with Grapefruit & Cherries

Ingredients are:

1 young wild turkey (6 to 8 lb.)
2 grapefruits, preferably pink
4 tsp. sugar
4 tsp. confectioner's sugar
½ cup dry white wine
¾ cup red port wine (of which 3 tsp. are to be used as cherry marinade)
1 tbsp. each of port, sherry, and brandy
1 medium can sour cherries
¼ cup sugar (for cherry syrup)
Pinch of paprika

Pare the skin from one grapefruit (avoiding any bitter white pith), and mince skin finely. In a small saucepan combine skin, dry white wine, and 4 tsp. sugar. Cook over moderate heat until sugar dissolves. Squeeze, strain, and save juice from this grapefruit.

Peel and section second grapefruit, and place sections in a small baking dish. Sprinkle with 4 tsp. confectioner's sugar, and glaze in a very hot oven.

Drain cherries (saving fluid), and marinate them in 3 tsp. red port wine. Make a syrup by boiling ½ cup cherry juice (from can) and ¼ cup sugar. Add 1 tbsp. each of port, sherry, and brandy, and let cool.

After turkey is cooked, discard all fat from pan. Then mix remaining red port wine (¾ cup less 3 tsp. already used in cherry marinade) with brown bits in pan bottom. Stir in white-wine-and-grapefruit mixture, grapefruit juice, and cherry syrup. Salt to taste, and add a pinch of paprika. Simmer until slightly thickened, and add the cherries.

Garnish the turkey with glazed grapefruit, and serve with sauce.

Turkey with Orange Sauce

You'll need:

1 10-lb. turkey
3 oranges (2 needed for juice)
1 large onion
2 tbsp. olive oil
Salt and pepper
¼ tsp. oregano
¼ tsp. rosemary leaves

1 clove garlic
1 chicken bouillon cube
$^2/_3$ cup dry white wine
¼ lb. butter, melted

For the sauce:

3 tbsp. butter
3 tbsp. flour
½ cup dry white wine
1½ cups turkey stock, pan juices

Dice unpeeled orange. Peel and dice onion. Mix in a bowl with olive oil, salt, pepper, and spices. Fill cavity of bird with this mixture, and roast in 325° oven.

Baste turkey frequently with a mixture made by combining dry white wine, melted butter, orange juice, garlic, bouillon cube, and salt and pepper. Discard onion and orange within bird before serving.

For the sauce, combine melted butter, flour, dry white wine, stock, and pan juices (without fat) in a double boiler and stir until smooth.

Another pro who should know plenty about cooking turkeys—wild and otherwise—is Tom Bates. Tom lives near Fort Deposit, Alabama, and has spent a goodly part of his life hunting wild turkeys and cooking tame ones. Tom's specialty is smoked turkeys. I've never asked him how many of these birds go through his plant in a single year, but they must run into tens of thousands. His smoked turkey is the best I have ever eaten anywhere, anytime.

Tom was generous enough to provide me with some of his unusual turkey recipes for this book.

Roasting the Turkey

To thaw turkey:

Leave turkey in original plastic bag, and use one of the following three methods:

(a) No hurry—place on tray in refrigerator . . . 3 to 4 days.

(b) Faster—place on tray at room temperature in a closed grocery bag (bag prevents skin of turkey from becoming too warm) . . . 1 hour per pound of turkey.

(c) Fastest—cover with cold water, changing water occasionally . . . one-half hour per pound of turkey. Refrigerate or cook turkey as soon as thawed. If you plan to stuff turkey, do so just before roasting.

To roast turkey:

Remove plastic bag, remove neck and giblets from cavities, rinse turkey, and pat dry. Boil neck and giblets for broth and for flavoring dressing and giblet gravy.

Fasten down legs by tying or tucking under skin band. Skewer neck skin to back, twist wings akimbo under bird.

Place turkey on rack in shallow roasting pan, breast side up. Brush with butter. If roast-meat thermometer is used, insert into the thick part of thigh.

Turkey is done when:

(a) Roast-meat thermometer registers 180° to 185°F.
(b) Thick part of drumstick feels soft when pressed with thumb and forefinger.
(c) Drumstick and thigh move easily.

Turkey Jumbos

¼ cup salad dressing or mayonnaise
2 tablespoons chunk-style peanut butter
12 slices unfrosted raisin bran bread, buttered
1 large banana (cut into 20 thin slices)
4 slices Swiss cheese
½ cup whole cranberry sauce
16 thin slices cooked turkey
16 wooden toothpicks

Blend salad dressing or mayonnaise with peanut butter. Spread salad dressing mixture over buttered bread. Arrange banana slices over 4 slices of bread, and cover with slices of Swiss cheese. Top with 4 more slices of bread and then cranberry sauce. Place turkey slices over cranberry sauce; top with remaining bread slices. Secure with wooden toothpicks. Cut each sandwich into 4 triangles. Makes 4 sandwiches.

Cornbread Stuffing

1 stick butter or margarine
1½ cups chopped celery
1 cup minced onion
2 tablespoons minced parsley
1 teaspoon dried sage
2 8-ounce packages cornbread stuffing mix
1 16-ounce can cream-style corn

In a large skillet, sauté celery and onions in butter until transparent. Add parsley and sage, mixing well and cooling for 2 minutes.

Mix in cornbread stuffing mix, blending thoroughly. Add corn and mix until moistened. Yield: Enough stuffing for a 14-pound turkey. *Note:* Stuffing can be baked in a greased casserole at 350°F. for about 30 minutes.

Turkey and Oysters in Cream Sauce

3 cups cooked turkey
1 pint oysters
6 tablespoons butter
6 tablespoons flour
3 cups rich milk
1 2¼-ounce can deviled ham

Cut turkey into chunks. Drain oysters, reserving liquid. Pick over oysters to remove any shell particles; set oysters and liquid aside. In medium saucepan, melt butter, blend in flour, add milk, cook and stir until smooth and thick. Blend in deviled ham. Add turkey, oysters, and liquid, over medium heat, gently stirring in. When thoroughly blended, turn to low heat to maintain serving temperature without boiling. Serve in pastry shells or toast cups. Makes 8 servings. Serve with cranberry relish.

Cranberry Relish: 4 cups (1 pound) fresh cranberries uncooked; 2 oranges, quartered and seeded; 2 cups granulated sugar. Grind cranberries and oranges coarsely. Stir in sugar and mix well. Chill in refrigerator several hours before serving. Makes 1 quart of relish.

Grilled Smoked Turkey

10- to 12-pound turkey
¼ cup vegetable oil
½ cup salt
1 cup vinegar
¼ cup pepper
Hickory chips, soaked in water

Rinse turkey; pat dry with paper towels. Make a paste of the vegetable oil and salt; rub ¼ cup of the mixture into large and wishbone cavities. Truss turkey and balance on spit; brush with oil. Prepare coals on charcoal grill or follow manufacturer's instructions for gas grill. Grill over medium heat for 1 hour. At the end of the first hour, brush bird with basting sauce prepared by mixing the remaining salt paste with the vinegar and pepper. Wrap hickory chips in small foil package, punch holes in foil and lay on coals or briquettes. Continue roasting, basting turkey every 30 minutes. Total cooking time will be 4 to 5 hours. To test for doneness, snip cord that holds drumsticks; test by moving drumstick up and down (protect hands first with paper towels). Legs should move easily or twist out of joint. Also press thick part of drumstick; meat should feel very soft. Allow turkey to rest at least 15 minutes before carving. Serve hot or cold. Makes 15 to 20 servings.

Turkey Chowder

1 large onion, thinly sliced
2 stalks celery, sliced
3 tablespoons butter or margarine
3 tablespoons flour
1 teaspoon salt
¼ teaspoon pepper
2 quarts turkey broth (see recipe below)
2 potatoes, pared and cubed
2 carrots, pared and cut in rings or strips
2 zucchini, cut in strips
1 10-ounce package frozen whole kernel corn
1 cup Sauterne or Chablis dry white wine
2 cups turkey pieces
2 tablespoons chopped parsley

Sauté onion and celery in butter or margarine just until tender-crisp in a large kettle; remove from heat. Blend in flour, salt, and pepper. Gradually stir in turkey broth. Heat, stirring, until mixture comes to a boil. Add potatoes and carrots. Cover and simmer 15 minutes, just until vegetables are barely tender. Add zucchini, corn, white wine, and turkey pieces. Continue simmering 15 minutes. Add parsley. Makes 8 servings.

To Make Turkey Broth: Break up turkey carcass to fit into a large saucepan. Add 1 quart cold water, 1 sliced onion, and a handful of celery tops. Cover and simmer 1 hour. Strain broth. Add enough water (or canned chicken broth) to make 8 cups.

We have come at last a full circle. As I said at the very beginning, your first job now is—to get the gobbler!

Bibliography

Bent, Arthur C. *Life Histories of North American Gallinaceous Birds*. New York: Dover Publications, Inc., 1932. 490 pp. 90 plates.

Brady, James F. *Modern Turkey Hunting*. New York: Crown Publishers, Inc., 1973. 160 pp.

Forbush, Edward Howe. *Birds of Massachusetts and Other New England States*. Norwood, Mass.: Norwood Press, 1925. 3 vols. 1,408 pp.

Groves, Earl. *Talking Tom Foolery*. Gastonia, North Carolina: Mason Athletic Co., 1977. 101 pp.

Hanenkrat, William Frank. *The Education of a Turkey Hunter*. New York: Winchester Press, 1974. 216 pp.

Harbour, Dave. *Hunting the American Wild Turkey*. Harrisburg, Pa.: Stackpole Books, 1975. 256 pp.

Hewitt, Oliver H., ed. *The Wild Turkey and Its Management*. Washington, D.C.: Wildlife Society, Inc., 1967. 589 pp.

Johenning, Leon. *The Turkey Hunter's Guide*. Waynesboro, Va.: The Humphries Press, 1962. 71 pp.

Kelly, Tom. *Tenth Legion*. Monroe, La.: Spur Enterprises, 1973. 119 pp.

Latham, Roger M. *The Complete Book of the Wild Turkey*. Harrisburg, Pa.: Stackpole Books, 1976. 228 pp.

Lewis, James C. *The World of the Wild Turkey*. Philadelphia: J.B. Lippincott Co., 1973. 158 pp.

Lignon, J. Stokley. *History and Management of Merriam's Wild Turkey*. Santa Fe: New Mexico Game and Fish Commission, 1946. 84 pp.

McIlhenny, E.A. *The Wild Turkey and Its Hunting*. New York: Doubleday and Co., Inc., 1914. 245 pp.

Mosby, Henry S., and Charles O. Handley. *The Wild Turkey in Virginia*. Richmond, Va.: Commission of Game and Inland Fisheries, 1943. 281 pp.

Rue, Leonard Lee, III. *Game Birds of North America*. New York: Harper and Row, Inc., 1973. 490 pp.

Schorger, Arlie William. *The Wild Turkey: Its History and Domestication*. Norman, Okla.: University of Oklahoma Press, 1966. 625 pp.

Turpin, Tom. *Hunting the Wild Turkey*. Delmont, Pa.: Penn's Woods Products, 1966. 64 pp.

Whittington, Charles S. *Tall Timber Gabriels*. Monroe, La.: Spur Enterprises, 1971. 100 pp.

Index